NEGOTIATING ACROSS CULTURES

International Communication in an Interdependent World

REVISED EDITION

RAYMOND COHEN

United States
Institute of Peace Press
WASHINGTON, D.C.

The views expressed in this book are those of the author alone. They do not necessarily reflect views of the United States Institute of Peace.

United States Institute of Peace
1550 M Street NW
Washington, DC 20005

Printed in the United States of America

The paper used in this publication meets the minimum requirements of American National Standard for Information Sciences—Permanence of Paper for Printed Library Materials, ANSI Z39.48-1984.

Library of Congress Cataloging-in-Publication Data
Cohen, Raymond, 1947–
    Negotiating across cultures : international communication in an interdependent world / Raymond Cohen. — Rev. ed.
      p. cm.
    Includes bibliographical references and index.
    ISBN 1-878379-72-0 (pbk. : acid-free paper)
    1. International relations. 2. Diplomacy—Cross-cultural studies. 3. Negotiation—Cross-cultural studies. 4. United States—Foreign relations—1945– I. Title.
JZ1305.C64 1997
327.2'0973—dc21   97-45198
                                                        CIP

Negotiating Across Cultures

revised edition

For Rivka

The Song of Solomon, iv. 6–7

Contents

Foreword by *Richard H. Solomon*   ix

Acknowledgments to Revised Edition   xiii

Acknowledgments to First Edition   xv

1   Prelude: The *Astoria* Affair   3

2   Negotiation: The Cultural Roots   9

3   Intercultural Dissonance: A Theoretical Framework   25

4   What Is Negotiable?   45

5   Setting Out the Pieces: Prenegotiation   67

6   Let the Contest Commence: Opening Moves   83

7   On Tactics and Players: Middle Game I   107

8   Sounds, Signals, Silence: Middle Game II   135

9   Under Pressure: End Game I   163

10   Face and Form: End Game II   183

11   When Is a Deal a Deal?   199

12   In Search of Harmony: Conclusions   215

Notes   227

Bibliography   249

Index   259

Foreword

In 1991, when the first edition of Raymond Cohen's *Negotiating Across Cultures* was published, culture seemed a lot less important to the conduct of international relations than it does today. Experienced diplomats and a growing circle of interested scholars may have recognized the power of cultural norms to influence negotiations and their outcomes, but most observers still understandably viewed international affairs through Cold War lenses, which highlighted the role of ideological differences and the military calculus of deterrence through the policy of mutually assured destruction. Following the demise of the Soviet Union at the end of 1991, there was at first a tendency to predict a world in which culture would become ever more homogenized among cooperative, peaceful nations and peoples bound by universal political and economic values.

Today, just half a dozen years later, the Soviet Union is extinct, the Cold War seems like ancient history, and large parts of the world are distinctly uncooperative and burdened with ethnic and religious violence. Furthermore, there is now wide agreement that when it comes to international relations, culture—and, more particularly, cultural difference—matters. In part, this growing appreciation of the role of culture is a consequence of the shrinking importance of ideology on negotiating agendas; with a few notable exceptions, ideological objectives and rhetoric no longer obscure the presence and interplay of other factors, including those based on culture. This enhanced recognition of the impact of culturally distinct modes of thought and behavior also stems from the fact that in so much of the violence of the 1990s, issues of ethnicity and identity—in which culture plays a large, even a defining role—have been used by political leaders to mobilize their followers for war.

If the first edition of *Negotiating Across Cultures* was thus somewhat ahead of its time in stressing the importance of culture in international nego-tiating, publication of this revised edition could not be more timely. Cohen offers not only a fascinating and fluent introduction to cross-cultural nego-tiation for readers new to the subject, but also a wealth of thoughtful com-mentary on the theory and practice of past and very recent negotiations that is likely to stimulate discussion among experts from both the diplomatic and the scholarly communities. Readers and critics alike responded enthu-siastically to the original book; *Orbis*, for example, dubbed it "a masterwork of cultural analysis applied to international politics," and the edition went through several printings. This new edition is significantly enlarged, updated, and reorganized.

As was the case in the first edition, Cohen here examines the ways in which cultural factors have affected the conduct and outcome of U.S. deal-ings with five increasingly significant nations: Japan, China, Egypt, India, and Mexico. For this expanded revision, Cohen has extended the already generous number and variety of negotiations that he analyzes with detailed discussions of such recent cases as the Clinton administration's policy toward China; NAFTA; disagreements in the 1990s over human rights and sovereignty; and developments in the ongoing trade talks with Japan. Thus, *Negotiating Across Cultures* now assesses a mixture of high-policy encounters (such as the drawn-out discussions with China that led to the breakthrough in Sino-American relations in the 1970s) and more typical but nonetheless important negotiations (such as air-transport agreements and water-rights disputes) over the course of almost half a century.

Moreover, Cohen goes beyond an examination of cases to present a theo-retical framework for his analysis. He argues that there is no single, univer-sal model for negotiation. On the contrary, he describes two quite different models, each equally valid in its own terms. Cohen defines the first model as "low context," the predominantly verbal and explicit style typical of indi-vidualistic societies such as the United States. The second model is "high context," a style associated with nonverbal and implicit communication more typical of interdependent societies.

For this new edition, Cohen has further refined this theoretical apparatus while also expanding its scope so that, for example, it offers new insights into a negotiation's "middle game" and takes a wholly new look at how dif-ferent cultures approach the process of implementing an agreement.

Whereas the impact on diplomacy of cultural factors received less attention than it merited at the start of this decade, there is today perhaps a tendency to err on the other side—to assign too much significance to cultural differences. Fortunately, Raymond Cohen puts matters into their proper perspective: "In most cases negotiation failure is more likely to be the result of divergent interests than of subjective misunderstanding. . . . It should not be thought that all international negotiation is a distressing saga of stumbling incoherence." Nonetheless, cultural factors do "on occasion complicate, prolong, and even frustrate negotiations where there exists an identifiable basis for cooperation." Cross-cultural disharmony, Cohen remarks, "is neither a trivial nor a negligible phenomenon. It is worthy of attention."

This is a judgment with which the United States Institute of Peace—mandated by Congress to strengthen the nation's capacity to promote peaceful resolution of international conflict—readily concurs. Indeed, this new edition of *Negotiating Across Cultures* is part of a wide-ranging research and training effort promoted by the Institute on cross-cultural negotiating behavior. In addition to Cohen's book, which casts its net widely in terms of countries examined and conclusions drawn, the work sponsored by the Institute currently includes a number of country-specific studies on Japan, North Korea, Germany, and Russia. The volume on Russia, *Russian Negotiating Behavior* by Jerrold Schecter, will be available from the Institute's press in the first half of 1998.

Like other works published by the Institute, *Negotiating Across Cultures* will significantly enhance our understanding of how to build bridges across, rather than tumble into, cultural divides. As such, it should help to minimize the mutual incomprehension and distrust that often lie behind or fuel heated disagreements and violent conflicts.

Richard H. Solomon, President
United States Institute of Peace

Acknowledgments to Revised Edition

During the course of revising this book I have incurred a number of debts of gratitude. The original idea of a revised edition came from Kay Hechler and Dan Snodderly, and I thank them for their unstinting encouragement. The idea would not have got off the ground if the president of the United States Institute of Peace, Richard Solomon, had not given it his support. During my 1996 return fellowship at the Institute to work on the revision I found the staff, as always, friendly, helpful, and efficient. My special thanks go to Joe Klaits, who brought me over, Jason Ellis and Frederick Williams, for their conscientious and enterprising research assistance, and Rebecca Caponi, for her thoroughly professional library help. Thanks, too, go to Nigel Quinney for his skill and tolerance as an editor.

While carrying out my further research in 1996 I was also helped by the following individuals who were kind enough to give of their time and wisdom: Henry Bassford, Walter Bollinger, Bill Breer, William Clark Jr., Sean Donnelly, Eliot Feldman, Chas Freeman, Karl Jackson, Brady Kiesling, Dan Kurtzer, James Lilley, Mike Mansfield, David Newsom, Ed O'Donnell, Robert Pelletreau, Charles Roh, Stanley Roth, McKinnie Russell, Teresita Schaffer, Jesus Silva de Herzog, Mike Smith, Richard Solomon, and Arturo Valenzuela. My sincere thanks.

To have been granted one Jennings Randolph Fellowship to the Institute (in 1988–89) was a privilege. To have received a return invitation in 1996 was a rare vote of confidence. On both occasions, I benefited greatly from the hospitality and excellent facilities of this fine institution.

Acknowledgments to
First Edition

The research and writing of this essay were carried out at the United States Institute of Peace, where the author was a peace fellow in the Jennings Randolph Program during 1988–89.

I am very grateful to the members of the Board of Directors of the Institute and its president, Samuel W. Lewis, for the opportunity to carry on my work in a congenial atmosphere. Michael Lund and his staff were, and are, instrumental in making the fellowship program a success. Kathleen Allison, Barbara Cullicott, Libby Diniak, Denise Dowdell, Darleen Hall, Gregory McCarthy, Charles Nelson, and Charles Smith gave me every administrative assistance. I would also like to thank the following friends and colleagues at the Institute for their help and advice: Hrach Gregorian, Priscilla M. Jensen, Gerry Jones, Paul Kimmel, Richard Lewis, David Little, Lewis Rasmussen, John Reinhardt, John Richardson, and Tim Sisk.

Many people in public life generously gave of their wisdom and assistance. Thanks are due to Adolfo Aguilar, Francesco Alberti, Diego Asencio, Lucius Battle, Timothy Bennett, Sergio Dias Briquets, Herbert Brownell, Carleton Coon, Martin Creekmore, Hermann Eilts, John Ferch, Roger Fisher, Joseph Friedkin, Robert Goheen, Herbert Hagerty, John Jova, Julius Katz, Herbert Kelman, Paul Kriesberg, Daniel Kurtzer, Steven Lande, Herbert Levin, Joseph Lorenz, Patrick Lucey, Thomas Mann, Doris Meisner, Joerg Menzel, Richard Parker, William Quandt, El Sayed Abdel Raouf El Reedy, Randy Ridell, Jeffrey Rubin, Nadav Safran, Harold Saunders, Robert Sayre, Howard Schaefer, Gordon Streeb, Lorand Szalay, Viron

Vaky, Christopher Van Hollen, Nicolas Veliotes, Pater Wallison, Robert Wilcox, and William Zartman.

Patricia Bandy, Mia Cunningham, and Dan Snodderly did a very professional editing and publishing job. My good friend Richard Smith read the manuscript and was particularly supportive during its preparation.

Negotiating Across Cultures

I

Prelude

The *Astoria* Affair

A study of the impact of cultural differences on international negotiation requires some explanation in an era said to herald the emergence of a global culture. With the end of the Cold War and the collapse of communism, Western culture appears everywhere on the ascendant. American popular tastes are ubiquitous: fast-food chains such as Kentucky Fried Chicken and McDonald's ply their wares from Bombay to Tokyo; Hollywood movies are as popular in Shanghai as in Cherbourg; T-shirts, jeans, and sneakers have become the universal uniform of the young; satellite television brings the same sitcoms, sports events, and news items into homes across the world. Nor is the phenomenon of globalization restricted to popular culture: the Internet, ease of international travel, an enormous proliferation of trade and professional ties across borders, and the adoption of English as a universal lingua franca facilitate the movement of people and the exchange of ideas and commodities as never before.

Yet the spread of mass artifacts and images, and the frequency of cross-cultural encounters, should not be confused with cultural homogenization at a deeper level. To speak in English is not always to think in English; to wear a three-piece suit rather than a *jalabiyya* is not the same as abandoning cherished Moslem values; to know the ways of the West is not necessarily to wish to emulate them. One of the characteristics of any vibrant society is its ability to assimilate foreign influences while remaining true to its essential beliefs and motifs. One need look no further than the United States to see how exotic imports—such as pizza, bagels, and chow mein—are subtly transformed into American food staples. The Tokyo landscape is a scene of striking cultural syncretism, yet it remains uniquely Japanese. Nor do even prolonged communication and contact across cultures obviate profound differences of outlook, as the English and French, Arabs and Persians, or Japanese and Koreans can readily testify. Culture is more than skin deep.

What, the reader may counter, of the increasing salience of transnational subcultures of professionals in areas such as business, engineering, and science? Do not such global elites, living a cosmopolitan lifestyle and sharing a common basis of technical expertise, "speak a common language" overriding their varied backgrounds? The argument to be developed in this book is that professional ties can ease, but in many cases—particularly when value-laden issues are being contested—not eliminate, cross-cultural dissonances grounded in profoundly contrasting views of the world, modes of communication, and styles of negotiation.

My own initial assumption, derived from an interest in diplomacy, was that shared expertise can indeed overcome obstacles to communication and negotiation grounded in cultural diversity. Such classic texts as Sir Harold Nicolson's famous study, *Diplomacy*, reinforced this view. According to Nicolson, there is a universal diplomatic language of specialized words and phrases used by diplomats when they communicate with one another.[1] Nowhere does he suggest that the polished and expert diplomat may ever be sucked into the whirlpools of miscommunication. Technical competence in conveying a message does not, however, ensure understanding of its content. But writing at a time when European diplomacy was still dominant, Nicolson could afford to pass over in silence the problem of East-West misunderstanding.

If mutual comprehension among diplomats can be assumed, an important conclusion inevitably follows: disagreement is invariably based on an objective conflict of interests; wherever else one may seek the sources of international dissension and misunderstanding, they are not to be found in any recurrent breakdown or failure of the communication process. Such a conclusion is reassuring; although the timber of international relations may be warped, at least the carpenter's tools are true and sure.

The first seeds of doubt about the completeness of this authorized version were sown in my mind by an account I came across of the *Astoria* affair. In October 1938, Hirosi Saito, a former Japanese ambassador to the United

States, died in Washington. As a mark of respect, President Franklin D. Roosevelt ordered the U.S. Navy to convey the late ambassador's ashes home to Japan. The cruiser *Astoria* was chosen for the mission. Roosevelt, whose enthusiasm for the Navy was famous, made the decision without consulting State Department experts and despite the grave state of U.S.-Japanese relations. Japanese aggression against China and infringement of American interests continued unabated. The president certainly did not intend to downplay these very real causes of friction, let alone hint at any new course in American foreign policy—which would have been quite unacceptable to public opinion, outraged as it was by Japanese atrocities against Chinese civilians and such incidents as the sinking of the USS *Panay*.

But Roosevelt had not reckoned on how the gesture would be viewed through Japanese eyes. Extraordinary importance is attached in Japanese culture to paying respect to the dead. Elaborate rituals are associated with the practice, and Japanese homes often contain a small shrine to family ancestors. Reverence for the deceased goes far beyond anything found in American culture. Against this background Roosevelt's act of courtesy acquired a resonance in Tokyo never intended in Washington. Joseph Grew, ambassador to Japan, wrote in his diary at the time:

> The reaction here was immediately and inevitably political. The Japanese interpreted the gesture as of deep political significance, and a tremendous reaction, both emotional and political, immediately took place. Not only did the Government and people of Japan assume that a new leaf had been turned in Japanese-American relations and a wave of friendliness for the United States [sweep] over the country, but there promptly developed a determination to express Japan's gratitude in a concrete way.[2]

The State Department and the Tokyo embassy were horrified and embarrassed by the whole affair. One cross-cultural complication followed another. A jeweler from Osaka gave twenty pearl necklaces for the wives of the officers of the *Astoria*. If they were accepted, American public opinion would be outraged; in American public life such a lavish gift has the connotation of a bribe. If the necklaces were rejected, Japanese opinion would be deeply hurt; gift giving is naturally accepted in Japan as part of that complex lattice of moral indebtedness, mutual obligation, and social duty that underpins the Japanese way of life; the direct refusal of a present may cause, as Ambassador Grew ruefully observed, "serious offense."[3]

As the *Astoria* approached Yokohama, Japanese excitement intensified. Plans went ahead for a mass rally of the kind beloved in Japan, replete with national anthems, waving flags, regimented students, speeches, a demonstration of martial arts, and a baseball game between a local team and the American crew. All this fanfare could only give an utterly distorted impression of the true state of diplomatic ties. Participation by representatives of the United States in such effusive ceremonial would hardly accord with the firmness that U.S. diplomacy sought to convey in the face of the ruthless expansion of Japanese power and influence on the Chinese mainland. The reaction of the American people to all the ballyhoo, Grew noted, would be, "Show us your appreciation in acts, not words."[4]

It required all of Grew's skills to disentangle the knot without causing an equally undesirable backlash in Japanese opinion. The episode posed "one of the most difficult problems" to face the ambassador since his arrival in Japan in 1932.[5] A tone of restrained dignity was tactfully insisted upon. Extraneous festivities were quietly canceled or toned down; the necklaces were held in safe keeping for a while, then returned. Even so, to the Japanese, the visit spoke for itself. Moving and elaborate funeral rites went ahead. A shrine had been erected at the harbor to first receive the casket; the funeral procession marched through the densely lined streets of Yokohama; a special train conveyed the ambassador's remains to Tokyo, where yet more intricate and ornate pageantry awaited. What had been intended as a simple mark of courtesy escalated into a major demonstration of international esteem. The Japanese foreign minister commended it as a "graceful act . . . an opportunity for the restoration of good relations." Emperor Hirohito himself received the bemused captain of the American vessel, informing him with emotion that he "had performed a great service which was deeply appreciated by himself and the nation."[6]

If, as will surely be agreed, interstate communication depends on governments conveying no more and no less than they intend, the dispatch of the *Astoria*, however well meaning, was a diplomatic blunder. Because of the quite different weight and significance attached in Japanese and American cultures to such seemingly universal human concerns as showing respect for the dead and giving gifts, a gesture that was intended to transmit one message inadvertently transmitted another one entirely. By innocently and unconsciously failing to take cross-cultural differences into account, the president, an international statesman with long experience of international affairs, sent a misleading diplomatic signal.

Was the *Astoria* episode perhaps an exception to the general rule of unhindered international discourse? The sad tale of persistent incomprehension marking U.S.-Japanese relations on the eve of Pearl Harbor suggests not. Nor do more recent disasters in American foreign policy, such as the Vietnam imbroglio and the Iran debacle, indicate that it was merely a curio from an age, happily long outgrown, of diplomatic inexperience. Robert McNamara, who was secretary of defense during the Vietnam War, bemoans, among other things, the cultural ignorance underpinning the miscalculations of the Kennedy and Johnson administrations.[7] The 1979 Iran policy failure was doubtless the result of various familiar pathologies, such as selective attention and wishful thinking in Washington. At the same time the American embassy in Teheran employed few officers who understood Farsi and the local culture. This not only inhibited the embassy's capacity to gather intelligence, but also meant that officials from Iran and the United States often unwittingly talked past one another.[8]

Have we now put this kind of conundrum behind us? Do modern business and other technical elites perform better across cultures than their diplomatic counterparts? The evidence presented in this book suggests a mixed picture: on occasion, an undoubted improvement; often, continuing cross-cultural discordance. The battle is far from won. Indeed, as the circle of international actors widens to include individuals from all walks of life, the possibility of misunderstanding may actually increase. Thus, unprecedented cooperation proceeds in tandem with important cases of confusion in the negotiation, not only of classic political issues, but also of matters touching on business, trade, air transport, aid, and so forth.

In a recent episode, neglect of local cultural factors and the subsequent forced renegotiation of a contract to build a power station in the Indian state of Maharashtra cost the American company Enron $400 million. U.S.-Japanese relations continue to be dogged by incompatibilities. Time and again stylized and damaging cycles of dissonance repeat themselves as U.S. trade representatives attempt to prize open Japanese markets. Similarly, U.S.-Chinese talks in the 1990s on subjects such as intellectual property rights have been marked by a revealing pattern of agreement and infringement. Even the United States and Mexico, despite the signing of the North American Free Trade Agreement and a web of entangling ties, continue to puzzle over features of each other's societies that hinder unencumbered cooperation in areas such as the prevention of narcotics trafficking, the protection of intellectual property, and the extradition of criminals.

Not that cultural dissonance explains everything; far from it. It should be emphasized from the outset that in most cases negotiation failure is more likely to be the result of divergent interests than of subjective misunderstanding. After all, for negotiators to have any prospect of success they must first and foremost identify shared interests. If these are absent, then even with the best intentions in the world the success of negotiations is in doubt. To claim otherwise would be naive and misleading. The thesis expounded in this book is more modest: it is that cultural factors may hinder relations in general, and on occasion complicate, prolong, and even frustrate particular negotiations where there otherwise exists an identifiable basis for cooperation. These cases of cross-cultural misunderstanding are certainly exceptional. The skill and experience of professional negotiators— diplomats and business people—will often prevent incipient misunderstanding from getting out of hand. Every so often, though, important talks are disrupted by cross-cultural disharmony. Appropriate examples, to be presented below, indicate that this is neither a trivial nor a negligible phenomenon. It is worthy of attention. Still, it should not be thought that all international negotiation is a distressing saga of stumbling incoherence.

For a fitting conclusion to this segment we may return to the hero of the *Astoria* affair, Ambassador Grew, whose memoir of his time in Tokyo contains many examples of the difficulties of communication, both verbal and nonverbal. In an address to the America-Japan Society, Grew reflected on the role of the ambassador. It was, he argued, to act first and foremost as an interpreter of the two countries to each other in a situation in which the written word was quite inadequate. "What really counts is the interpretation of the written word and of the spirit that lies behind it," he wrote. With an extraordinarily modern insight Grew then submitted the following radical proposition: "International friction," he suggested, "is often based not so much on radical disagreement as on nebulous misunderstanding and doubt."[9] It is in this spirit that we shall turn to consideration of the effects of cross-cultural differences on international negotiation.

2

Negotiation

The Cultural Roots

NEGOTIATION DEFINED

Diplomatic negotiation, in its strict sense, consists of a process of communication between states seeking to arrive at a mutually acceptable outcome on some issue or issues of shared concern. On the spectrum of diplomatic activity it is to be distinguished, on the one hand, from the simple exchange of views and, on the other hand, from the practice of coercive diplomacy by which one party attempts to impose its wishes unilaterally.

In an anarchic world without any overarching international authority that can resolve disputes and allocate resources among contending powers, it may be useful to think of negotiation as the primary mechanism for achieving peaceful and legitimate change. Indeed it might even be described, in quasi-anthropological terms, as the procedure legitimating the transition of nations from one state of affairs in their relationships to another. Put another way, diplomatic negotiation can be thought of as a kind of rite of passage, analogous to the ceremonies by which societies celebrate the transition of individuals or groups from one status to another. The relevance of negotiation in the transition from war to peace is self-evident: the choreography of the exchanges, implying mutual recognition and acceptance after the dislocation and alienation of war, may be no less momentous than the content of the settlement itself. But even in less momentous situations it is the mutuality, the reciprocity, of the negotiation that is required to cast

9

the mantle of authenticity over the whole business. An arrangement reached by negotiation, and hence by joint consent, is absolutely different from one arrived at by the crude imposition of one party's will on another.

Usually, but not always, diplomatic negotiation is made up of a rather structured exchange of proposals between accredited representatives. This exchange may be conducted formally or informally, verbally or nonverbally, tacitly or explicitly. What cannot be disputed is that the goal of the process is an agreed rearrangement (prospective or retrospective) of some element of the relationship. As we shall see, this rather abstract definition is necessary because different cultures may disagree on important details of the nature and mechanics of the negotiating process.

As well as discussing diplomatic negotiation in its narrow sense of face-to-face meetings between individuals or delegations acting under government instructions, this book will also cast its net more widely to touch upon relevant communications and contacts outside the structured diplomatic setting. As we saw in the *Astoria* affair, gestures without specific diplomatic intention may still have diplomatic consequences. Even internal actions and statements by public figures may impinge on the diplomatic process. Though delivered to domestic audiences, inept articulations and gestures risk being misunderstood by audiences abroad, hindering both specific negotiations and wider international relationships. It is probably too much to expect local figures to be always sensitive to foreign concerns, especially when xenophobic rhetoric still tends to be confused with patriotism. But in an age of global communications and growing economic interdependence, it is not only the professional diplomat who has to be attuned to the sensibilities of other cultures. An intercultural contretemps, as in the Enron case, may easily spill over from the foreign to the domestic scene and result in the loss of valuable foreign contracts and local U.S. jobs, not to mention the harm to national security.

THE NATURE OF CULTURE

The problem to be explored in this book concerns the effect of cultural differences on diplomatic negotiation between the negotiating parties. We must first clarify just what we mean by culture. Any visitor to foreign parts is struck by the remarkable variety of customs, manners, and forms of social organization developed by the human race in the conduct of its everyday affairs. In essence, the concept of culture was developed by anthropologists as a way of accounting for this extraordinary richness. It has been argued since the time of such pioneers in anthropology as Edward

Tylor that the lifestyle of a collectivity is not the result of random and arbitrary accident. Rather, it is the outward expression of a unifying and consistent vision brought by a particular community to its confrontation with such core issues as the origins of the cosmos, the harsh unpredictability of the natural environment, the nature of society, and humankind's place in the order of things.[1] Human heterogeneity results when alternative answers are proffered to invariant questions.

DEF. OF CULTURE

A neat, one-sentence definition of culture can only mislead. More helpful is an ostensive definition, intended to draw attention to the main features of the concept. Amid the welter of formulations put forward in the literature, three key aspects of culture have gained general approval: that it is a quality not of individuals, but of the society of which individuals are a part; that it is acquired—through acculturation or socialization—by individuals from their respective societies; and that each culture is a unique complex of attributes subsuming every area of social life.

From the first feature we may conclude that culture is not to be confused with innate personality, let alone with "national character." Take, for example, the institution of the vendetta or blood feud, the obligation found in clan-based societies to avenge a loss of honor to one's kith and kin perpetrated by members of another group. The duty is remorseless: a family member is killed, a woman dishonored, a relative abused. Whatever an individual's personal propensities, whether he is peaceably or violently inclined, he has no choice in the matter; he must join his fellow clansmen in the act of retaliation or be ostracized by the group—and in collectivistic societies ostracism is an unthinkable deprivation. Thus character has nothing to do with it. In societies where the feud is endemic, even the most outrageous homicide statistics cannot form the basis of conclusions about the personal traits of the individuals who make up that society.

The second feature of culture places emphasis on the methods by which a society implants its way of life in its members. Partly, these mechanisms are formal and conscious—education both religious and secular, creation of role models, propaganda and advertising, military service or its absence, and systems of reward and punishment (widely defined to include not only the courts and prison system, but also the salary scale and the ways communities honor their distinguished citizens, past and present). But, of course, the informal modes of influence that are present in the family home, playground, street corner, and workplace may be no less important.

From the third ostensive feature of culture it follows that the concept is not restricted to exotic artifacts or rituals but equally subsumes material, intellectual, and organizational dimensions. The objects, decorations, homes, buildings, and towns we surround ourselves with are only part of the story, albeit a revealing part. How much about a culture can be learned from the things that are cherished, the spaces that are lived and worked in, the styles of dress and deportment! No less important, however, are a culture's intangibles: the etiquette of personal encounter, the manner in which relationships are conducted (the structure of the family and the obligations it entails, the nature of friendship, the way in which the multitude of social roles is defined), and, perhaps most important, the assumptions inculcated about how life's activities should and should not be conducted.

Culture is fundamentally a property of information, a grammar for organizing reality, for imparting meaning to the world. As Clyde Kluckhohn argues, it "consists in patterned ways of thinking, feeling and reaction, acquired and transmitted mainly by symbols, constituting the distinctive achievements of human groups, including their embodiments in artifacts; the essential core of culture consists of traditional (i.e., historically derived and selected) ideas and especially their attached values."[2] Humankind can be thought of as displaying a rich selection of physical "hardware." We come in a variety of shapes, sizes, and shades, but our capacities and potentialities are astonishingly similar. It is the programming of the human system, the "software," that translates potential into actuality, converting the American ideals of freedom, individuality, and migration into an inanimate object like a mobile home.

Human software, then, is made up of ideas, meanings, conventions, and assumptions. It is the syntax that governs the creation and use of symbols and signs, rather than a collection of items in a museum of anthropology. As Avruch and Black point out, culture is not something tangible, a "thing"; it is not a commodity possessed uniformly by every member of a community, nor is it a set of quaint customs to be learned before a trip abroad.[3] Rather, it can be thought of as the shared "common sense," in Geertz's words, "the realm of the given and the undeniable" that shapes a group's view of the world, enabling it to live together and survive in a certain habitat.[4] Indeed, culture permits community, because without it communication, coordinated activity, social life itself, would be impossible. Culture, in short, rests on shared meaning, permitting members of a group "to perceive, interpret, evaluate, and act on and in both external and internal reality."[5] Cultural analysis proceeds by examining the way symbolic systems—such as the stylized interplay that is negotiation—work.[6]

Since culture forms meaning, it also necessarily lends significance to our perceptions, so that where the city dweller sees only sand, the nomad picks up a host of clues about the nature of the terrain, the presence of wildlife, the weather, the availability of pasture, and the proximity of other tribes. It structures our ideas, so that one group sees work as the fulfillment of human destiny while another sees it as a curse. It shapes our actions, among other things defining the rules of interaction for meeting, parting, bestowing hospitality, trading, begging, giving, and negotiating. Whereas artifacts and buildings are observable, the substructure of principles that underpins thought and behavior is less accessible to the casual observer. Because most social interaction takes place within, rather than among, cultures, we usually take all those assumptions and conventions for granted or assume they are of universal validity. "Surely," we tell ourselves in the West, "all men and women are self-evidently created equal." What a shock to discover societies dominated by caste, social class, or stratification on ethnic or sexist grounds!

A starting point for discerning cultural differences is language: the dominance of rank in Korean society can immediately be inferred from the conjugation of the verb in Korean; the extensive vocabulary in English associated with fair play is a telling clue to American expectations of bargaining behavior. Grasping the central role of language is essential in order to clarify the two key premises of this book: the connection between culture and negotiation, and the validity of talking of culture in the singular— as in "American culture"—when we can all observe a heterogeneous and changing social tapestry. Without overlooking nonverbal forms of communication and solidarity, language is pivotal to cultural identity, since it acts as the communal archive and conveyor belt by which shared meanings are stored and transmitted within human groups down the years from one generation to the next. However, it is its remarkable capacity to actively imprint and purvey changing experience and shifting knowledge throughout society and its component communities that distinguishes language from more static and specialized symbolic systems. Language is a dynamic medium of social evolution as well as of record. It is therefore a powerful centripetal force binding together the subcultural atoms that form the molecule of a national culture. Without it each subgroup would fly off into a different direction. For the focused purposes of this monograph, language has a particular importance as the repository of that shared common sense directing a culture's conduct of negotiation. It is the link between culturally embedded meaning and practice.

Finally, it should be emphasized that the domestic bureaucratic and political loom on which negotiation is usually weaved can hardly be supposed to be beyond the scope of culture. I refer here not so much to the formal institutions established to govern (often copied from foreign role models, such as the British Parliament or the U.S. Constitution) but to the substance of civil behavior. After all, communist states had parties, national assemblies, and constitutions. More consequential are such factors as the prevalence of bribery, the ethics of public officials, the existence of trust in interpersonal relations, the real basis upon which representatives serve (whether to promote the interests of a constituency, clan, or ethnic group), how fresh blood is brought into the system (by co-optation, family ties, success in business, or military record), models of patron-client relations, expectations of leadership, acceptance or rejection of the adversarial system, and so on. Political culture, in brief, cannot be understood in isolation from the wider culture.

PROBLEMS OF INTERCULTURAL RELATIONS

It is not, however, the linear impact of culture on diplomacy as such that concerns us here. The emphasis of this book is not on culture as a simple determinant of behavior but on the effect on bilateral negotiation of the cultural gap (often detectable at the linguistic level) between the negotiating parties. The problem is one of relative, not absolute, values. Of interest is the chemistry of the combination: what happens when culturally dissonant traits react with one another? Take the concept of "face," a prominent feature of both Chinese and Japanese cultures. In a Sino-Japanese negotiation, misunderstanding based on disparate assumptions about face is unlikely to loom large.[7] Not so in a Sino-American negotiation, where the relative gap is much wider. Although the need for saving face is more or less appreciated in the West, the equal imperative in transactions with China of honoring or giving face is almost certainly less familiar; we hardly even have a satisfactory term to express the idea.[8]

A growing literature in the social sciences suggests that intercultural communication may be strongly influenced, and even hindered on occasion, by the confrontation of disparate assumptions, not only about the role of language and nonverbal gestures, but also about the nature and value of social relationships.[9] Unencumbered discourse, it is argued, rests on the interlocutors' possession of a complex and extensive body of shared knowledge, conscious and unconscious, of what is right and fitting in human communication and contact. When this knowledge is absent, inadvertent confusion may result.

Many aspects of cross-cultural activity have been helpfully illuminated by this approach. The use of cross-cultural insights and findings in eminently applied fields such as medicine, psychiatry, education, social work, and marketing suggests that the perspective is of more than purely academic interest. For example, Michael Weingarten, for over twenty years a general practitioner in a Yemenite-Jewish township in Israel, attests to the way in which culture molds the presentation of illness, description of pain, expectation of right treatment, and appropriate setting for care.[10] Failing to understand these differences, Western-trained doctors often are not able to function effectively or communicate intelligibly with their non-Western patients. For the student of diplomacy, studies on the effect of cultural differences on conflict resolution[11] and business negotiations are of particular interest.[12]

In recent years there have also been a number of suggestive applications of the intercultural communication approach to the field of international negotiation. One application has taken the form of the detailed, historical case study. Marie Strazar examined the effect of cross-cultural elements in the negotiation of the 1951 San Francisco peace treaty between the United States and Japan. Her conclusion was that an important contribution to the success of the talks was made in this particular situation by the complementarity of cultural traits. The willingness of the Japanese to adjust uncomplainingly to their surroundings, an acceptance of hierarchy in social life, and familiarity with dependency *(amae)* relationships proved compatible, she argued, with the optimistic and manipulative American approach to nature, egalitarianism in relationships, and readiness to accept a role of responsible leadership.[13]

Another noteworthy case study was Hiroshi Kimura's analysis of the Soviet-Japanese fisheries talks held in Moscow in 1977. He argued that it was not just the objective intractability of the issues involved that weighed on negotiations; the clash of "culturally conditioned patterns of behavior and thought" also complicated matters. Whereas cultural differences acted complementarily in San Francisco, they proved antithetical in Moscow. Japanese status consciousness and acceptance of dependency evoked not indulgence and sympathy but exploitative and brutal treatment by a Soviet Union preoccupied with rank, power relationships, and the establishment of its own superiority.[14]

A second approach to culture and negotiation focuses not so much on the bilateral chemistry of a negotiation as on national negotiating styles taken as subjects of investigation in their own right. Michael Blaker published a good historical study of Japanese negotiating behavior in the twentieth century.[15] Richard Solomon's more conceptual account of Chinese negotiating style is also particularly enlightening given the author's practical experience on the National Security Council.[16] Originally published by the RAND Corporation, Solomon's analysis has also been included in a survey of the negotiating styles of six countries put out by the Foreign Service Institute of the U.S. Department of State.[17]

Another example of the national style approach is a 1989 analysis of Soviet diplomacy written by a former diplomat, Raymond Smith, who had extensive hands-on experience dealing with Soviet negotiators. In a nutshell, Smith argues that Soviet negotiating behavior was marked by three dominant features: preoccupation with authority, avoidance of risk, and imperative need to assert control. These features, he maintains, "provide the context within which specific issues on the table are negotiated, whether the negotiators are two Soviet citizens at the collective market" or Soviet and American diplomats in Geneva." He goes on to make the original observation—usually overlooked by negotiating theorists—that negotiating style is not something neutral, like a golfer's putting technique. On the contrary, the clash of negotiating styles between Americans and Russians may even lead talks to "break down in mutual bafflement and anger." Once this point is realized, it may be possible, by studying the differences between the two countries' approaches to diplomacy, to negotiate more effectively in the future.[18] This assumes, of course, that the parties are negotiating in good faith. As Ambassador David Newsom points out, this might be an unwarranted assumption. When the Soviets saw diplomacy as war by other means, part of an effort to wear down an enemy, negotiations could be dragged out endlessly.[19] It will be interesting to observe the extent to which features of Soviet negotiating behavior have carried over to the new Russia.

Although we tend to think of nations conforming to a fixed negotiating style, we should again beware of viewing the question deterministically. Negotiators can draw on a repertoire of approaches according to need, partner, and subject matter. Negotiating style may be best thought of as a family of possibilities rather than a rigid and invariant preselection. Both William Breer, former deputy chief of mission, Tokyo, and William Clark, former ambassador to India, emphasized this point.[20] Samuel Lewis, former ambassador to Israel, has indicated in this context that Egyptian negotiating behavior varies from region to region. Overbearing in Africa, where they draw on long institutional experience and prestige, Egyptian diplomats tend to deal with other Arabs in a special if superordinate way. Americans and Israelis come in for a quite different treatment.[21] Indian diplomacy exhibits a similar range of behavior. Domineering in its treatment of small regional partners like Nepal and Sri Lanka, India has displayed a painful and defensive sensitivity in matters of pride and status in relations with the United States. When one or both of the parties has a strong sense of hierarchy in international affairs, derived from social stratification at home, the relative status of the parties is likely to influence strongly the ambience of negotiations.

A third approach to culture and negotiation is provided by Glen Fisher, a former foreign service officer with a background in social anthropology and sociology. His work was a pioneering attempt to construct a systematic, theoretical introduction to the subject. The more pronounced the cultural contrasts between the negotiating parties, he argues, the greater the "potential for misunderstanding" and the more time they will lose "talking past each other." Different values, mannerisms, forms of verbal and nonverbal behavior, and notions of status may block confidence and impede communication "even before the substance of negotiation is addressed." Within negotiation itself, he believes, culture impinges on negotiation in four crucial ways: by conditioning one's perception of reality, blocking out information inconsistent or unfamiliar with culturally grounded assumptions, projecting meaning onto the other party's words and actions, and possibly impelling the ethnocentric observer to an incorrect attribution of motive. Fisher compares and contrasts American, French, Japanese, and Mexican assumptions about such issues as the nature of the negotiating encounter; the importance of form, hospitality, and protocol; the choice of delegates; decisionmaking style; national self-image; methods of persuasion; and linguistic conventions.[22]

METHODOLOGY

In this book I have attempted to integrate elements of the case study, national negotiating style, and theoretical approaches described in the preceding section. Within the loose framework of a process model of negotiation (preparatory phase, opening moves, intermediate phase, final rounds, and postnegotiation/implementation), I examine the encounter and interplay of contrasting approaches to negotiation with reference to detailed

historical examples. This historical material was obtained from the recon-
struction and analysis of bilateral international negotiations over a range of
subjects, political and non-political, in the postwar and post–Cold War
periods between the United States and some important, non-European
bargaining partners. Where possible, documentary evidence has been
drawn upon, but secondary sources and also the autobiographical accounts
of participants have proved indispensable. When requested, I have withheld the identity of my interviewees. I also refrain from giving the names
of past or present State Department officials when to do so might cause
embarrassment.

A methodological word of caution: my only criterion for selecting a case
was adequacy of information. The closer the researcher approaches the
present day, and the more relevant the instance for mapping current trends,
the harder it is to find definitive material. Any negotiation that could be
reconstructed in sufficient detail to bear historical analysis was therefore
deemed worthy of inclusion. Obviously, the set of cases finally gathered is
in no statistical sense representative. It is up to the reader to judge whether
my findings are helpful. No exaggerated claim of infallibility is made for
this book. Because the events under investigation were unique historical
occurrences, they can never be replicated in the laboratory, nor surrounding
circumstances held constant while variables are manipulated. No control
group of duplicate negotiations, with only the identity of the parties changed,
is available.

It should be clear that it is sometimes hard to disentangle the precise
impact of culture on a negotiation from other influences. Negotiators tend
to be more conscious of the impact of culture when talks fail than when
they succeed.[23] Nor are participants necessarily the best judges of these
matters. A variety of factors clearly impinges on any diplomatic encounter,
such as system of government, individual psychology and belief, ideology,
public opinion, power, circumstances, and so forth. Thus in any single case
the decisive influence on the course and outcome of events is a question of
judgment, and some may dispute my call.

Nevertheless, examining a range of cases and cross-checking the
accounts of participants makes it possible to point out suggestive trends.
Atypical occurrences are to be sifted out and only those tendencies noted
that repeat themselves over time, in varying situations involving a changing
cast of actors and a repertoire of shifting issues. If a peculiar reaction is
observed to recur, even though circumstances and participants change, one

is justified in inferring that some underlying pattern is present that is a property of the relationship rather than of the individual situation.

Note that there is no pretension here to demonstrate the existence of "laws," in some positivistic sense, of diplomatic behavior. All I am trying to do is to propose more or less convincing explanations of otherwise puzzling phenomena. The student of culture is concerned with interpretation, unraveling meanings, not with providing causal explanations. "Cultural analysis is not causal analysis," argue Avruch and Black, but "the searching out of meanings in . . . systems of symbols."[24] "What is happening here and what does it mean?" is the question, not "What are the correlates of this class of phenomena?"

This study takes the United States as the baseline culture against which other cultures are compared and contrasted. My reasons are practical, not ideological; this is not meant to imply that American culture is considered superior or normative. The project was funded by an American institution and was largely conducted in Washington; and material on contemporary diplomacy—archival, published, and oral—is much more accessible in the United States than in most other countries. The openness of American public life facilitates political research to a degree hardly found elsewhere. As a citizen of none of the states mentioned in this book (and obliged to learn about American culture "on the job"), I did my best to avoid egregious ethnocentrism or cultural bias. Occasionally, where I have come across a particularly apt exhibit not engaging the United States, I have presented it to the jury.

The partners of the United States in the bilateral negotiations discussed in this study (China, Egypt, India, Japan, and Mexico) were chosen as regional great powers with cultural identities quite distinct from those of the United States and its North Atlantic allies and cultural siblings. For convenience, and for reasons that will shortly become obvious, I call them collectively "high-context" states. From the outset, the checkered history of their relations with the United States over the years qualified them as potentially rewarding subjects of investigation. My initial plan was to present each relationship in a separate chapter. Unexpectedly, as my research progressed, the cultural dissonances that have marked U.S. negotiations with one or another of the five states were observed to recur with others as well. It turned out that shared cross-cultural contrasts underpinned U.S. diplomatic dealings across the board. Without ignoring individual variants, therefore, I decided in the end that it would be most interesting to weave my material together into an integrated narrative.

AN "INTERNATIONAL DIPLOMATIC CULTURE"?

A final crucial issue to be considered is the argument that although culture undeniably affects the customs and habits of society at the grassroots level, it does not necessarily influence the behavior of foreign service officers (and other well-traveled elites). Highly educated and cosmopolitan, should not diplomats, irrespective of their countries of origin, be considered members of an international diplomatic fraternity with its own distinctive subculture? Indeed, may not diplomats from different countries be more like one another than like the fellow citizens they ostensibly represent?

In making precisely this case, William Zartman and Maureen Berman argue that "idiosyncratic differences" can be accommodated within a general model of negotiation. They readily accept that there are "national differences in negotiating behavior" and that culture affects "the perceptions and assumptions of negotiators." However, they maintain that "cultural aspects of communication" are "peripheral to the understanding of the basic negotiating process." They suggest two reasons for this: first, "that negotiation is a universal process, and that cultural differences are simply differences in style and language"; and second, "that by now the world has established an international diplomatic culture that soon socializes its members into similar behavior."[25]

A good argument can certainly be made, not only for a single diplomatic culture, but increasingly for a set of functional cultures governing defined multilateral regimes, such as those concerning ocean issues, telecommunications, aviation, trade, arms control, and so on. When technical experts work together over extended periods, become personally acquainted, and develop a strong stake in the success of their joint endeavors, there is every likelihood that they will indeed acquire a common language, a sense of belonging to a professional community.[26] However, although the evidence for the emergence of elite subcultures is clear enough, it would be rash to conclude that this therefore eliminates the effect of cross-cultural differences.

Diplomats themselves are frankly divided over the problem. Some already quoted, such as Grew, Smith, Lewis, and Fisher, are clearly convinced of such effects from their personal experience. As Robert Goheen, former ambassador to India, said in a speech: "There are vast differences in the cultural background of Americans and Indians, which sometimes lead to differing expectations and ways of interpreting experience."[27] However, other diplomats take the Zartman-Berman view and minimize dissonance.[28]

Partly, the debate stems from the varied backgrounds and professional experiences of the diplomats themselves. Service in Bonn or Vienna predisposes one to a more sanguine view of cultural differences than service in Baghdad or Beijing. Another source of disagreement lies in contrasting understandings of the meaning of culture. Zartman and Berman mistakenly equate culture with national character, an outdated and unhelpful concept. While they are right to reject "ridiculous stereotypes," such as inscrutable Orientals and haggling Arabs, no serious student of culture would really propose such travesties. A related error is to identify culture with traditional, but also outmoded, customs and modes of dress. As foreigners acquire a Western education and adopt "modern" habits, it is taken for granted in this version that they shake off the mind-set of the "tarbush generation."

From all that has been said so far it should already be clear that this is an unsustainable way of looking at culture. It assumes, ethnocentrically, that Western behavior is modern and value free, while that of other societies is old-fashioned and idiosyncratic. Culture, seen in this light, is a feature of "backward" societies that they grow out of when they come into contact with the more advanced West, an offensive and patronizing idea. This view also lacks self-awareness of unique features of American culture and negotiating style. Suffice it to say at this point that non-Americans can be as puzzled by Americans as the reverse. Modernity has nothing whatsoever to do with such key questions as whether negotiation is results oriented or relationship oriented, or whether disputes are best settled by confrontation or a more indirect approach. As noted above, sensitivity to cross-cultural distinctions in the language of negotiation, revealing differences in the way each society thinks about the process, can be an excellent corrective to ethnocentrism.

In the final analysis the debate over culture can be settled only by empirical investigation. Nevertheless, one may anticipate findings by suggesting that the true problem is not deciding whether cultural dissonance impinges on negotiation, but determining when it may be more or less salient. The more committed the political leaderships of the parties to any course of action, the greater their convergence of interests, and the greater the power differential, the less likely are cultural factors to hinder talks. The North American Free Trade Agreement negotiations between Mexico and the United States are a case in point. Conversely, the lower the level of political engagement, the more troubled the relationship, the greater the power symmetry, and the more ambiguous the interests at stake, the greater the scope for cultural antinomies. U.S.-Chinese negotiations in recent years over an entire range of matters exemplify this tendency. In between these two extremes one can observe an indeterminate area where much depends on contingent factors such as the insight of participants, the issue under discussion, and surrounding circumstances.

Why, in spite of their worldliness and expertise, diplomats should be influenced by their cultural backgrounds can be accounted for in various ways. Glen Fisher suggests three possible answers. First, no officials can ever completely escape the mind-set of the parent society; it is too deeply woven by socialization into the warp and weft of their thinking. No amount of professional training in later life can wipe away the deep-seated assumptions of childhood. Second, diplomats are not free agents: they cannot stray beyond "the public's [or organization's] tolerable limits of morality or self-image." Were they to do so, they would soon be looking for other work. Diplomacy is about the means, not the ends, of foreign policy. Values, often the crucial barrier between negotiators, are outside their jurisdiction. Finally, it should be emphasized that negotiation is on the whole a collective rather than individual activity and is therefore subject to group norms.[29] We might add that positions evolve within and between various government agencies, and negotiators continually refer to their home base for instructions. The idiosyncratic character traits of individual delegates, as Gilbert Winham demonstrates, play much less of a role than is popularly assumed.[30]

An additional, perhaps decisive, consideration is that in the modern world professional diplomats are no longer the only, or even the main, actors in the conduct of foreign relations, broadly defined. In short, the diplomatic guild has lost its monopoly over negotiation. Such agencies as the Arms Control and Disarmament Agency (ACDA), the Office of the U.S. Trade Representative (USTR), the Treasury, the CIA, the White House, and so on all perform critical diplomatic roles, strictly speaking, outside the auspices of the State Department. Officials from other domestic agencies such as Commerce, Defense, Agriculture, Customs, Justice, Science and Technology, Drug Enforcement, and many others are also just as likely to be involved in major or minor negotiating roles in present-day diplomacy.

Even when "experts in foreign affairs may lead or be present on U.S. delegations," Ambassador David Newsom reports, "such delegations often contain those from other agencies with less diplomatic experience who can be brakes on efforts to accommodate—even by gestures—another culture." In military base negotiations led by Ambassador Newsom of the United States, "negative attitudes of military representatives and their separate communications to Washington were obstacles to agreements that might accommodate cultural sensitivities." A related problem arises when a "drop-in delegation" is sent out from Washington to wrap up an agreement prepared by local embassy officials. Members of such a team hardly have time to acclimatize, let alone learn the local culture.[31]

Private business and nongovernmental organizations are other major actors on the contemporary international stage. Some officials and executives doubtless have broad experience in dealing with foreigners; many do not. Elected representatives, political appointees, and temporary migrants from the private sector are even less likely to reflect the norms of a diplomatic set. How can one speak of a modern select club of international negotiators when the membership is so diverse and turns over so frequently? When Harold Nicolson was an official in the service of His Majesty's Foreign Office (in the 1920s), diplomacy might have been restricted to an elite. Those days are long since gone.

3

Intercultural Dissonance

A Theoretical Framework

So far, I have suggested that intercultural negotiation may be prone to mis-understanding. Some initial confirming testimony has been offered. But before I proceed to the empirical material that is at the heart of my case, it will be useful to present a more systematic analysis of intercultural communication to show why dissonance should occur at all. For this purpose I will use a particularly helpful model proposed by Lorand Szalay.[1] With very little modification it can provide a theoretical underpinning for my study. If it is accepted that a communicatory interaction—the exchange of messages, or proposals, to be more exact—lies at the heart of negotiation, then it follows that negotiation can be considered a special case of communication. Hence obstacles to communication in general may constitute hindrances to negotiation in particular.

THE SZALAY MODEL

Szalay's point of departure is a distinction between the form or code in which a message is sent, and its content or meaning. Our use of modern communication technology, with its mechanical vocabulary (such as "bits" or "packages" of information), may lead to the tempting but deceptive conclusion that communication simply involves the transfer of hard, indubitable packets of data—like so many billiard balls—from a sender to a receiver. According to this analogy, the main factor likely to compromise understanding is the physical quality of the message: Is reception affected by "noise" on the line? Has part of the message been lost in transmission?

The trouble with this simile is that it overlooks the problem of decoding, peeling away the outer husk of a message to reveal its inner meaning. Let us assume that a message has been successfully transmitted at one end and picked up at the other, with no loss of information and no noise to confuse the issue. Is communication now complete? Of course not. Once a message has been physically received, it still has to be comprehended—and comprehension is a matter of psychology, not mechanics. Between human beings, unlike computers or radios, the difficult question is whether the receiver is able to discern the ideas contained within the message, the intention behind the words.

After all, as Szalay points out, "The idea itself does not really travel, only the code; the words, the patterns of sound or print. The meaning that a person attaches to the words received will come from his own mind. His interpretation is determined by his own frame of reference, his ideas, interests, past experiences, etc.—just as much as the meaning of the original message is fundamentally determined by the sender's mind, his frame of reference."[2]

For a message to be correctly understood there must be sufficient similarity, if not identity, between the intention of the sender and the meaning attributed by the receiver. Put another way, the content encoded by the sender must be consistent with the content decoded by the receiver. If the parties involved are able to draw upon similar semantic assumptions, if they both use the same sort of code to convey a certain meaning, then they will be able to communicate successfully with each other. "Since the encoder and the decoder are two separate individuals," Szalay continues, "their reactions are likely to be similar only to the extent that they share experiences, that they have similar frames of reference. The more different they are, the less isomorphism there will be between encoded and decoded content."[3]

Szalay now arrives at a key contention, which is also crucial to my own argument: for there to be real understanding—true communication in the normative sense of the term—the parties engaged must be able to draw upon matching semantic assumptions. And this ability occurs optimally within the boundaries of a common culture or language. As long as activities resting on the precise coordination of message and response, like negotiation, are governed by common knowledge—assumptions and meanings shared by both participants and observers—culture can be largely ignored as a pertinent factor. This is not because culture is absent but because it is understood. Rules of the game construct the game, but players and commentators rarely refer to those rules in order to explain outcomes. If everyone is playing by the same rules, then it is clearly not the rules that account for variance in performance. Because most communication does indeed take place within a given community, this condition of rule conformity usually holds. This is not to say that everyone within a particular community must possess an identical outlook on life; within any group many factors go into forming an individual's lexicon of subjective meanings. However, intimate acquaintance with a culture presupposes reasonable familiarity and the ability to work with a wide range of possible subjective variations—"alternative lifestyles"—on the dominant cultural theme.

But what if, to return to our game metaphor, contestants are playing by different rules, that is, operating on the basis of dissonant assumptions, or systematically violating the rules as the other side understands them? In this case the communication "game," whether the practice of medicine, marriage, or dispute resolution, is put into jeopardy. And this is precisely the problem with cross-cultural negotiation: the "rules" cannot simply be taken as common knowledge and subsequently ignored. Within a given society it is hard enough to reach beyond the imaginative constraints of generation and class. How much more difficult to communicate across cultural boundaries, where there is no organic compatibility between the frames of reference and the semantic assumptions of sender and receiver? Cultural strangers can rely on no shared experience of family, church, schooling, community, and country. Their national histories, traditions, and belief systems may or may not concur. When they communicate there can be no guarantee that the meanings encoded by one and decoded by the other will be at all related. In Szalay's words: "Cultural meanings are basically subjective meanings shared by members of a particular cultural group. People in each country of the world develop their own particular interests, perceptions, attitudes, and beliefs, which form a characteristic frame of reference within which they organize and interpret their life experiences . . . Different cultural experiences produce different interpretations not shown in conventional dictionaries."[4]

Szalay goes on to show how spontaneous word association tests can uncover cross-cultural differences in the meaning and connotations of key terms. Simple, tangible concepts limit the scope for discrepancy. Words attached to basic objects such as foot, sun, and tree translate without much loss or distortion of meaning from one language to another. However, more complex, abstract nouns like justice, soul, sovereignty, and leader are embedded within overall signification systems and possess special associations that may be conveyed only with difficulty, if at all. Szalay contrasts the meaning of the English word "corruption" with its Korean equivalent. In both languages the word has negative connotations. But at a more subtle level the word evokes very different associations to the two sides. For Americans, corruption implies immoral and criminal behavior. For Koreans, Szalay demonstrates, corruption is not considered morally wrong, although they accept that its social consequences are unfortunate. The explanation for this critical distinction lies in differing conceptions of public service. In the United States a civil servant is supposed to be impartial, not to take bribes, and to serve the whole community. In Korea it is accepted that one gives gifts to officials, who have obligations to friends and relatives that take precedence over any abstract duty to society. When Americans and Koreans talk to one another about corruption, therefore, they are unlikely to attach the same range of meanings to the word, even if it is correctly translated. This divergence is not accidental: it is a logical consequence of the different cultural frameworks within which the word is embedded.

In the area of international negotiation the potential for discordance inherent in intercultural communication takes concrete form. Not the simple, unmediated conversation of tourist and local here, but a complex and sustained interchange of proposals over time, overlaid by level after confusing level of interagency consultation, political supervision, and media and legislative oversight. Here is not one game, but a set of games, linguistic, procedural, ritual, each one of which rests on certain conventions or rules. At every step of the way the possibility for a failure of coordination exists.

INDIVIDUALISTIC AND INTERDEPENDENT ETHOSES

To apply and extend the Szalay model to the specific problem of intercultural negotiation between the United States and non-European societies, we have to establish a matrix of cross-cultural antinomies (contradictions) relevant to the diplomatic encounter. A good place to start is the fundamental antithesis hinted at in Szalay's discussion of corruption: that between the individualistic and the communal, collectivistic or relationship-oriented ethoses. Geert Hofstede, in his encyclopedic study of the influence of national culture on management, provides considerable evidence to suggest that many aspects of organizational behavior can be grouped ("loaded") around the two poles.[5] Harry Triandis and his colleagues have also written extensively on the individualism-collectivism dichotomy, demonstrating its practical applicability in training and other contexts.[6]

(I readily admit that the following framework neglects the very considerable differences within the category of relationship-oriented cultures. India and Japan may be as culturally remote from each other as each one is culturally remote from the United States. There is no suggestion that this rather stark, simplified classification has validity outside the context of this analysis. Obviously, in analyzing the various different cultures in their own right one would wish to present a much more variegated and complete picture, while inserting many reservations and glosses. But when individualistic and communal-minded impulses confront each other across the negotiating table, there are sufficient recurrent and characteristic dissonances to suggest the existence of a gap about which it is possible and useful to generalize.)

The American stress on individualism is, as Edward Stewart points out, so deeply ingrained that Americans rarely question it.[7] But emphasis on the individual is an exceptional rather than universally accepted ethic. Individualism is grounded in the Protestant concept of predestination, which emerged in Northern Europe at the time of the Reformation and assures salvation to a predetermined elect who have been granted the gift of divine grace. Because salvation is assured and unconditional, there is no call for the intercessionary services of a priestly authority. Morally autonomous, the chosen individuals need resort only to their own conscience and their personal reading of the Holy Scriptures for guidance to the right and true path.

Individualistic cultures, of which the United States is a paradigm, hold freedom, the development of the individual personality, self-expression, and personal enterprise and achievement as supreme values. Individual rights, not duty to one's family or community, are paramount. Affiliation with a group or enterprise is based on personal choice. Typically, members of individualistic cultures belong to many different groups and associations, each catering to a different set of needs—professional, religious, and recreational. Personal relationships embrace all these areas of activity. Colleagues, friends, and coreligionists all have their separate place in the shifting mosaic of one's life. Mobility is highly prized, and if one social setting loses its enchantment, the individualistic citizen goes elsewhere.

Equality is the prevailing ethic in society and politics. Status is acquired, rarely inherited. Authority is a function of office and, although respected, may be freely questioned. Rights and duties are defined by law, not ascription. Contract, not custom, prescribes the individual's legal obligation to a given transaction, role, or course of action. Similarly, conflict is resolved through the courts rather than by group opinion or informal methods of conciliation. Litigation is frequent. The adversarial approach to debate, in which both sides plead their cases on an equal basis, marshaling their arguments in a logical and persuasive manner, is ubiquitous in politics, education, and business—indeed, wherever opinions differ.

Of course, individualism, particularly its encouragement of mobility and personal initiative, proved to be highly functional and adaptive for opening up and developing the United States (and other "Anglo-Saxon" immigrant societies like Australia and Canada). Its flexibility and openness also permitted the nation to absorb immigrants in a way no relationship-oriented society, trammeled by hierarchy and tradition, could have. Finally, the economic and political dimensions of individualism (the free market and representative democracy), which were imported from Enlightenment Europe and which were so effective in unlocking the natural resources of the country, have become almost categorical ideological imperatives. Their demonstrable success has convinced Americans of the universal applicability of their way of life and their duty to spread its benefits around the world.

The communal ethos, exemplified by the other states examined in this study, reflects quite different assumptions about the relationship between individuals and society. Its origins are to be sought in the historical predominance of the rural village community (and the need for partnership in harvesting crops or irrigating fields); the primacy of the extended family, clan, or caste; and rigid, stratified forms of social and religious organization. The concept of a personal, unmediated relationship between human being and deity is foreign. The collectivistic ethic has the welfare of the group and cooperative endeavor as its guiding themes, and it subordinates individual wishes and desires to that leitmotif. Indeed, the individual is identified on the basis of group affiliation and individual needs defined in terms of communal interests.

Face (one's standing in the eyes of the group) must be preserved at all costs. Dishonor (the loss of a good name) is a fate worse than death. The honor of one's family has equivalent priority; the family name is sacrosanct. In the face-to-face society, where all transactions are personal and anonymity is not an option, no humiliation is ever forgotten. Because the social disruption caused by loss of face is likely to be severe—in some of these societies the feud is still endemic—elaborate mechanisms have evolved to protect not only one's own face, but also that of others.

Within this system individual freedom is constrained by duties to family and community. Group affiliation is acquired by birth and is not subject to personal preference. One's primary relationships and loyalties, therefore, are inherited, in-group, and often lifelong. The abstract concept of duty to the wider community, let alone government or state, is quite unfamiliar. Law, as some disembodied notion of justice, is meaningless. All decisions are personal decisions made on the basis of group affiliation and past favor. Transactions are conducted not within the protective framework of contract, but on a personal, face-to-face basis. "Frontality"—here understood as the quality of unmediated contact with another person—is a word aptly applied (originally by the French) to this kind of relationship.

Within the family the authority of the father is unquestioned, and this model of superior-subordinate relations is replicated at all levels of society and politics. Roles are ascribed. Consequently, members of communal-minded societies accept hierarchy as part of the natural order of things and are strongly status conscious. Education fosters not individual autonomy, but respect for tradition and authority. Truth reposes in the traditions of the group and is not to be uncovered by lone intellectual inquiry or the give-and-take of debate. Wisdom and disputation, an essentially Western conjunction, are viewed as antithetical. Actions likely to disrupt group harmony are to be shunned and those that promote it, highly valued. Confrontation is anathema. Conflict is resolved not by resort to formal processes of law, but by mechanisms of communal conciliation, concerned less with abstract principles of absolute justice than with the requirements of continuing harmony.

THE CONTRASTING ROLES OF LANGUAGE

The contrast in use of language by Westerners and non-Westerners follows directly from the individualism-collectivism distinction and has far-reaching implications for intercultural communication. Basing her thesis on Edward Hall's famous dichotomy,[8] Stella Ting-Toomey sees interactions across the divide between low-context and high-context cultures as particularly prone to confusion.[9] While such a model involves simplifications and stark contrasts, it is nevertheless highly suggestive for an understanding of many of the problems that have emerged in U.S. negotiations with its non-European partners. High-context communication is associated with key elements in the communal ethic described above: the requirements of maintaining face and group harmony. A high-context culture communicates allusively rather than directly. As important as the explicit content of a message are the context in which it occurs, surrounding nonverbal cues, and hinted-at nuances of meaning. Communally minded persons are vitally concerned about how they will appear to others. There is no more powerful sanction than disapproval. Loss of face (humiliation before the group) is

an excruciating penalty to be avoided at all costs. On the other hand, pro-
hibitions tend not to be internalized and may well be evaded if nobody is
watching. For this reason collectivistic cultures may also be categorized as
shame oriented rather than guilt oriented.

Given the importance of face, the members of such societies are highly
sensitive to the effect of what they say on others. Language is a social
instrument—a device for preserving and promoting social interests as
much as a means for transmitting information. High-context speakers
must weigh their words carefully. They know that whatever they say will be
scrutinized and taken to heart. Face-to-face conversations contain many
emollient expressions of respect and courtesy alongside a substantive element rich in meaning and low in redundancy. Directness, and especially
contradiction, are much disliked. It is hard for speakers in this kind of culture to deliver a blunt no. They wish to please their interlocutors, and they
prefer inaccuracy and evasion to painful precision. Truth is not an imperative when a lie avoids unpleasantness. Sometimes the necessary link
between subjective truth and empirical validity may also become blurred,
intention being assimilated to accomplishment, the statement of a fact
being taken for the act itself. Finally, the concern with social effect and not
just the transmission of information results in a propensity for rhetoric and
verbal posturing. Public discourse may be rich in invective, but nothing
personal is meant or perceived in the hyperbole.

Since communal affiliation looms large in any interaction, it is hard for
members of a collectivistic culture to deal with a stranger from outside
their circle. Where the in-group/out-group division is crucial, confidence
can never be assumed; an outsider owes you nothing. Before a frank
exchange becomes possible, let alone the conduct of business, a personal
relationship must be cultivated. But relationships are not simply instrumental; they are, profoundly, ends in themselves. (Not surprisingly, this a
central feature of collectivistic negotiating styles.)

Timing is also important. Much probing and small talk precede a
request, because a rebuff causes great embarrassment. To an outsider, the
high-context individual may appear insincere, suspicious, and devious, but
these traits are simply part of the veneer of courtesy and indirection essential to preserve social harmony. Nor is mistrust a deviant characteristic but
the manifestation of an ingrained caution required for dealing with members of other groups. In their own societies, relationship-oriented people
are justifiably receptive to hidden meanings, always on the alert for subtle
hints known from experience to be potentially present in the tone of a

conversation and the accompanying facial expressions and gestures (body language) of their interlocutors.

The low-context culture, exemplified by the United States, reserves a quite different role for language. Very little meaning is implicit in the context of articulation. On the contrary, what has to be said is stated explicitly. Indirection is much disliked. "Straight-from-the-shoulder" talk is admired. "Get to the point" is the heartfelt reaction to small talk and evasive formulations. People have little time or patience for "beating around the bush" and wish to get down to business and move on to another problem. Why waste time on social trivialities? Doing business should not require the interlocutors to be bosom friends. Clearly, this propensity is associated with individualistic people's relative freedom from group constraints and niceties, and their ability to distinguish between professional and social role-playing. In business, results are definitely more important than relationships.

Language, then, performs on the whole an informational rather than socially lubricative function. Accuracy (the "truth ethic") is the highest virtue. Lying is certainly not unknown, but is guaranteed to seriously undermine personal trust and professional confidence. Politeness is obviously not precluded, but low-context culture hardly sees the need for contrived formulas and verbal embellishments. Refutation is not felt to be offensive. The reverse is the case, because society flourishes on debate, persuasion, and the hard sell. Subtlety and allusiveness in speech, if grasped at all, serve little purpose. Nor does "face" possess the crucial importance it has for the high-context culture. An internalized sense of responsibility, rather than a concern with outward appearances, is the rule. Guilt, not shame, is the psychological price paid for misdemeanor. One is therefore less sensitive to what others say; little importance is attached to hint and allusion. Suspiciousness and an excessive preoccupation with hidden meanings are seen as morbid. Nonverbal gestures are paid little attention. In public discourse, although there are variant traditions, language remains factual and is intended to inform, not impress. Content is taken seriously and rhetoric found tedious. Invective is not easily dismissed as a lot of hot air.

MONOCHRONIC VERSUS POLYCHRONIC CONCEPTS OF TIME

Time is crucial in diplomacy. Major tactical and strategic judgments hang on assumptions about history, ripeness, timing, tempo, and duration. Preparing for a negotiation, one might ask such questions as these about the opponents: How heavy does historical grievance weigh on relationships? How important to them are short-range considerations versus long-range considerations? Indeed, to what extent do they plan for the future? Do they keep appointment books? Is punctuality important to them? How do they perceive the future—better than the past, the same as before, teleological, or cyclical? How do they perceive time—as a road stretching off purposefully into the future, or as an ocean lapping in on all sides, directionless? Is "time on their side"? Do they see it as a sequence or a confluence? At what point should a negotiation be initiated? When do they consider a dispute ripe for resolution? When do they think proposals should be made and at what tempo should concessions be offered, if at all? How patient are they? Can they postpone agreement, and if so, for how long? Do they consider the expeditious treatment of business desirable or undesirable? What do they believe is the optimal point at which to make their truly final offer? What, in fact, is the "end" for them (if any!)—or the "beginning," for that matter?

Traditional societies have all the time in the world. The arbitrary divisions of the clock face have little saliency for cultures grounded in the cycle of the seasons, the invariant pattern of rural life, and the calendar of religious festivities. For peasants, work begins at sunup, when they walk out to their fields, and it continues until sundown, when they trudge their weary way home. Nature, not human will, determines their day; every task—plowing, sowing, reaping—has its due season. Timeliness is measured by days and weeks, not hours and minutes (let alone seconds). Personal encounters are not ruled by mechanical schedules; no conceivable activity could be more pressing or important than human contact. Steadiness, not haste, is the cardinal virtue. What has to be done will get done in the end. And in the overall scheme of things, where the individual counts for so little in the face of much greater, inexorable forces, what could be more futile than urgency?

In some areas of the United States this more leisurely approach to time can still be found, but in the modern metropolis quite different habits prevail. These days even industrialized agriculture demands as rigorous a production schedule as the factory. From the womb of individual freedom and endeavor has emerged a society governed by a ruthless taskmaster—the clock. The posttraditional, corporate person is at its service, his or her day segmented into tasks. The ticking of one's wristwatch regulates all work, play, family life, and social life. Even a meeting between friends is measured and limited by the imperatives of one's calendar. "Time is money," a quantifiable commodity to be allotted with miserly pedantry. In an individualistic culture like that of the United States, grounded in personal fulfillment and the work ethic, "getting things done" is the prevailing value, and life is a treadmill of achievement.

Schedules and deadlines loom over everything. "Once set," Edward T. Hall writes about the American approach to time, "the schedule is almost sacred, so that not only is it wrong, according to the formal dictates of our culture, to be late, but it is a violation of the informal patterns to keep changing schedules or appointments or to deviate from the agenda." Enlarging on the latter point, Hall suggests that American negotiators set particular stock by the arrangement of an agenda and are thrown off balance by a less meticulous negotiating partner.[10] He also contrasts the related American monochronic assumption that it is better to deal with one thing and one person at a time, with the Latin American or Middle Eastern polychronic willingness to handle several tasks in parallel. Just as the latter habit may be unnatural and annoying to Americans, the need to plan everything ahead of time may appear very peculiar to many non-Americans.

Alongside this regimentation of the present, Hall draws attention to features of the American attitude to history that are quite different from those found in communal-minded (and indeed almost all other) cultures. The United States—to state the obvious—is not a traditional society. Americans take great pride in their past. But it is a past usually re-created noncontroversially in the image of the present. The slave cabins are tidied up at Mount Vernon and entirely absent from the spotless lanes of Williamsburg. Traditions tend to be contemporary. If the past obstructs progress, it is to be discarded. Tomorrow is more important. Americans, Hall comments, "are oriented almost entirely toward the future. We like new things and are preoccupied with change. We want to know how to overcome resistance to change."[11]

Americans, then, are mostly concerned with addressing immediate issues and moving on to new challenges, and they display little interest in (and sometimes little knowledge of) history. The idea that something that occurred hundreds of years ago might be relevant to a pressing problem is almost incomprehensible. A sense of history is in no way a qualification for public service. In marked contrast, the representatives of more antique societies possess a pervasive sense of the past, of the long run. They are likely to harbor enduring memories of their treatment at the hands of the United States and the West in general. This preoccupation with history, deeply rooted in the consciousness of ancient civilizations, cannot fail to influence diplomacy. Past humiliations for these societies (which are highly sensitive to any slight on their reputations) are not consigned to the archives but continue to nourish present concerns. To anticipate one of my findings, American diplomats are often astonished at what seems to be the inappropriate and irrelevant obsession of others with "ancient" history. For the Chinese the opium wars of the nineteenth century and the Boxer rebellion are still relevant to and come up in the discussion of contemporary issues. Mexican, Egyptian, Indian, and Japanese negotiators are also conscious to varying degrees of the racist and imperialist outrages to which their countries were subject in the colonial era.

In American society, with its calendars and timetables, the business of government is a regimented affair. Monochronism—one thing at a time—reigns supreme. Despite the concern of the White House and Congress with public relations, there is often disregard for the messages time conveys. In 1989 the *New York Times* published a telling photograph showing President François Mitterrand of France seated at a podium, having just finished reading a statement at the conclusion of a summit conference. At his side President Bush has just sprung to his feet and is anxiously eyeing his wristwatch.[12] Time beckons; on to the next capital. If it's Tuesday, it must be Bonn. A few extra moments would have made for a more graceful parting.

LOW-CONTEXT VERSUS HIGH-CONTEXT NEGOTIATING STYLES: RESULTS VERSUS RELATIONSHIPS

The cultural, linguistic, and temporal dichotomies described above can be seen to generate two quite different negotiating ethoses, both at the conceptual and practical levels: the low-context (individualistic) and the high-context (relationship-oriented) styles. As I have argued at length, unhindered communication rests on sender and receiver possessing matching assumptions. Exactly the same principle applies to unhindered negotiation: negotiation proposals are simply a special case of communicated messages.

Just what obstacles have actually hindered negotiation will be discussed in the following chapters. But first, it will help to point out the characteristic feature of the American approach to negotiating that most distinguishes it from others. Mushakoji Kinhide, a noted Japanese political scientist, believes that the basic incompatibility between American and Japanese negotiators (which he, like many other Japanese observers, takes to be virtually axiomatic) derives from a fundamental philosophical difference in views about the relationship between humans and their environment. The American *erabi* (roughly, "manipulative," can-do, or choosing) style, he argues, is grounded in the belief that "man can freely manipulate his environment for his own purposes. This view implies a behavioral sequence whereby a person sets his objective, develops a plan designed to reach that objective, and then acts to change the environment in accordance with that plan." Little attention is paid by the *erabi* negotiator, according to Kinhide, to the need to cultivate personal ties or to special circumstances. Choices are "either-or" and are made on the basis of instrumental or ends-means criteria alone.[13] In short, results rather than relationships are paramount.

In opposition to the can-do spirit stands the Japanese *awase* (roughly, "adaptive") style, which "rejects the idea that man can manipulate the environment and assumes instead that he adjusts himself to it."[14] Oversimplified, dichotomous choices are eschewed. The world is seen as a complex, ambiguous place. Disembodied generalization bows to the imperatives of personal relationships. Subjective factors—the appeal to past obligation and request for present favor—may figure prominently. An *awase* negotiation, therefore, exemplifies the quality of frontality that we have seen to be such an important element of interdependent cultures. Social realities and concrete circumstances loom large. Negotiation is not an end in itself, to be treated in isolation, but simply one episode in an ongoing relationship. The implication is that short-term wisdom may be long-term folly.

Given that Kinhide was particularly addressing himself to U.S.-Japanese relations (and some features of Japan's negotiating behavior are unique to that country), the contradiction he posits between results-oriented and relationship-oriented negotiating styles truly reflects important features of the U.S.–non-European negotiations examined below. As we shall see, many difficulties, at both detailed and principled levels, derive from this pivotal dichotomy. Reconciling the contradictory requirements of the two impulses may be one of the greatest challenges facing American diplomacy.

Kinhide's characterization of the U.S. negotiating style is certainly consonant not only with the main features of American culture, but also with that ubiquitous pragmatism that Stanley Hoffmann found to be characteristic of U.S. foreign policy. Grounded in the pioneering experience of a young, expanding nation that had taken on and subdued the natural might of a continent, Americans saw every problem, material and social alike, as amenable to an engineering or technological solution. For a society supremely confident of its goals and values—indeed these were self-evident truths—means, not ultimate ends, became the focus of attention. In the foreign policy sphere, Hoffmann believes, "political issues tend, first, to be fragmented into components each of which will be susceptible to expert techniques and, second, to be reduced to a set of technical problems that will be handled by instruments which are equipped to deal with material obstacles but much less so to cope with social ones."[15]

Hoffmann's characterization of the American national style is exemplified by the theoretical literature on negotiation produced in the United States. An entire "how to negotiate" literature, the guiding principle of which is instrumental and manipulative, crowds the bookshelves. Howard Raiffa, whose *Art and Science of Negotiation* is the best of its type, demonstrates how negotiators can break down a problem into its component parts, evaluate the relative costs and benefits of various negotiating options, and arrive at a solution that may maximize the payoffs to both sides.[16] Roger Fisher and William Ury, in their immensely successful *Getting to Yes*, propose a variety of "creative problem-solving" techniques intended to facilitate efficient and expeditious outcomes that will leave everybody better off.[17] Zartman and Berman, emphasizing the distinction central to the manipulative style (and alien to the adaptive approach), ask us to "remember that the problem, not the opponent, is the 'enemy' to be overcome. It is the problem that prevents good and beneficial relations and sours the other party's perception of things (including yourself), so the other party needs help to solve the problem, often against his own will and perception."[18]

For cultures preoccupied with relationships, "payoffs" cannot be detached from the relationship they derive from and must ultimately serve. To separate people from a problem can mean little if issues are always seen through the prisms of relationships. What price a good result or an "optimal solution" if the cost is the ruin of the attachment? Between individuals, companies, or nations, communal cultures believe, the benefits of a long-term, healthy relationship must always outweigh short-run considerations.

THE CASE OF THE "RECALCITRANT" PRIME MINISTER

The 1993 case of the "recalcitrant" prime minister, drawn from Australian-Malaysian relations, nicely illustrates the major themes of this chapter. The background to the affair was the redrawing of the map of institutional affiliations under way in the Pacific region since the end of the Cold War. On the one hand, Australia sought to redefine its international identity, realigning itself away from Europe to Asia. On the other hand, Malaysia feared being dominated by a powerful and culturally alien neighbor whose real orientation was to the Western world.

The occasion for the incident was the refusal by Prime Minister Mahathir Mohamad of Malaysia to attend a trade summit in Seattle in November 1993 of the Asia-Pacific Economic Cooperation forum

(APEC).[19] Mahathir explained his decision on the grounds that the United States and its partners had been unenthusiastic about the idea of an ASEAN-type trading group (ASEAN, the Association of Southeast Asian Nations, established in 1967, then consisted of Indonesia, Malaysia, the Philippines, Singapore, and Thailand). Reserved for Asians only, such a body would have excluded Western states such as Australia, Canada, and the United States, and would have allowed Malaysia to play a central regional role. Mahathir was a major advocate of this policy.

Asked in Seattle about the Malaysian prime minister's absence, Prime Minister Paul Keating of Australia gave the following reply:

> I don't know and I don't care. I am sick of asking [sic] questions about Dr. Mahathir. Everyone has a chance to come here. If he didn't come, that's his business. The thing about it was there was just a very historic meeting. Please don't ask me any more questions about Dr. Mahathir. I couldn't care less, frankly, whether he comes or not. APEC is bigger than all of us—Australia, the U.S., and Malaysia, and Dr. Mahathir and any other *recalcitrants*.[20]

These remarks infuriated the Malaysian government, drawing bitter recriminations and sanctions in their wake. The subsequent diplomatic crisis dragged on for almost three weeks and threatened a dislocation of relations and full-scale trade war.

The immediate response of the Malaysian government was that the kind of outspoken language acceptable in Australian society was utterly out of place in Asia. Prime Minister Mahathir said that "Australians do not have the values of respect and manners that Asians do." Therefore, Australia's claim that it was an Asian country was meaningless.[21] Information Minister Mohamed Rahmat added: "In the Australian context it is all right to be blunt but when you deal with Asians you have to be extra careful. If you want to be part of Asia you have to be sensitive to the Asian way of life and Asian culture."[22]

At one level the dispute was clearly a classic cross-cultural clash between high- and low-context cultures. In Geert Hofstede's work on cultural differences, Malaysia and Australia are shown to be virtually polar opposites in their ranking on two central cultural dimensions: "individualism" (as opposed to "collectivism") and "power distance," defined as the acceptability of inequalities in society.[23]

If overall cultural dissonances in the Australian-Malaysian relationship provided fertile ground for misunderstanding, the episode in question also exemplifies the potential for abrasion when loaded terms are translated from one language and cultural context to another. According to the *Oxford English Dictionary*, the word "recalcitrant," which so offended Dr. Mahathir, means "'kicking' against constraint or restriction; obstinately disobedient or refractory." It is not a complimentary word, certainly, but neither does it sound particularly abusive to the Anglo-Saxon ear; indeed, it can possess a wry flavor of grudging admiration. Like other words referring to willful, individualistic behavior such as stubborn, hard-nosed, or aggressive, it has come to acquire the added sense of standing up for oneself in a competitive world, where it is "each man for himself." These positive connotations, however, were entirely absent from Malaysian equivalents of "recalcitrant." Two expressions were used to translate the term: *kurang ajar* and *keras kepala*. The semantic fields they cover include an entire area of denigration entirely absent from the original English. *Kurang ajar* means not just disobedient in Malaysian, but also ill-educated. In Malaysia's collectivistic, family-oriented society, where the reputation of the individual casts shame or honor on one's kinship group, such an implication carried a grave imputation. This disobedient person, it suggested, the prime minister of the country no less, had not been brought up properly; his conduct brought discredit on his family and community.[24] Similar pejorative associations are attached to *keras kepala*. Seen in this light, it is less surprising than appears at first sight that Information Minister Rahmat might conclude that Keating's comments "had humiliated Dr. Mahathir and the Malaysian nation."[25]

The sort of behavior expected of an ASEAN member is described by Thambipillai and Saravanamuttu.[26] Relations within ASEAN, they argue, are modeled on the system of consensual decisionmaking through discussion and consultation *(musyawarah)* found in village politics in Indonesia, Malaysia, and the Philippines. Because, as is typical of a high-context culture, open disagreement and controversy must be avoided at all costs in the intimate face-to-face society of the village—as potentially disruptive of communal life—an elaborate system of prior consultation, mutual adjustment, and synthesis has become ingrained, intended to lead eventually to a unanimous decision known as *mufakat*. The effective leader is one who is able to meld together contrasting viewpoints into a single, generally accepted conception. Projected onto the international arena, *musyawarah* requires that negotiations be conducted in a face-saving manner that ensures continuing harmony among the participants. Confrontation is avoided at all costs; rather than register a blunt contradiction of others' positions, postponement and further attempts at conciliation are preferred.

Aggressive behavior, outspokenness, and crude directness are completely unacceptable. Unfortunately, these were precisely the qualities displayed by Prime Minister Keating in his "recalcitrants" outburst. In this he was doing no more than acting in conformity with the accepted, low-context norms of Australian public life.

It proved extraordinarily difficult to retrieve the situation following the Seattle incident. Just as Keating had stumbled inadvertently into a trap for which sound Australian common sense had hardly prepared him, so did his cultural conditioning deprive him of the tools of reparation obvious to Malaysians: as far as Mahathir was concerned, the appropriate remedy for insult was a *public apology*, and this was soon made clear by the Malaysian government and media.[27] For a time, Keating rejected this out of hand, going so far as to suggest that it was Australia that was the injured party.[28] Following warnings and a verbal protest from Kuala Lumpur, Keating then wrote a letter to Mahathir putting the incident "in some sort of context" and claiming "that what I said was not calculated to offend him." The issue had been blown out of proportion, it was not in the long-term interests of either party for it to continue, and they should put it behind them.[29] Mahathir's reaction was that the letter was "not in the least . . . an apology," and did "not even appear conciliatory." Though Keating's words "were not meant to be offensive . . . they cannot but be interpreted as being offensive." The Malaysian foreign minister concluded that the letter had actually made things worse. "The letter sent by Keating to Dr. Mahathir Mohamad does not come from a person who appears to be sorry and regrets what happened as a result of his own remarks which went beyond extreme [*sic*] . . . what disappoints us most is that his letter neither offers an apology nor shows any interest to be friendly."[30] There were implied threats of trade sanctions and a downgrading of relations.[31]

Only now did Keating take the step called for all along. Appearing on television on December 5, the Australian prime minister stated: "If my remarks were not intended to offend him and he has taken offence, naturally one would regret that." This albeit backhanded apology was repeated by Foreign Minister Gareth Evans in Parliament and by Federal Trade Minister Peter Cook on a mission to Kuala Lumpur.[32] Mahathir quickly pronounced himself satisfied with Keating's expression of regret and declared the quarrel at an end.[33]

One does not need to be a conflict resolution expert to see that some kind of apology was the fitting antidote for the insult to Dr. Mahathir, whether real or imagined. Why, then, was the Australian government unable to arrive at an elegant solution much sooner? Partly the responsibility must lie with Mr. Keating personally. In the end he was the truly "recalcitrant" prime minister. But it is also possible to interpret the affair as a cross-cultural misunderstanding over the form apology should take. The *Oxford English Dictionary* defines "apologize" as "To speak in, or serve as, justification, explanation, or palliation of a fault, failure, or anything that may cause dissatisfaction; to offer defensive arguments; to make excuses." As the dictionary definition makes clear, it is an act undertaken by the wrongdoer; something that the one who apologizes bestows on the aggrieved party. It would probably not be considered appropriate for remedying a serious grievance, but rather seen as a supplementary device or one used for making rather minor amends.

Within societies—like Malaysia's—organized on hierarchical, kin-based lines, apology is an important way of disposing of a dispute. When a conflict occurs that threatens relationships within the community, apology, taking an elaborate, stylized form of entreaty and deference, enacts the humble status of the petitioner and the superior status of the forgiver. In this way honor is requited and hierarchy reaffirmed. Anger cannot be maintained and retribution inflicted when the injured party's superior rank has been recognized and mercy requested.[34] A lexical analysis may further clarify the difference between Malay and Anglo-Saxon sensibilities: Malay has no exact words to denote "apology" or "apologize." The expressions commonly used are *meminta maaf, menuntut maaf,* and *meminta ampun,* meaning to ask or pursue forgiveness or pardon from someone who has been wronged. Unlike English, where apology is framed as an action taken by the apologizer, Malay places the onus on the aggrieved party to absolve the offender as an act of grace. The Malay does not "apologize," he begs for pardon.

Because Mahathir felt that he had been slighted in public and his family background impugned, it was natural for him to expect a public acknowledgment of contrition on Keating's part accompanied by an appeal for forgiveness. At first, Keating completely failed to grasp the unavoidable need to express regret in order to restore harmony to the relationship, and clumsily transformed the dispute into an irrelevant contest of wills, in the polemical, confrontationary tradition. When he finally understood the need to apologize he did so in the exact manner surrounding the usage of the term in English: he *explained* what had gone wrong, shifting the blame on extenuating circumstances ("putting it in some sort of context"), and even suggested that the ostensibly injured party was partly responsible in that he had misunderstood remarks that were not intended to offend.[35] It should be noted that it was just this parade of excuses and self-centered claim to have been misinterpreted that so annoyed Mahathir. If Keating absolved himself of all responsibility there could be no true appeal for forgiveness. "Intention alone will not suffice," the Malay leader complained. "If our intention is good but we utter bad words, people will only remember our words and not our intentions."[36]

In the end, the message that Malaysian diplomacy had been hammering home for almost two weeks finally got through and Keating used the magic word "regret" on television, a public apology. Mahathir, his superior status symbolically acknowledged, could now graciously grant pardon, canceling planned punitive action against Australia. "The Government is of the view that the matter has brought about greater Australian appreciation of the sensitivities of Malaysians, which should help prevent similar incidents in the future."[37]

4

What Is Negotiable?

Behind every negotiation there must be a prior agreement to negotiate in the first place. Unless the wider relationship permits it and the parties agree to discuss a certain matter, there can be no detailed negotiation at all. Before considering the mechanics of negotiation, then, it is necessary to ponder the taboo areas in high-context–low-context negotiating. Two broad topics have proved especially delicate for U.S. diplomacy in its dealings with non-European countries: status and sovereignty. The fact that these themes are particularly (though not exclusively) loaded for communally minded societies, with their preoccupation with relationships and hierarchy, should come as no surprise in light of the discussion so far. Given American power, U.S. relations with China, Egypt, India, Japan, and Mexico have been inevitably marked in the past by greater or lesser degrees of inequality. Although regionally dominant and possessing great pride in their ancient civilizations, the latter have often been cast in the role of supplicant or dependent.

Regrettably, some American officials and public representatives have made their own sense of superiority only too obvious. For instance, as director of the Office of Management and Budget under President Nixon, George Shultz was present at a meeting in Tokyo in 1970 between U.S. ambassador Armin Meyer and Minister of International Trade and Industry Kiichi Miyazawa. He describes Meyer berating the Japanese minister in such an offensive manner that the latter threatened to walk out! Toughness, Shultz reflects, is one thing; "bashing" quite another. "It is visceral and transmits a sense of disdain and dislike, if not hatred. It can lead to a reciprocal sense of distrust and distance that is entirely counterproductive."[1]

For an Egypt of almost sixty million people, the historic leader of the Arab world, it is galling to depend on the United States for its daily bread, let alone economic assistance, and to be treated as a second-rate nation, increasingly sidelined by regional developments. For India—soon to be the most populous nation on Earth—humiliation by British rule and a continued obsession with caste make subordination (and, maybe worse, diplomatic neglect) hard to swallow. China finds it insufferable to be lectured to on human rights, excluded from the World Trade Organization, and generally not given what it considers its due. Mexico has had the special problem of living in poverty in the shadow of a mighty neighbor: "Poor Mexico," as that country's nineteenth-century president Porfirio Díaz famously observed. "So far from God, and so close to the United States." Japan for long presented a rather different picture: cast adrift by defeat in the Second World War it did welcome the security of protection, recognizing in it the familiar and reassuring Japanese *amae* relationship of benefactor and dependent.

In all these cases the touchy questions of recognition and respect are, if anything, becoming more sensitive than ever as the relative status of the parties changes, as the unchallenged supremacy of the United States is widely perceived to erode, and especially as other countries grow richer. Japan has recently found a more independent voice and lays claim to being treated as an equal partner. China, with annual growth rates of 9 percent over the past fifteen years, considers itself, in Lucian Pye's term, "a superpower-in-waiting."[2] Suddenly, it awaits with keen and pleasurable anticipation the prospect of righting the wrongs that were its humiliating lot in unequal relations with the West over the past one hundred fifty years. Egypt and India continue to express resentment at what they feel is their unjustified neglect, but there is not as yet much they can do about it. Only relations with Mexico, since the conclusion of the North American Free Trade Agreement (NAFTA), display far-reaching changes, but here, too, great sensitivities remain. The January 1995 U.S. rescue of the Mexican peso was a graphic reminder of the fundamental asymmetry of the partnership.

But where, the reader may wonder, does cross-cultural dissonance enter the picture? Is the United States not equally sensitive to issues of status and sovereignty? It is true that the United States has taken immense pride in being "number one" in the postwar world and has displayed resentment at such perceived intrusions as Japanese real estate purchases and corporate acquisitions (while, significantly, ignoring the extent of British and Dutch equity in the U.S. economy). However, compared with the inordinate sensitivity of its collectivistic partners on these matters, the United States is relatively relaxed. It has attached great importance to military capability but not to the outward trappings of prestige for its own sake. No, the main source of dissonance lies elsewhere—in the belief of many Americans (to quote the title of a best-selling book on negotiation) that "you can negotiate anything."[3] The fact is that, in international relations, you cannot. To believe otherwise is a recipe for disappointment. McGeorge Bundy, a national security adviser in the 1960s, criticized President Johnson for precisely this culture-bound illusion. "Johnson treated Third World leaders like Senators," Bundy later observed. "He presumed that they were all reasonable men who could be persuaded to compromise on almost any issue if the right combination of threats and incentives was employed."[4]

PRIDE AND STATUS

The major obstacle to negotiation may lie, then, not in some vagary of the negotiating process, but in the inability of the parties to get to the bargaining table at all or, once there, to get the negotiations off the ground. This inability may simply arise from a hard-nosed calculation that no benefit is to be gained from negotiation. On the other hand, in a number of cases investigated during this study, negotiations bogged down for more subjective reasons.

Indian pride, I was told by diplomats, has long hobbled ties with the United States. Time and again Indian officials and leaders have taken umbrage at real or imagined insults to their national dignity. Indeed, my interviewees were outspoken. One U.S. Foreign Service officer suggested that Indians walk around with a "chip on their shoulder" and suffer from a melancholia derived from the thought that the world is looking down on them. Another senior official, not long back from the subcontinent, mused in contrast that Delhi's problem was that it looked down on U.S. diplomats, with a sort of "Anglophilic snobbery," as a bunch of "country bumpkins—brash and crude, if well meaning." A third official identified a "Krishna Menon syndrome" (after the prickly Indian foreign and defense minister) compounded of a mixture of arrogance and hypersensitivity and found in certain quarters (by no means all) of the Indian foreign ministry from junior official to minister. A perceived imputation on their intellectual ability, any sign of arrogance or superiority, would produce an explosion.

Since the early 1990s, with the breakup of the Soviet Union and liberalization of the Indian economy, U.S.-Indian relations have greatly

improved. Increasingly, since the 1970s and early 1980s, American companies, including PepsiCo, Kellogg, and General Electric, have been investing
in India in growing numbers. Nevertheless, acute sensitivities dating back
to India's independence in 1947 have not disappeared. This was graphically
brought home in a 1993 diplomatic crisis when the new U.S. assistant secretary for South Asia, Robin Lynn Raphel, was ruthlessly pounced upon
for an injudicious remark at an off-the-record, background briefing for
journalists. Replying to a question, Raphel noted—accurately—that the
United States did not recognize the 1947 document by which the local
prince ceded Kashmir to India "as meaning that Kashmir is forevermore
an integral part of India." A hysterical Indian reaction followed: the press
was vitriolic; the issue was brought up in local elections; parliamentarians
accused the United States of sinister motives; a strong protest was lodged
by the Indian government; the Indian president, reverting to the language
of anticolonialism, rejected foreign "interference." Anti-American sentiment was so strong that acting U.S. ambassador Kenneth C. Brill felt
obliged to answer charges in a statement published in a leading newspaper.
The crisis was then exacerbated in February 1994 when President Clinton
expressed concern at "the abuse of human rights [by the Indian army] in
Kashmir." Threatening to disrupt administration policy in other areas, the
dispute was terminated only by a conciliatory visit to Delhi in April 1994
by Deputy Secretary of State Strobe Talbott.[5]

What had gone wrong? Obviously, Raphel's remark was tactless, and
she should have known how paranoid India tends to be about anything
related to Pakistan, Kashmir, or the integrity of the Indian union. There
was, though, an underlying source of Indian grievance—the sense that the
Clinton administration was indifferent to India and systematically failed to
acknowledge its leading international standing. In April 1993 Thomas
Pickering, the senior U.S. ambassador, was transferred, after only a few
months in Delhi, to Moscow. As if this was not bad enough, the nomina-
tion of his projected successor, former New York congressmen Stephen
Solarz, was held up for over a year, reportedly by FBI background checks.
As John Anderson rightly noted: "Indians, whose society is based on a
caste hierarchy, see the year-long absence of a U.S. ambassador in Delhi as
a sign of their low status with Washington."[6] The choice of Raphel herself
as assistant secretary of state compounded the perceived slight, because
before her appointment she had been simply a senior political officer in the
Delhi embassy. "What in hell gives some pup of an American officer the

right to question the boundaries of our country?" was the way a leading Indian columnist put it.[7]

As with so many disputes over prestige and hurt feelings the antidote to the crisis lay in a symbolic remedy. The Strobe Talbott trip was a signal that the Clinton administration did not after all intend to neglect the region. Talbott invited Prime Minister P. V. Narasimha Rao to Washington, and requested approval of top diplomat and Defense Under Secretary Frank Wisner as new ambassador. Talbott's manner was exemplary: "He said things like, 'I've come to consult,' 'I've come to ask,' 'An invitation has been extended,' instead of it being presented, as it had till then, as a sort of summons."[8] Sticklers for European-style protocol, this was the kind of deference that the Indians yearned for.

None of the other relationships examined here reflected quite this intensity of psychological ambivalence, but a concern that the outer trappings of equality be meticulously respected was ubiquitous. When the United States intercepted an Egyptian airliner carrying suspected Palestine Liberation Organization (PLO) terrorists over the Mediterranean in October 1985, old resentments were aroused. President Mubarak talked of an injury to "the pride of every single Egyptian." Memories of the British occupation flooded to the surface. "We are a nation of over 40 million, with 7,000 years of history behind us, not a bunch of 'coolies' to be pushed around by colonial masters," remarked an *al Ahram* newspaper commentator. "Don't think that because we are a poor country we are not a proud country. Even if we starve, our national pride will not be for sale."[9]

Since the restoration of diplomatic relations in 1974, American officials in Cairo have been well briefed on Egypt's sore points. It was not always so. After the 1967 Arab-Israeli war, prospects of negotiation hinged on the restoration of Egypt's shattered pride. Yet Mohamed Riad, who was Egyptian foreign minister at the time, recalls that Secretary of State William Rogers cautioned one Egyptian diplomat not to "forget that you have lost the war and therefore have to pay the price."[10] In contrast, the breakthrough in U.S.-Egyptian relations following the 1973 October war was facilitated by Secretary of State Henry Kissinger's grasp of the need to establish President Anwar Sadat's status as an equal. At their very first meeting Kissinger did so by first addressing Egypt's military achievements in the recent war. The Egyptian president, it was implied, "was not negotiating from weakness; he was not a supplicant; he had earned Egypt's right at the conference table; he had, in short, restored Egypt's honor and self-respect."[11]

Recently, Egypt has felt itself less central to U.S. policy. Talk of a "new Middle East" based on economic cooperation threatens to downgrade Egypt, given its weak economy. In May 1995 a multilateral conference, following a major U.S. diplomatic effort, permanently extended the Nuclear Nonproliferation Treaty (NPT) barring the spread of nuclear arms. Yet for many months Egypt had resisted direct American appeals to cooperate, including a visit to Cairo by the secretary of state, and had waged an international countercampaign to link extension of the treaty to Israel's signature of the pact. Israel declined to sign the NPT in the absence of peace treaties with all its regional opponents, including Libya, Syria, Iraq, and Iran. Egypt had originally joined the NPT in 1968—and indeed Sadat had made peace with Israel—despite Israel's nuclear program.

Just as in the Raphel affair, Egypt's position on the NPT, which complicated relations with its superpower patron over a long period, derived from considerations of status even more than of substance. As a senior state department official indicated, Egypt's self-perception since 1993 was that it was being marginalized, that it no longer had a "best buddy" in Washington to look after its interests, and that it had been consistently ignored on a string of regional issues. As a result Egyptians were afraid that they had lost their premier position in American eyes. Egypt's foreign minister, Amr Moussa, half-hinted that the NPT dispute and his coolness toward Israel were really about primacy in the Middle East: "If people say relations between us are at their most tense, fine, we have to live with that," he told an interviewer. "Egypt will not say yes to everything Israel says." He was particularly annoyed at the suggestion that the Israeli economy, far larger than that of Egypt, would become a regional magnet. "It cannot happen, because Egypt is half of the Arab world!"[12] But this was true only in demographic, not economic terms.

In the end, the NPT dispute was resolved by a direct appeal from President Clinton on an official visit by President Mubarak to Washington. Pulling out all the pomp and protocol stops at his disposal to emphasize his guest's stature, Clinton succeeded, like Kissinger in his time, in symbolically affirming the equality of his Egyptian counterpart.

China has been quite explicit in its demand for equal treatment in relations with the United States, a desire fueled by recollections of the unequal treaties foisted on it during the nineteenth century and heightened by exclusion from a seat in the United Nations Security Council in the 1950s and 1960s. Pointing out this background, Kenneth Young rightly notes that "a century of humiliation at the hands of the Western powers, including

Russia, has made the 'Central Country' unusually sensitive to slighting and disrespectful treatment."[13] In 1954–55, U.S. acceptance of the "principle of equality and reciprocity" was a fundamental Chinese condition for the repatriation of American civilians held in China after the revolution, even though Chinese citizens were free to leave the United States at any time (most did not wish to).[14] In February 1970, on the eve of the breakthrough in Sino-American relations after a generation of dislocation, China made it known through the good offices of Pakistan that it was prepared to accept a U.S. envoy. The vital proviso was added that "they would, however, be upset if the United States were to give the impression that Chinese overtures derived from weakness or from fear." Kissinger immediately passed on the desired assurance.[15]

Although President Bush, having served as U.S. envoy to Beijing under Nixon, had a very clear sense of China's strategic importance to the United States, during the first years of the Clinton administration the need for a steady, long-term relationship as befits two great powers tended to be obscured. The two sides found themselves embroiled in a series of quarrels over human rights, trade policy, arms proliferation, and the status of Taiwan. In fact, at the very first meeting of President Clinton and President Jiang Zemin at Seattle in 1993, the Chinese leader had returned to the old theme of the need to establish a relationship based on full equality. In his presentation Jiang spoke for fifteen unbroken minutes on the two countries' complementary futures, "China as the biggest developing country, the United States as the biggest developed country." Moreover, deeply unhappy at being chastised on various matters—as though China was the pupil and the United States the teacher—Jiang pointedly remarked in public, "When the leaders of two of the largest countries in the world get together, we should talk about bigger problems."[16] Unfortunately, this message was not at first heard by Clinton and over two years later Jiang was obliged to remind a U.S. Senate delegation that the basis of relations could only be mutual respect, the search for common ground, and equal treatment.[17]

The Mexican sense of pride and honor is well known and never far from the surface in dealings with the "colossus to the north." Injuries to national pride have often been placed at the door of the United States. Old wars, interventions, and occupations can still rankle. Offended pride has prevented or aborted negotiations in the past: postwar civil aviation negotiations failed for this reason. "We have failed," wrote a senior State Department official in 1950, "to appreciate and understand Mexico's desire to be treated on a basis of equality."[18] However, although Mexican sensitivity remains, most American diplomats today are only too conscious of the need for tact. Former ambassador John Jova (1974–77) noted that he had always borne in mind the need to avoid "humiliating them." Any issue might trigger a sense of offended pride and public criticism was usually counterproductive.[19] President Reagan's ambassador to Mexico, John Gavin, hardly endeared himself to his hosts with his proconsular propensity to preach. Even since the successful negotiation of NAFTA, and the undoubted, dramatic change for the better in relations, Mexico remains sensitive. At an international conference held in Mexico City in 1996, Drug Enforcement Administration director Thomas Constantine got into hot water for warning of increased efforts by drug traffickers to launder money through the Mexican banking system. Although he chose his words carefully, and apparently had good reason to believe his allegations to be accurate, they aroused the ire of the Mexican Foreign Ministry, which accused him of "making unfounded allegations against Mexican bankers" and striking a combative tone. For a short time this seemingly unwarranted and inflated incident diverted attention from the real problems.

Among the cases considered here, Japan's has unique features by virtue of its defeat and occupation at the hands of the United States. Like other collectivistic societies, Japan has viewed the international community, by analogy with domestic society, in hierarchical terms. Confirming this basic point, Kano Tsutomu perceives a national preoccupation with Japan's ranking in the world pecking order, which goes together with "hypersensitivity about international reputation and image." He argues that, as a consequence, the search for national identity has been a "traumatic experience." Shocked out of centuries of self-imposed international isolation by the arrival of Commodore Perry, uninvited, in the Bay of Yedo in 1853, Japan "became plagued with a strong sense of inferiority regarding the West." Once an unparalleled national effort at modernization had raised Japan to the ranks of the great powers, it then acquired a sense of superiority toward its Asian neighbors.[20]

After the catastrophe of defeat in the Pacific War, the Japanese, with resignation in the face of the inevitable, "accepted the fact that they had been put into a secondary position in the world."[21] Japan was bluntly informed in September 1945 by the occupation authorities that "the Allied powers do not regard Japan as an equal in any way. Negotiations take place among equals—and the Japanese are not to be led to believe that they have already gained the respect of the world or a status where they can 'negotiate' over orders of the Supreme Commander," General Douglas MacArthur.

For years Japan was content to accept, at the international level, a relationship of ward and guardian vis-à-vis the United States (without necessarily agreeing on what this relationship implied). But the unequal provisions of the 1951 security treaty were rapidly overtaken by events as Japan recovered its economic strength and national self-confidence. Revision of the treaty so that it reflected, at least in form, an appearance of mutuality became vital to the preservation of the alliance. This revision was successfully carried out in 1960. Even then, unprecedented public emotion in Japan over the issue resulted in the last-minute cancellation of a visit by President Eisenhower and the resignation of the Japanese prime minister.[22]

Culturally grounded differences about the obligations imposed on the two sides by the partnership were at the root of another traumatic episode in postwar U.S.-Japanese relations, the notorious "Nixon shock" of 1971, when the decision of the American president to visit Beijing was announced without prior consultation with Japan. Observers believe that long-term damage was done to the relationship by this episode—which was, it should be stressed, one of form, not substance. Japan was unquestionably the major ally of the United States in the Far East; the implications of the American breakthrough to communist China would be momentous for Tokyo. But the worst feature of the American omission was its disregard for the outward form of the relationship. Was this the way to treat a partner? For Prime Minister Sato, the episode was a public humiliation. Moreover, it could not fail to be interpreted "as evidence that the United States placed a low value on its relationship with Japan as a whole." It also made it more difficult politically for Japanese negotiators to make concessions in economic talks then in progress.[23]

As Japan has achieved the stature of economic superpower, enjoying huge surpluses, year in, year out, in its balance of trade with the United States, the postwar older brother–younger brother syndrome no longer reflects either psychological or material reality. Of course, in the strategic domain history teaches Japan that reliance on a great Western protector is a better option than going it alone. However, as a new generation grows up old habits of compliance inevitably fade. In the end, the brutally confrontational tactics chosen by Clinton's trade representative Mickey Kantor became not only ineffective but also gravely counterproductive in terms of the wider partnership. When Japanese prime minister Morihiro Hosokawa "just said no" to Kantor's ultimative demands on the opening of the Japanese market to American products, it was viewed in Japan as a coming of age. "The U.S.-Japan relationship has matured," commented a senior Japanese government official. "No longer does the Japanese prime minister have to bring an *omiage* [gift] with him every time he visits the United States as if he were some kind of feudal subordinate."[24]

SOVEREIGNTY

Culture is expressed not only in the way a society sets about ordering its existence, but also in the structuring of its priorities, that is, the goals or values it seeks to promote or defend. This structuring crucially determines what a society is or is not prepared to negotiate about. Each of the countries studied had its own area of inviolability—issues it was unhappy to discuss and which, if discussed, proved invariably contentious. For a culturally dominant power like the United States, whose movies are shown all over the world, culture is not something to be protected but rather promoted. Indeed, Americans thirst for variety and innovation. Not so societies that fear that their traditional way of life is under attack from "modern" values (which are usually identified with the United States). An otherwise innocuous project may become the focus for acute controversy the moment it is branded an "instrument of American cultural imperialism."

Differing conceptions of history also have a profound effect on relations. Tainted by association with past episodes of perceived injustice, which still rankle for traditionalist societies, certain topics come to symbolize the national sense of wounded pride and resentment. It takes little to stir up such historical hornets' nests. For a future-oriented society like the United States, such preoccupation with the past seems irrational, even pathological.

Egypt's sore spot has been anything suggesting a restoration of a foreign military presence, with its evocation of the colonial experience. A series of attempts by the West in the early 1950s to bring Egypt into the Western alliance system was abortive. Prime Minister Nasser of Egypt spelled out why assistance tied to a foreign military presence was unacceptable:

> Because of our history we have complexes in this country about some words—especially those that imply that we are being tied to another country. Words like "joint command," "joint pact," and "training missions" are not beloved in our country because we have suffered from them . . . I think your men who deal with this area should understand the psychology of the area. You send military aid, but if you send ten officers along with it, nobody will thank you for your aid but instead will turn it against you.[25]

By the 1980s circumstances had clearly changed and the rawness of the colonialist wound had somewhat eased. The fall of the shah of Iran in 1979 and associated events rendered a military association with the United States more acceptable—provided it was based on the appearance of full equality and did not involve a massive, high-profile U.S. military presence. But old lessons had to be relearned in the Ras Banas affair. In the period of anxiety following the Soviet invasion of Afghanistan, the idea of a U.S. "facility" on a peninsula jutting into the Red Sea opposite Saudi Arabia was conceived of as a contribution to the rapid deployment force. The camp would have consisted of an airstrip, warehouses for the prepositioning of materiel, and some residential quarters. The initial suggestion came from President Sadat, who was interested in cementing a flattering strategic alliance with the United States. He envisaged the camp not as an *American* base, but as an *Egyptian* facility put at American disposal—ostensibly quite a different thing.

Accepted enthusiastically by Secretary of State Alexander Haig and the U.S. Air Force, the suggestion was viewed with foreboding by the State Department. Typically, Sadat had not thought through the details of his scheme. A great deal hung on the terminology and on the way the camp could be presented to the Egyptian military and public opinion. A "base" would be unacceptable, evoking memories of the British, and then the Soviet, presence. A "facility" under Egyptian control would not be perceived as an intrusion on sovereignty. On the contrary, an arrangement of mutual benefit freely entered into would enhance, not detract from, Egyptian status.

Regrettably, the Pentagon either failed to grasp, or was insufficiently flexible to meet, Egyptian requirements. Much of the subsequent negotiation concerned such loaded issues as U.S. military demands for uniformed Americans to be permanently stationed at the site, a transit facility at the port of Alexandria, and an extraterritorial road to Ras Banas. All these proposals were viewed with grave suspicion by the Egyptian army. As the negotiations proceeded, obstacles piled up: although Egypt wished to handle construction and payments, funds appropriated by Congress for military construction purposes legally entailed the use of the U.S. Army Corps of Engineers; and even if the United States gave up its request for an American troop presence, a stockpile of degradable aviation fuel necessitated the presence of trained technicians.

Finally, after negotiations on the original scheme had ended in deadlock, agreement seemed to have been reached on a significantly scaled-back effort. There would have been an emergency "pass-through" facility involving minimal prepositioning. But when a thick U.S. Army Corps of

Engineers specifications manual asking for bids from contractors thudded on his desk, President Mubarak called it a day. Overcoming national sensitivities demanded a lighter touch than this.[26]

Although there are no sovereign American bases on Egyptian soil to this day, close military cooperation, reaching its height during the 1991 Gulf War, has developed. As part of this tacit alliance the United States has been granted selective access to Egyptian military facilities and some prepositioning of military equipment. William Quandt quotes without comment newspaper reports of "secret" air operations and a small "secret base" in Egypt. The vigilance of the Egyptian press on sovereignty issues would preclude anything with a higher profile.[27]

For Japan the question of the Okinawa bases has encapsulated two resonant themes: lost territories and nuclear weapons. The "particular potency," as Dr. Kissinger puts it, of the nuclear issue "in the land of Hiroshima and Nagasaki" need hardly be stressed. Occupied by the United States long after the military administration of the main islands had ended, Okinawa has long been considered one of the most important American bases in Asia. It was also a storage site for nuclear weapons in the past (they have now been completely withdrawn), although these were not permitted on U.S. bases in Japan proper.[28]

When the demand was raised in Japan in the mid-1960s for the reversion of Okinawa to Japanese sovereignty, a diplomatic collision seemed inevitable. Ignoring Japanese sensitivity at first, the joint chiefs of staff argued that conceding to Japanese requests would threaten vital American security interests. Fortunately, it was eventually realized in Washington that the basic issue was nonnegotiable and that U.S. obduracy would simply threaten the whole future of the alliance. Either Japanese wishes might be conceded with good grace or the United States could look forward to the unhappy prospect of a replay of the anti-American rioting that had forced the abandonment of the 1960 Eisenhower visit. President Nixon decided to bow to reality. By agreeing to restore Japanese rights over Okinawa and accepting "the particular sentiment of the Japanese people against nuclear weapons," he succeeded in preserving both the alliance and the bases.[29]

Okinawa, where two-thirds of the 47,000 U.S. troops on Japan continue to be located, remains a sensitive issue. This became only too clear in September 1995 when an Okinawan schoolgirl was raped by three U.S. servicemen. Local feeling against the U.S. military presence ran high, with demands for the removal of the bases. This could not be done without jeopardizing American commitments to both the defense of Japan and the stability of the entire region. Following negotiations between the two parties, the United States agreed on the return and reduction of various facilities including the important Futenma Marine Airfield. Accepting that the airfield had become, as Japanese foreign minister Ikeda put it, "a symbolic issue," both sides saw this as the best way to rescue the overall alliance.[30]

If a Japan chastened by defeat and ruin had made a virtue of necessity and fully aligned itself with the West in the postwar world, India—like Egypt of the 1950s and 1960s—resolutely set its face against such a course. The policy of nonalignment, defined as India's right to determine its foreign policy orientation freely and without duress, became sacrosanct. After all, Indian forces had fought and died in two world wars without even being consulted on the decision to go to war. Not only was alignment in the Cold War rejected, but fierce opposition was consistently expressed to anything that smacked of limiting Indian sovereignty. Even apparently secondary restrictions, such as conditions on the receipt and distribution of aid or the end use of U.S. technology, were taken as implying American trespass on Indian domestic prerogatives. However, in time of dire need India was able to overcome its distaste and displayed considerable pragmatism in negotiations. In recent years a steadily growing economy and increasing interest in Western technology and investment have also blunted the sharp edges of Indian concerns.

India's first crisis of conscience in relations with the United States came in 1951 at a time of famine in India and a desperate need for grain. From the beginning Prime Minister Jawaharlal Nehru was far from "happy about accepting favors from the U.S." and "agreed to request food aid only because he could see no other way for India to surmount the crisis." Even so, he and his colleagues were distraught when the U.S. Congress conditioned assistance on the dispatch of a mission to observe the distribution of the grain and to supervise the disbursement of counterpart funds (U.S. funds held in India in the local currency, to be spent in a way agreed upon by the two governments—in this particular case, Indian development projects). In a defiant speech Nehru rejected help with "political strings attached" as "unbecoming for a self-respecting nation." But in the end he found himself with no choice.[31]

What was to become a question of perennial concern, namely, the end use of materials and technology, first arose two years later when the U.S. government was upset to discover that India was selling thorium nitrate to the People's Republic of China. Under American law, a recipient of U.S. aid could not export this product, which has nuclear applications, to a communist country. Although this provision was not put in writing in 1951, the Indians had been officially informed of the U.S. position. When Ambassador George Allen brought the matter to the attention of the Indian minister of finance, the latter denied that India had ever requested U.S. aid. Then followed long and fruitless American attempts to persuade India to accept some kind of formal commitment to restrict its trade with communist countries if it were to continue to receive assistance. In an amazing scene, Allen asked Prime Minister Nehru whether the Indian government would be at least prepared to inform Washington in advance of future decisions to ship strategic commodities to barred areas. The prime minister wrapped himself in a proud and eloquent silence; he was not even prepared to answer the question. "Nehru," Allen reported home, "stared at the ceiling for a full minute, smiled, turned to Ambassador Donovan, who was present, and asked if he had ever been to Thailand before."[32]

During the 1962 emergency, with Indian and Chinese forces fighting along their common border, India had no alternative but to modify its nonalignment principles and accept military assistance from the West. It also agreed to American legal requirements for inspection of the use to which the arms were put. India went so far as to request U.S. transport aircraft with pilots and crews. But when Ambassador Galbraith decided to press the government of India "to promise a more cooperative role elsewhere" the effort failed. Sensing that they were being drawn into a "virtual alliance," the Indians retreated.[33]

In recent years the end use question has emerged as a central issue in U.S.-Indian diplomacy. Talks in 1981–82 on the supply of nuclear fuel to the Indian reactor at Tarapur were complicated by American demands for externally imposed constraints on the disposal of spent material. Looking back, Ambassador Robert Goheen believed that American negotiators had been excessively optimistic about the possibility of the Indian government accepting the limitations of a safeguards regime (presumably nobody had bothered to look up the thorium nitrate case). President Carter was particularly slow to appreciate the intractability of the problem. Eventually, however, an agreement was concluded based on the supply of French, not American, nuclear fuel.[34] Moreover, in later—albeit protracted—negotiations for the sale of U.S. Cray supercomputers, the government of India, under pressure from its own scientific community, accepted more far-reaching safeguards on end use than ever before.

In the Tarapur and Cray cases the parties were able to conclude compromise agreements that met their minimal needs. This new flexibility over sovereignty issues was exemplified during the 1990–91 Gulf War. The V. P. Singh and Chandra Shekhar governments both secretly agreed to allow U.S. military aircraft on supply missions to Saudi Arabia to refuel at Indian airports. However, both Indian Muslims and Hindu nationalists expressed sympathy for Iraq and opposition to "superpower domination." When an Indian journalist discovered a U.S. military plane at Bombay airport taking on fuel, most of the Indian parties, with Rajiv Gandhi of Congress in the lead, leaped at the opportunity to embarrass the government and make political capital. Chandra Shekhar, cornered by the opposition, was obliged to terminate the refueling arrangement. The affair had demonstrated a lag between government and mass perceptions of Indian interests in the 1990s.[35]

Despite its propinquity to the United States and the enormous range of issues of mutual concern, Mexico has for long tenaciously sought to defend its sovereignty and independence from its great neighbor. Three U.S. invasions in 150 years and the loss of half the national territory have left deep scars. Significantly, Mexico was the only Latin American country to refuse to sign a military assistance agreement with the United States during the Cold War. Washington's request in 1948 for permission to use Mexican territorial waters for defense purposes was turned down on the spot. In 1978 Mexico went so far as to rebuff a modest offer of aid for hurricane damage. Ambassador Patrick Lucey pleaded with the Mexican foreign minister to be allowed to help, but to no avail. Mexico has never accepted Peace Corps volunteers under the Alliance for Progress.

NAFTA, which came into force in 1994, and the 1995 peso bailout changed the game in many respects. The Mexican economy has opened up as never before and the Mexican authorities are cooperating in an unprecedented manner with their U.S. counterparts. Nevertheless, the United States has to tread carefully in its treatment of lingering Mexican concerns. Since 1938, when Mexico nationalized the oil industry and expropriated powerful U.S. companies in the process, oil has been a symbol of national pride and independence—part of the patrimony. The anniversary of the 1938 expropriation is still celebrated as "a day of national dignity." In the NAFTA talks, U.S. negotiators, under pressure from American oil companies, were eager to see Mexico open up its huge oil fields and distribution business to investment and risk-sharing arrangements. Reflecting domestic opinion, the Mexican side remained obdurate on the issue and the United States had eventually to accept that oil would be outside the scope of free trade.[36]

In other fields Mexico has shown a capacity "to break out of historical shibboleths," in the words of a senior U.S. official.[37] Within bounds that the United States has had to discover, there is no longer a strict Mexican military embargo on contact with the U.S. armed forces. In October 1995 Secretary of Defense William Perry made an unprecedented visit to Mexico to discuss military cooperation, especially in combating narcotics. As a result, the Mexican army requested a package of high-technology military equipment, including advanced satellite tracking systems. In addition, the two countries agreed on a training program for Mexican officers in U.S. military schools and a joint working group on security matters. Perry was particularly circumspect during the course of his visit, taking pains to emphasize the sovereignty and independence of Mexico.[38]

The former defense secretary was continually being reminded about Mexican touchiness. Because of dissatisfaction with the handling by Mexican personnel of U.S.-supplied helicopters, American officials suggested that it might be better to have American pilots fly them. The proposal was predictably rejected out of hand by the Mexicans. Then in March 1996 Perry discovered the limits of the possible when he informed the press that he had proposed joint exercises with the Mexican armed forces involving the presence of U.S. soldiers on Mexican soil. He had struck a raw nerve; the Mexican public continues to view the United States as the historical aggressor. Thus the proposal was quickly disavowed by the Mexican government: "We remain firmly tied to the fundamental argument of Mexico's foreign policy, which is strict respect for the sovereignty of nations and the principle that only our armed forces can operate on our national territory," declared a senior foreign ministry official.[39]

HUMAN RIGHTS

What national dignity is to a nation that has suffered occupation or loss of national territory, human rights are to the United States. It is an axiomatic value, beyond argument, whose importance to Americans often puzzles and infuriates others for whom it is not the measure of all things. It is not, one hastens to add, that only the United States has discovered the Just and the Good; these concepts are present in all ethical systems, Eastern and Western. Rather, the concept of human rights is taken by the United States to be synonymous with its own particular legalistic and individualistic formulation of liberty as meaning freedom from oppression as opposed to freedom from deprivation. Moreover, human rights activism (political action to promulgate human rights beyond national boundaries) is a particularly North American and North European preoccupation. Many other societies bitterly resent such activity both as interference in internal affairs and as reflecting a holier-than-thou attitude.

In a sustained critique of the International Bill of Human Rights, Surya Prakash Sinha excoriates it for ignoring "civilizational pluralism." As it stands, he argues, it reflects values and assumptions that simply do not apply universally. "Techniques of the West and even its life styles have been adopted by the world in varying degrees. Nevertheless, there continue to exist various value systems among various peoples of the world, manifesting different approaches to human emancipation."[40]

The bill, he continues, regards "the individual as the fundamental unit of society and the nuclear family as its fundamental group unit. This is an eloquent expression of individualism, which is fine. But the provisions stop there. They do not go any further in taking an adequate account of, say: the hierarchical family of China or Japan; the Hindu joint-family; or . . . African lineage and kinship systems." For example, the bill defines the choice of marriage partner in utterly culture-bound terms; its provision that marriage be based on the consent of the partners can apply only in societies where young men and women mix freely. It is meaningless in village communities, such as in India, where free association between the sexes is deplored and marriage is arranged by the families.[41] Sinha brings many other examples of this kind to demonstrate his case. Other areas of the bill that reflect ethnocentric assumptions are those dealing with social assertion, economic well-being, and conflict resolution.

Different perspectives of human rights have particularly affected U.S. relations with Egypt and the People's Republic of China. Hermann Eilts, ambassador to Egypt from 1974 to 1979, remarked that Egyptians were "indifferent" to the issue of human rights. "Given the life and death problem" of this sorely overpopulated country, many of whose people live in a state of poverty, disease, and undernourishment unknown in the West, there was a degree of "callousness" about compassionate issues. For example, an Israeli request for the return of bodies of troops lost in the 1973 Yom Kippur War, passed on by Ambassador Eilts to the Egyptian government, was turned down. The Egyptian government was not motivated by "spite" but was simply "indifferent" to the issue.[42]

President Carter's emphasis on human rights was greeted with open skepticism. Ismail Fahmy, former foreign minister of Egypt, dismisses it contemptuously in his memoirs as "a pompous and empty slogan."[43] This blatant incomprehension of a leading motif of U.S. foreign policy, the true expression of the American view of the world as a place to be perfected, not viewed with fatalism, can hardly fail to lead to dissension. It can be seen to underlie the 1985 *Achille Lauro* affair, which resulted in the worst crisis in U.S.-Egyptian relations since their restoration in 1974. The crisis came about when an Italian cruise ship, the *Achille Lauro*, was seized in the Mediterranean by a group from the PLO, and an elderly disabled man named Leon Klinghoffer was murdered and thrown overboard. The PLO men handed themselves over to Egypt, which then, rather than complicate relations with the Arab world, put them on a plane for Tunis. President Mubarak claimed ignorance of the murder and then added insult to injury by saying to reporters: "Maybe the man [Klinghoffer] is in hiding or did not board the ship at all." The United States, which had requested extradition of the murderers, ordered its fighters to intercept the Egyptian airliner, which was escorted to an Italian air base, to the chagrin of both the Egyptians and the Italians.[44]

A senior U.S. diplomat who played a key role in the affair mused (in a classic description of cross-cultural dissonance) that "the United States and Egypt looked at the same set of facts and came out with diametrically opposing judgments." Just as "corruption" means one thing for Koreans and quite another for Americans, "human rights" evokes quite incompatible meanings for Egyptians and Americans. The main Egyptian concern was to get the problem out of the way, precisely in order to restore relations with the United States and return to business as usual. Egypt never grasped the meaning for U.S. opinion of the death of an elderly, disabled American. Then, in an atmosphere of mutual recrimination, President Mubarak, reacting as the true son of a shame culture, "wrapped himself in Egypt's dignity," arguing that the PLO men had been guests of the Egyptian government. In this way, the United States was presented as violating Egypt's sacred Middle Eastern obligation of hospitality.

Nothing is more calculated to infuriate Egyptians than Western reports on human rights violations in Egypt. In the 1995 annual U.S. State Department survey, for example, Egyptian security forces were accused of arbitrary arrests, torture, extrajudicial killings, and other abuses in their campaign against Muslim extremists. The reaction of the Egyptian Interior Ministry was to denounce the report as consisting of "lies and fabrications. Upon close reading, the deliberate intention to do harm to Egypt becomes clear."[45] It is not a comfortable posture to be caught between Islamist terrorism and American criticism. This does not mean that it is not possible to promote human welfare in Egypt. The United States Agency for International

Development (USAID) has been able to use the leverage of foreign aid in limiting the practice of female genital circumcision. However, the condition for success has been a meeting of minds and a willingness to work discreetly with the Egyptian authorities (and, implicitly, a sympathetic middle class). Broadcast by CNN in 1994 of a segment showing the performance of an operation on a young Egyptian girl was counterproductive, infuriating Egyptian opinion that deeply resented being publicly held up to disrepute. Although Egyptian minister of health Ali Abdel Fattah then prohibited the practice, he was soon obliged to backtrack under pressure from parts of the Islamic establishment. It then took another substantial diplomatic effort to persuade Fattah to restore the original ban.[46]

China and the United States possess strikingly different interpretations of the meaning of human rights—a source of unending contention. On both sides there are those who fully understand the existence of a gap, but this is not sufficient to bridge it. A Chinese foreign ministry official explicitly put the dispute down to a confrontation between the individualistic and communal ethoses. Asians, he asserted, "give greater emphasis to the rights of the people rather than the privileges of a few. Those who criticize human rights in China fix their eyes only on a small number of people."[47]

Developments since the June 1989 suppression of the democracy movement in Tiananmen Square indicate that no other subject is quite so intractable, with America accusing China of inhumanity and China charging America with meddling in other people's business. Time and again the two sides have reenacted their allotted roles in arguments that often take the form of a cat-and-mouse game in which China arrests dissidents on the eve of visits by U.S. officials and the United States demands their release. The Chinese authorities act to demonstrate their autonomy and indifference to American pressure; the United States, impelled by domestic opinion, is unable to remain indifferent to the challenge. The dispute almost has an element of ritual inevitability, as if neither party can escape its deepest impulses. Many in the United States still seem moved by that old, nineteenth-century missionary vocation to bring God to the heathen. For a Chinese leadership that knows from history that their country is quite capable of falling into appalling chaos, the smallest whisper of dissent is viewed as a threat to the regime. Seen in this light, American support for the democracy movement and solicitude toward dissidents seems motivated less by human rights and more by a wish to undermine the regime, thereby preventing China from regaining its rightful place in the world.

Negotiations over human rights have had a prominent place in U.S.-Chinese relations since the communist accession to power. Three themes have been prominent: the insistence of the United States that the matter involved an ethical imperative, whatever its capacity for political disruption, where China adopted a position devoid of moral content; the willingness of the Chinese side to use internees as pawns in a game in order to extract concessions in other areas, and the U.S. high-minded unhappiness about engaging in profane haggling on a sacred issue—but ultimate readiness to pay a high trade-off price; and the infinite capacity of a negotiation on the subject to generate great mutual ill-will, whatever the outcome. Human rights can never be a win-win subject.

Little has changed over the years. In 1954–55 civilian repatriation talks, the two sides had completely different views of the point of the exercise. The United States envisaged that its representative would meet with a Chinese delegate merely in order to work out the technical details of the release of American citizens held since the revolution. In document after document the State Department repeated the view that to "bargain" over the Americans would be "dubious morally and legally," tantamount to "bartering in human lives." China could not be permitted to obtain "political advantage" from the affair.

From the Chinese point of view, the handful of American citizens was of no inherent interest. The taking of hostages is an ancient practice. China's only concern was to extract an agreement establishing China's symbolic equality of status and obtaining various other U.S. concessions. From the moment the issue was raised, the Chinese government made clear that any accord would have to be based on the principle of mutuality. When the formal talks started in Geneva in August 1955, the American representative, Alexis Johnson, found himself in an invidious position. His mission was to get the captured Americans out, but without haggling over a price. Accordingly, his opening position was not a negotiating proposal in the usual sense but a call for the redress of a moral wrong. No negotiation can be conducted on this basis. This approach left the initiative in the talks to Chinese delegate Wang, who had every intention of bargaining for all he was worth and was able to set his own terms from the outset.

Only at the very end did it dawn on Johnson that the political hostage aspect did not shock the Chinese and that they regarded the release of the Americans as a "political act of grace and therefore directly related to other political factors in relations between the two countries."[48] China's adroit use of the American internees as a bargaining chip demonstrated an understanding of the value the United States placed on human rights. The cross-cultural error was that of the State Department, which failed to see that moral rectitude may not be enough. Nevertheless, the Chinese strategy ultimately backfired. Determined to wring every drop of advantage out of having the Americans in its hands, China declined to release them all at once and dribbled them out over the years, thereby providing a permanent irritant for public opinion and reinforcing its image of inhumanity, whereas a prompt release might have served it better.[49]

Relations between the United States and its high-context interlocutors have often threatened to run aground on the twin rocks of pride and sovereignty. Status consciousness and historical grievance have produced an acute sensitivity on the part of these societies to any issue perceived to encroach on their sovereign rights and possessions. This sensitivity repeatedly influenced, and on occasion aborted, negotiations. Today, on the whole, the parties are more skilled at anticipating and skirting problems than previously. With Mexico, territorial issues or questions of the national patrimony, such as oil and fish (believed to have been long exploited for U.S., rather than Mexican, benefit), were sure to be highly controversial. With Egypt it was anything that evoked associations of the hated British bases or the capitulations (extraterritorial legal rights for foreigners). In the case of India, nonalignment was a touchy issue. For China, a nineteenth- and twentieth-century victim of aggression and occupation, the issue of Taiwan released deep emotions, and legal prerogatives were to be jealously guarded. In Japan's relationship with the United States, a strain of historical resentment persists in public opinion. The Okinawa bases continue to be a sore spot, but the parties have learned together how to conciliate local anger. For many years, Japan's conditioning by *amae* gave it a lopsided view of the obligations of partnership. Of necessity this is giving way to a more balanced relationship.

Collectivistic cultures attach to the issues of sovereignty and national pride the same importance that they associate with questions of honor and status at the individual level. Similarly, form may overshadow substance. Finally, all of the nations discussed here have undergone wrenching changes and severe soul-searching in their common effort to modernize and catch up with the West. They have been forced to ask painful questions about the validity of traditional beliefs and seen cherished values threatened by a seemingly irresistible tide of Westernization. Whereas a new generation of leaders has mostly made its peace with this tendency (at least with its economic dimension), major sectors of the public remain unhappy about manifestations of American influence, whether Kentucky Fried Chicken in Bombay or U.S. troops training on Mexican soil. The domestic gap between elite and mass opinion, revealed most fatefully in prerevolutionary Iran, should not be underestimated. In these circumstances any hint of an American intrusion into the jealously guarded realm of sovereign prerogative—about which non-Western nations tend to have old-fashioned views—may seem to threaten their very identity and self-respect as human beings.

5

Setting Out the Pieces

Prenegotiation

In the following chapters I shall examine the effect of cross-cultural differences on the process of negotiation, drawing on examples from the recent history of American diplomatic exchanges with China, Egypt, India, Japan, and Mexico. Various schemes have been suggested for breaking the negotiating process down into its component parts. One of the most original is that of Zartman and Berman, who conceive of diagnostic, formula, and detail phases.[1] Another imaginative model is that of Daniel Druckman, who sees turning points and crises taking negotiators over a series of negotiating thresholds.[2] With due respect to these valuable contributions, it is doubtful whether they can be considered free of culturally grounded assumptions and therefore universally applicable. Certainly, Japanese analysts of negotiation would find it difficult to agree on the constructive function of either general formulas or crises. On the contrary, the instinct of the Japanese is to make every effort to sidestep confrontation and crisis, and to avoid what they see as the peculiarly American propensity to formulate general rules to cover specific cases.[3]

The framework to be used here (in order to avoid as much as possible the more blatant kind of cultural bias) divides, for technical reasons, negotiation into five rough-and-ready phases: preparation, beginning, middle, end, and implementation. This division is not intended to make any analytical point about negotiating but merely to act as an organizing device.

The reader will discover that even the concepts "beginning" and "end" are not culture free. For high-context societies the ideal negotiation may be one in which all has been agreed upon, informally, before the principals ever meet. Similarly, the conclusion of the negotiation and drawing up of a contract may not be quite as final as their low-context partners might wish, since talks about the meaning of just what has been agreed tend to continue into the implementation stage. Nevertheless, the Japanese, for their part, are certainly aware of the meanings Western negotiators attach to those terms.[4]

The first phase to be discussed is the preparatory one. In recent years the idea of *prenegotiation*, the work of overcoming long-standing, principled obstacles to negotiation, has rightly been emphasized. In the Panama Canal and Arab-Israeli negotiations, for instance, it was excruciatingly difficult for Presidents Johnson and Sadat to agree to sit down and actually talk with the other side. The prior acknowledgment that *the issue under contention was negotiable* involved much soul-searching and swallowing of pride. The major work on the subject, *Getting to the Table*, defines prenegotiation, very broadly, as the phase beginning "when one or more parties considers negotiation as a policy option and communicates this intention to other parties. It ends when the parties agree to formal negotiation . . ."[5] This definition covers developments both at home and abroad, internal and bilateral, including the entire area of domestic politics, foreign policy decisionmaking, and the evolution of public attitudes. While accepting the importance of the home front in conflict resolution, in the following account I shall restrict the discussion to the diplomatic interaction between the parties. Attention will be paid, therefore, to the preliminary contacts, direct or indirect, initiated to prepare for a negotiation that the parties have already agreed to undertake.

Adopting this approach, Brian Tomlin examines the prelude to the negotiation of the U.S.-Canadian Free Trade Agreement. His analysis of the episode provides a very clear expression of the North American *erabi* (instrumental or outcome oriented) mode of negotiation. Preparation for the negotiation, according to Tomlin, was very much a problem-solving exercise, a search for "joint solutions."[6] It involved "inventing and choosing among alternative definitions of the problem, inventing and choosing among alternative ways of handling the problem so defined, and setting the themes and limits—parameters and perimeters—that are necessary to guide a solution."[7]

Now it is clear that this approach is excellent in clearing the way for a U.S.-Canadian negotiation. It is doubtful whether it is equally applicable in negotiations involving the representatives of high-context cultures. All negotiations involve a problem-solving element and a relationship element. But if individualistic, low-context negotiators can be described as primarily outcome oriented and have the definition of the problem and the clarification of alternative solutions uppermost in their thoughts, high-context negotiators are seen to be predominantly relationship oriented. For them, negotiation is less about solving problems (although, obviously, this aspect cannot be dismissed) than about attending to a relationship. For communally minded cultures it is not a conflict that is resolved but a relationship that is mended. And when a problem does arise—a trade dispute, a financial crisis, the threat of famine—it cannot be solved in isolation, like a crossword puzzle, but only within the context of the given relationship. In international relations the consequence is concern both with the international relationship and with the personal ties between the interlocutors.

ESTABLISHING A PERSONAL RELATIONSHIP

For high-context negotiators, then, the initial concern is to exchange the sterility of the business files that are tossed on their desks for a tangible sense of the humanity of the other side. One of the threads running through the negotiating practice of interdependent cultures is a discomfort with purely technical, "let's not waste time but get right down to business" attitudes. Frontality, not anonymity, is the dominant ethic. For the smooth conduct of affairs in these societies, partners need to establish warm, personal ties. Reared in a setting where the intimacy of the extended family or peer group is the norm, high-context persons do not compartmentalize their relationships. They cannot relate successfully to cold and faceless partners. Thriving on personal attention as a plant thrives on sunshine, they are uncomfortable without it and unable to relate to the issue at hand. The consequences of this need for affiliation are felt at every stage of the negotiating process. It should therefore be immediately clear that a priority of the prenegotiation phase is to create an affinity between the negotiating partners. This affinity, better than anything else, will facilitate the later conduct of business.

Mushakoji Kinhide, in his study of Japanese diplomacy, is in no doubt that "the first order of business in Japan is the establishment of a personal relationship between the parties which will allow them to speak frankly and to give and receive favors."[8] For a low-context individual it is hardly customary to view negotiation as an exercise in ingratiation. In the cases of negotiation studied here, it is difficult to assess the consequences of

American negotiators' neglecting personal ties in the prenegotiation phase. What is clear is that success in negotiation is invariably assisted by careful attention to just this factor.

The 1971 U.S.-Japanese monetary crisis was the result of a rising imbalance in trade between the two countries and a large U.S. balance-of-payments deficit, matched by ballooning Japanese foreign currency reserves. Among the various measures called for by the Nixon administration was an upward revaluation of the Japanese currency, the yen. An adjustment in exchange rates, it was hoped, would stimulate American exports to Japan and dampen Japanese imports to the United States. Japan was far from enthusiastic at this prospect, favoring the existing state of affairs. In November 1971, Treasury Secretary John Connally arrived in Tokyo. Japanese ministers, who had awaited the outspoken former governor of Texas with some trepidation, "were treated to a generous serving of Texas charm." From the moment of his arrival at the airport, Connally set out to impress his hosts. Finance Minister Mikio Mizuta was complimented on his legislative skill and took away an abiding impression of the Texan's "courtly manners." Other concerned members of the Japanese cabinet were considerately visited in their own offices (rather than being invited to come to meet Connally).

Wisely, Connally made no attempt on this visit to negotiate, let alone put pressure on his hosts, but insisted that his aim was to exchange opinions and, picking up a phrase used by Japanese diplomats, "to improve mutual understanding." In private he set out American needs—not demands—for monetary adjustments and trade liberalization. This low-key, relationship-oriented approach was precisely the right strategy to adopt. The Japanese do not react kindly to pressure, faits accomplis, or heavy-handed attempts at bludgeoning them into submission. They do need a great deal of time to achieve their famous domestic consensus. Summing up the achievement of Connally's prenegotiating visit to Tokyo, Robert Angel writes: "He left his negotiating counterparts in the [Ministry of Finance] and the [Liberal Democratic Party] in a better position to compromise with American demands than they had been before he arrived—perhaps his primary objective."[9]

Connally's gracious approach is not always followed. During 1984 negotiations over reforms in Japan's financial markets, the abrupt manner of U.S. negotiators is thought to have affronted many Japanese and been self-defeating. Treasury Secretary Donald Regan, his Japanese counterparts complained, behaved as if he were cutting a deal on Wall Street, rather than engaging in delicate diplomatic negotiations with the representatives of a sovereign state "known to need gentle persuasion."[10]

Chinese negotiating behavior can be seen to reflect a similar attention to the long-term dimension of relationships rather than just short-term issues. In an interesting comparison of American and Chinese managers, unambiguous differences in work-related priorities were uncovered. U.S. executives were found to score dramatically higher than their Chinese counterparts in their emphasis on job performance as opposed to the maintenance of harmonious working relationships. Whereas the Americans were *task oriented*, the Chinese were *people oriented*.[11] Chas Freeman, who was Nixon's interpreter in 1972 and has negotiated on and off with the Chinese for many years, believes that personal relations are vital. Without the confidence born of a long acquaintance, a Chinese negotiator could not know whether or not he would be hurt by his interlocutor. He would never make concessions to you if he could not trust your discretion and integrity. The key term, Freeman points out, is *guanxi*, literally "connections and access," more subtly, the character and quality of the personal relationship.[12]

As a negotiating ploy the Chinese are adept, as many observers have noticed, at manipulating friendship for negotiating gain. (Paul Kreisberg, though, explains that *lao pengyou*, "friend," is better translated by the American term "old buddy" than "bosom companion"; it is possible to exaggerate the depth of the relationship implied.)[13] Richard Solomon argues that "the most fundamental characteristic of dealings with the Chinese is their attempt to identify foreign officials who are sympathetic to their cause, to cultivate a sense of friendship and obligation in their official counterparts, and then to pursue their objectives through a variety of stratagems designed to manipulate feelings of friendship, obligation, guilt or dependence."[14] Bette Bao Lord agrees, describing how it is done: "At the first meeting the Chinese would be politely warm; at the second meeting you would be an 'old friend'; then the Chinese would start to 'reel you in,' because in China an old friend could be expected to make concessions."[15]

Solomon notes that on several occasions Chinese officials implied that unless the United States showed flexibility in negotiations, its friends in the Chinese government would be harmed. In 1972, when normalization of relations was being discussed, Zhou Enlai's standing was suggested to be on the line. In 1981–82 Deng Xiaoping repeatedly told American visitors that he would be in trouble if the question of U.S. arms sales to Taiwan was not satisfactorily resolved. The Chinese government has also been skillful in giving privileged access to, or lobbying, officials known to be

sympathetic to their cause, avoiding those who were felt to be more critical.[16] In 1978, for example, during the normalization negotiations, Chai
Zemin, head of the liaison office of the People's Republic of China in
Washington, met with National Security Adviser Zbigniew Brzezinski, an
enthusiastic and vociferous proponent of U.S.-Chinese strategic cooperation, and told him: "The U.S. bears the major role in reaching a successful
conclusion," meaning that U.S. concessions were required.[17]

China made especially skillful use of the "old friends stratagem" after its
fall from grace following the June 1989 Tiananmen massacre and suppression of the democracy movement. That December, General Brent Scowcroft, President Bush's national security adviser, was sent to Beijing to
mend fences. Eager to prove to all that they were no longer being given
the cold shoulder, the Chinese authorities orchestrated a lavish reception
for the U.S. delegation in front of the cameras, and General Scowcroft was
received by all of the major Chinese leaders, including Deng Xiaoping in
retirement. At a banquet in the American delegation's honor, Foreign
Minister Qian Qichen toasted General Scowcroft, calling him "an old
friend very familiar to us all," and pointed out his contribution over the
years "to removing obstacles to Sino-U.S." relations. The presidential envoy
himself was photographed raising a champagne glass in a toast to his hosts,
and was reported telling Deng that President Bush still regarded him "as a
friend forever."[18] However, although President Bush was concerned about
getting Sino-U.S. relations back on track, the ostentatious warmth of the
reception, choreographed by the Chinese for their own purposes, was
counterproductive given Deng's responsibility for the very recent and tragic
events in Tiananmen Square. The Scowcroft visit came in for damaging
criticism, infuriating American opponents of the Chinese regime and sup-
plying them with ready ammunition with which to attack Bush's conciliatory policy. A low-key, correct, but not effusive visit would surely have
been in both parties' better interests.

The personal touch is equally important in preparing the ground for
negotiations with Mexico. Glen Fisher points out that the various ongoing
commissions within which American and Mexican officials tackle common problems provide ideal frameworks for productive cooperation. Such
commissions include the U.S.-Mexico Commission for Border Development
and Friendship, and the International Boundary and Water Commission.
"By being continuing bodies with members working with each other over
time, an essential personal rapport can be generated, and a familiarity with
the other side's decision-making process can be gained and appreciated."[19]

Since the 1993 conclusion of NAFTA, the number of joint frameworks of various kinds has greatly increased. The value of such standing bodies, working in a collegial spirit out of the limelight, can hardly be exaggerated. In the 1962–63 resolution of the Chamizal boundary dispute, the long-standing friendship of the two principals, Ambassador Thomas Mann for the United States and Ambassador Manuel Tello for Mexico, proved invaluable. At the technical level, significant work was also performed in the commission. Over the years U.S. officials such as Boundary Commissioner Joseph Friedkin had established close ties with their counterparts that facilitated the quiet resolution of many problems.[20]

Good personal chemistry was instrumental in preparing the groundwork for NAFTA. During the Reagan–De la Madrid years, the presidents of the two countries cultivated sound relations, while the long-running saga of Mexican debt brought together government officials on a regular basis. During the Bush administration a conscious effort was made by the United States to develop "strong working relationships with key Mexican players." Secretary of State James Baker raised the profile of the Binational Commission, a meeting of cabinet members from the two countries. President Bush, for his part, agreed to meet with President Carlos Salinas de Gortari of Mexico even before his own inauguration, establishing what was called the "Spirit of Houston," and continuing throughout his term in office to foster an atmosphere of close friendship.[21] All of these efforts were crucial in generating the political commitment that fueled the entire process. However, at the negotiating level personal relationships took time to cultivate. Charles Roh, who as assistant U.S. trade representative helped to draft NAFTA, commented that the negotiation would have gone more smoothly had the two sides been better acquainted at the outset. U.S. trade representative Carla Hills and her Mexican counterpart, Jaime Serra Puche, tended to harangue each other at first and only later developed mutual trust.[22]

As for U.S.-Egyptian relations, Ambassador Hermann Eilts believes that personal relations are essential throughout the Arab world and that the success of his Cairo embassy was related to his ability to establish close personal ties with key Egyptian leaders. Without a strong basis in convergent interests, however, these personal ties would not have helped. As valuable as more formal representations, he added in an interview, were the hours spent in informal conversation with his counterparts. Not only was this time well spent from the point of view of cultivating contacts, but information acquired on such occasions might also come in useful in the future. ("Look here, don't you remember saying to me . . .")[23] A predecessor of Eilts, John Badeau, agreed that the way to get along best in Egypt was "to practice a fairly personal diplomatic stance." He made a point of seeing President Nasser regularly, fostering a mutuality of interests.[24] The personal approach to Egyptian leaders became the hallmark of the Kissinger period of Middle East diplomacy, was inherited by President Carter, and was passed on to Secretary of State George Schultz in the 1980s and Presidents Bush and Clinton in the 1990s. Former senior State Department official Joseph Sisco believes that Americans have a special gift for friendship with Egyptians, derived from the egalitarian tradition of U.S. culture, which contrasts, in Egyptian eyes, with the arrogance remembered from the old days of British imperialism.[25] Unfortunately, the retirement of the Sisco-Eilts-Saunders generation has left a gap in U.S.-Egyptian relations not easy to fill and has impeded on occasion the ongoing dialogue between the parties.

It is hard to exaggerate the benefits U.S. diplomacy derived from the remarkably warm relationships cultivated by Kissinger and Carter with President Sadat. In her essay on the role of prenegotiation in the American mediation of the 1978 Camp David Accords, Janice Stein quotes the following significant extract from President Carter's memoirs: "In my private visits with Sadat he emphasized again and again that his main concern was about me . . . It was imperative to him that the United States and Egypt stand together."[26] Stein convincingly demonstrates the use made of prenegotiation by the United States to define the problem, delimit the agenda, select participants, and shape a negotiating strategy. She pays rather less attention to Israeli and Egyptian preparations (which did not fit this pattern). But surely the single most noteworthy feature of the Camp David conference of September 1978 was Sadat's willingness to place his own fate and that of his nation in the hands of the leader of a foreign power—President Carter. Having gone to Jerusalem and stated his case before the Knesset, Sadat was at a complete loss on what to do next. Apart from characteristic, face-to-face attempts to woo such Israeli politicians as Defense Minister Ezer Weizman and opposition leader Shimon Peres, Sadat's main tactic was simply to rely on "my friend Jimmy Carter." Rarely can a patron-client relationship have achieved such pronounced expression.

From the start, Sadat's negotiating strategy for achieving a settlement of the Egyptian-Israeli dispute (a conflict that had been pursued in five wars) was to put himself completely into American hands, displaying utter trust in American fair-mindedness. It was a remarkable conception, unintelligible unless the networks of mutual obligation that prevail in Egypt as in other relationship-oriented societies are taken into account. Patron-client relationships are based on long-lasting, affective ties between a powerful protector and a loyal ward. Under Sadat the circle of friends, or *shilla*, became a key instrument in the exercise of power in the face of the "hydra-headed" Egyptian bureaucracy.[27] For a man who was notorious for personalizing the conduct of international affairs (as Foreign Ministers Ismail Fahmy and Mohamed Kamel confirm),[28] it was quite natural to project assumptions about the value of client status onto his relationship with the United States.

The first strands in the fabric of friendship were woven by Sadat in the aftermath of the 1973 Yom Kippur War. He told Secretary of State Kissinger, in Cairo to consolidate the cease-fire, that "he was determined to end Nasser's legacy. He would reestablish relations with the United States as quickly as possible and, once that was accomplished, he would move to friendship." Sadat did not quibble over details but concentrated on essentials: establishing a personal relationship. Astonishingly, he left it up to the secretary of state to decide how best to deal with Jerusalem.[29]

Sadat, Kissinger recalls, "had an uncanny psychological discernment," handling each American president he knew with skill, gaining the confidence of each. "He worked at identifying Egypt's interest with America's own. He repeatedly challenged us to enter the negotiations not as mediator but as participant, or else he offered to accept what we put forward."[30] Sadat's trusting and open-hearted manner greatly appealed to President Carter, who writes in his memoirs: "There was an easy and natural friendship between us from the first moment I knew Anwar Sadat. We trusted each other. Each of us began to learn about the other's family members, hometown, earlier life, and private plans and ambitions, as though we were tying ourselves together for a lifetime."[31] Observing the bonding between the two men, Secretary of State Cyrus Vance confirms that they achieved a "sincere and real" rapport. He adds: "Because Sadat trusted Carter, he was repeatedly willing to take Carter's word that a given step was necessary."[32] Later, at Camp David, Carter put this trust to excellent use, although not quite in the way Sadat may have expected. The U.S. president, it turned out, was better able to separate business from friendship than was the Egyptian leader.

PREVENTING SURPRISES

High-context cultures are also shame cultures. Standing, reputation, and honor are paramount. Outward appearances are to be maintained at all

costs. Thus the high-context negotiator has an abiding nightmare: loss of
face. Face may be lost as a result of many developments: a premature or
overeager overture that is rebuffed by one's opponent; exposure to personal
insult, in the form of either a hurtful remark or disregard for one's status;
being forced to give up a cherished value or to make a concession that will
be viewed by the domestic audience as unnecessary; a snub; failure to
achieve predetermined goals; the revelation of personal inadequacy; damage to a valued relationship. The list is endless, for in the give-and-take of
a complicated negotiation on a loaded subject, anything can happen.

The high-context negotiator seeks, insofar as possible, to ensure that
"anything" will not happen. The more uncertainty, abrasion, the risk of the
unexpected, and the shadow of failure can be removed from the impending
encounter, the better. An ideal negotiation would be one in which every
move was foreseen and choreographed in advance. Contrast this aversion
to risk with the propensity for crisis of a typical low-context negotiator such
as Mickey Kantor, former U.S. trade representative. Far from deploring the
unforeseen and the abrasive, the latter relished the prospect of cut-and-
thrust, the exploitation of an unexpected opportunity, the pressure-cooker
atmosphere of short time and taut nerves in which innovative solutions
unexpectedly emerged. What matter if egos were bruised? The main thing
was to solve the problem. Glen Fisher recalls a State Department official
who was accused by his staff "of being prepared to create crises when none
existed because he so enjoyed meeting crises."[33] The general truth of this
observation will be apparent not only to the observer of American politics
but also to the student of American political science. The discipline has
developed an entire subfield of crisis studies.

High-context cultures have evolved a variety of prenegotiation stratagems
intended to head off just such crises, with their unwelcome potential for
loss of face. The Japanese style is to engage in informal talks prior to formal meetings in order to gather information about the other side's requirements and views. *Nemawashi*, "testing of the water," according to tradition,
is intended to enable thorough preparation of a proposal that is seen as
more definitive than in the Western tradition, because it will take both
sides' needs into account.[34] By extracting prenegotiation assurances and
commitments, negotiators can reduce the risk of failure in the impending
negotiations to a minimum. "For Japan," Michael Blaker argues, "efforts to
secure opposing commitments through understandings *(ryokai)*, consultations *(uchiawase)*, and preconditions *(senketsu joken)* are central to its pre-
bargaining approach."[35]

While learning as much as possible about the opponent's likely position in the forthcoming negotiation, the Japanese themselves avoid striking a premature posture, retaining flexibility while they develop their own reflexive proposal. "React, do not initiate!" might be their motto. In the *awase* tradition Japanese negotiators adapt to reality rather than pit themselves against it. (Michael Blaker notes that the Japanese use about forty different terms for "situation" in their negotiating discourse, such is the importance of circumstances or context in their approach.)[36] At the same time, consideration for the opponent can be built into the meticulous process of consensus building *(ringisei),* both within and between agencies, that famously characterizes decisionmaking in Japan.[37] As a Japanese colleague, the head of a research institute in negotiation, explained it, "We Japanese really don't like negotiating at all!" Informal contacts permit one to "negotiate without negotiating." Christopher Wendel believes it significant that the Bush administration's "structural impediments initiative (SII)"—negotiations about obstacles to bilateral trade inherent in the structures of the U.S. and Japanese economies—were referred to in Japanese as the *nichi–bei kouzou mondai kyougi* or "structural problem discussion."[38] In other words, they were conceived of as nonthreatening talks, not disputatious negotiations.

A typical example of Japanese prenegotiation can be found in the instructions sent to the Japanese delegate to the Versailles conference following World War I: "Before presenting our already established demands to the Allied Powers," Foreign Minister Uchida Yasuya wrote, "we should first exchange views with them, altering our demands somewhat by deleting or abbreviating sections, while we continue to work on those policies as yet not completely decided upon."[39] This pattern of behavior remains intact. At the preparatory stage of textiles negotiations in 1970, Prime Minister Sato ("in good Japanese fashion," as Dr. Kissinger wryly records) sent ahead a mutual friend to reach agreement on "basic issues of principle" with President Nixon's national security adviser. Without official standing in the Japanese government, the intermediary "could easily be disavowed" if necessary.[40] This maneuver has become the stock-in-trade of U.S.-Japanese trade negotiations in recent years. In former Tokyo deputy chief of mission Bill Breer's experience, the Japanese prime minister would invariably send "trusted friends in advance to sound things out."[41]

In the 1989–90 strategic impediments initiative, no informal sessions were arranged at which the parties might raise ideas ("brainstorm") without commitment. Nor were low-level advance teams sent ahead to raise talking points in preparation of their principals' meetings. This neglect of *nemawashi* meant that the Japanese went into formal negotiations unsure of U.S. intentions, what topics would be raised or tactics adopted. Wendel suggests that the pressure to improvise inherent in such a situation was bound to spawn "misconceptions and misunderstandings." It is notable, therefore, that on at least two occasions the talks were saved from complete collapse only by informal, behind-the-scenes contacts.[42]

Whereas the Japanese prefer to determine the position of their adversary in advance of the actual negotiation, the Chinese tend to adopt the reverse technique: they establish ahead of time a number of irreducible principles that are their own preconditions for entering talks. These principles may be insisted on for years. Once the other party agrees to negotiate, it will have implicitly conceded the essentials of the Chinese position from the outset. Although the Japanese and Chinese styles are apparently contradictory, they surely perform the same purpose: to avoid surprises—the intimidating uncertainty of a leap into untested waters.

Long before the United States entered into negotiations with the People's Republic of China in 1978 for the normalization of relations, it was aware of three Chinese conditions: cessation of diplomatic relations with Taipei, withdrawal of U.S. military forces and installations from Taiwan, and abrogation of the U.S.-Taiwanese defense treaty. Under the circumstances Washington did not challenge the principles directly, probably correctly viewing any such effort as an exercise in futility, but sought to modify them to suit the special relationship between the United States and Taiwan after normalization.[43] Years later, the People's Republic of China still views the "three principles" as applying. Thus the granting of a visa by President Clinton in 1995 to President Lee Teng-Hui of Taiwan to enable him to attend a class reunion at Cornell was angrily condemned by Beijing as undermining the very foundations of the U.S.-Chinese relationship.

One of the great diplomatic achievements in U.S.-Mexican relations was the 1963 settlement of the Chamizal boundary dispute. The dispute arose in the mid-nineteenth century when the Rio Grande changed its course and a small parcel of land shifted from the Mexican to the U.S. side of the border in the area of El Paso/Ciudad Juarez. The United States rejected an arbitration award made in 1911, and since then the issue had festered, impeding the settlement of other nonrelated boundary problems. Prenegotiation was probably decisive in the 1963 success. It was an irreducible matter of pride to Mexico that the Chamizal be transferred from El Paso to Ciudad Juarez in conformity with the 1911 award. The Mexicans believed it was their rightful property and they wanted it back.

Before entering into detailed negotiations, therefore, the Mexican government insisted on prior assurance of satisfaction and received it at two levels. At the actual negotiating level Mexico could be reassured by the known position of the U.S. ambassador to Mexico—and chief negotiator—Thomas Mann. He and his Mexican counterpart, Ambassador Manuel Tello, had been friends for years. Indeed, their involvement with the Chamizal dispute went back to the early 1950s when Mann actually worked with Tello unofficially on the problem. All told, Mann made five trips at that time to El Paso and several to Mexico City. He did not conceal his personal view, which became the basis for the final accord, that the United States would have to honor the 1911 award and that one possibility was to reroute the course of the river. (This idea was to form the basis of the final, ingenious technical solution.) At that time, political circumstances were unpropitious, and these unofficial soundings never acquired an official character. However, they did play a role in preparing the ground for the successful 1962–63 talks.[44]

But Mexico's principal guarantee against embarrassment came at the U.S.-Mexican summit of June 1962 between Presidents John F. Kennedy and Adolfo López Mateos. The Mexican delegation insisted that reference to the Chamizal in the final communiqué contain words to the effect that the whole area would revert to Mexico. Given Texan public opinion, this insistence was domestically very difficult for the United States. One meeting between Ambassador Mann and the Mexican foreign minister broke up on just this point. The solution came in the classic diplomatic shape of an ambiguous formula. Both presidents agreed to "instruct their executive agencies to recommend a complete solution to this problem."[45] This instruction was taken by Mexico to mean that Mexico would get all the Chamizal back, and by the United States to mean that difficulties "on the ground" would be taken into account. But the decisive consideration was that there had been a commitment of political will at the highest level, and that Mexico had good reason to think that it would not be disappointed.

Another important dispute between the United States and Mexico in which prenegotiation proved its worth was over the pollution of the Colorado River. The actual negotiations, which took place in 1973, are described in greater detail in chapter 6. Of interest at this point is the prenegotiation strategy that was adopted to facilitate the forthcoming formal talks. The two preparatory moves exactly paralleled those made in the case of the Chamizal. First, at a meeting of the presidents of the two countries a solemn commitment was made "to find a definitive, equitable, and just solution to this problem at the earliest possible time." Second, President Nixon designated a special representative for the negotiations, former attorney general Herbert Brownell, who engaged in extensive preparatory contacts with all interested parties in Mexico City and on the spot, in the Mexicali valley.[46]

Neglecting prenegotiation is a tried-and-tested method for ensuring negotiation failure. Besides being well advised to consult meticulously with Mexico in advance of a formal negotiation, the United States has to take care that any initiative appear to come from the Mexican side and not be an American imposition. There was full understanding of this requirement at the outset of the NAFTA negotiations, which were thoroughly planned in advance. It was realized that the very prospect of negotiating a free trade agreement with an economic giant like the United States would be disturbing to many Mexicans. However, the problem was involuntarily solved, since the United States was anyway prevented from proposing a bilateral trade agreement under the terms of the congressional "Fast Track" proceedings that governed the negotiations. At the same time the United States was careful to accept in advance that the hypersensitive oil and energy issues would be off the agenda, and would be addressed, if at all, only in a low-profile manner.[47]

Most important, there must be no surprises. Infringement of any of these rules may prove fatal. Their importance was stressed by several sources, including Steve Lande, chief U.S. trade negotiator with Mexico from 1976 to 1982.[48] In the American system of government, negotiating positions have to evolve from a painstaking process of interagency consultation to be acceptable to concerned domestic players. This practice may foster a propensity on the part of U.S. delegations to view an opening proposal as an end in itself—while leaving the other side out of the equation.

American negotiators have indeed displayed this tendency on numerous occasions. In 1946 U.S.-Mexican negotiations on an air transport agreement ran aground on this very reef. "Shortly after the beginning of the negotiations," Ambassador Thurston reported, "it became increasingly apparent that the Mexican delegation felt that the United States had not come to Mexico to negotiate, but to implement the decisions previously arrived at by the U.S. Civil Aeronautics Board" authorizing five American airlines to operate in Mexico. He had no doubt about the Mexicans' patent resentment and "feeling of imposition." Under the circumstances "it was agreed that no purpose would be served by further discussions at the present time." Thurston concluded that there was a substantive dispute between the two sides (Mexico demanded a prior division of the traffic, the United States favored free competition). Nevertheless, he was "particularly struck by the need for evolving some method for preventing the wounding of Latin American sensibilities by prior decisions of the Civil Aeronautics Board in cases involving routes which are to be the subject of later negotiations with them."[49]

There have been other virtually identical cases over the years. In June 1969 U.S. and Mexican representatives met in Mexico City to discuss the drug problem. A rumor that Washington was considering a passport requirement for Americans traveling to Mexico did not create an atmosphere of trust and confidence. The head of the U.S. delegation, Attorney General Richard Kleindienst, also annoyed his hosts. Stressing the need for greater cooperation between the two countries, he confronted the Mexicans with a set of formal proposals earlier recommended by a presidential task force. Attorney General Julio Sánchez Vargas of Mexico was taken aback. One American suggestion for the direct aerial application of herbicides on Mexican territory produced the polite but tart rejoinder that they be tested first in the United States. At the end of the talks, which were supposedly informal, no agreement whatever had been reached on new means to intensify the Mexican antidrug campaign. Moreover, a large-scale and highly publicized U.S. drive against drugs—Operation Intercept, spearheaded by laborious, disruptive (and fruitless) searches at the border—was a complete debacle because the United States had failed to ensure prior Mexican cooperation.[50]

During Patrick Lucey's term as ambassador (1977–79), exactly the same error was repeated. The United States proposed a twelve-point program on immigration. There had been no advance consultation with the Mexicans, and the foreign minister was "livid." At a meeting Lucey agreed to change a couple of the program's minor points, but this step was insufficient to placate his colleague.[51] Strictly speaking, the issue was a domestic American one and not dependent on Mexican consent. Still, Mexican cooperation was essential in a wider sense if progress on the problem was to be made. During Lucey's tenure of office, Robert Wilcox served as science counselor in the Mexico City embassy. He was adamant that initiatives, to get anywhere, had to be "fronted as their own" by the Mexican government, and negotiating strategies had to take this need into account. Thus American proposals on the development of solar energy got nowhere. The only projects adopted were those submitted by the Mexicans.[52]

As recent research suggests, prenegotiation may contribute to the success of negotiations. By the same token, neglecting it may impede success. However, consistent with the American tendency to view negotiation as primarily a problem-solving exercise, the literature tends to pay insufficient attention to the interpersonal side of the activity. When negotiations involving the United States and high-context, communal-minded nations are examined, the importance of cultivating relationships in the preparatory phase clearly emerges. It is not that high-context negotiators ignore the problem at issue; rather that they decline to disentangle it from the wider, long-term framework of affective relationships within which it is lodged.

A similar difference in focus can be discerned in the way the issues at stake are addressed. Janice Stein, summing up the findings of *Getting to the Table*, concludes that "in every case, prenegotiation framed the problem and set the limits of the negotiation to follow. Without an analysis of the process of getting to the table, we cannot explain the shape of the table, who gets there and who doesn't, what is on the table and, equally important, what is kept off."[53] To that summary I would add the need for face-salient, shame cultures to set parameters, not so much on the process of negotiation as on the configuration of the final outcome. In the Anglo-Saxon tradition, great stress is laid on creating the conditions for an equitable contest. A whole vocabulary, redolent with approval, exists to describe this state of affairs: fair play, level playing field, rules of the game, due process, and so on. Face-salient cultures, in contrast, are less enthusiastic about competition, with its potential for affront and painful confrontation, than about ensuring a result that will protect their cherished dignity.

6

Let the Contest Commence

Opening Moves

With the formal opening of negotiations the contrasts and contradictions between the individualistic and the interdependent models of negotiation begin to take practical effect. Dichotomies appear at the levels of philosophy, procedure, and tactics. At a general level, the United States emphasizes immediate issues rather than long-term relationships, as already observed in the prenegotiation phase. And in the American tradition of egalitarianism (whatever the power discrepancy between the parties), interlocutors are treated as equals, deserving no more and no less respect than is due all men and women. Due process, rather than personal preference, is what counts. For a negotiated settlement to be valid, Americans expect it will be arrived at in conformity with certain objective rules of equity and fair play. The concept of reciprocity has a prominent place in this design. Mutual benefit is a value very much at the heart of the contract-based, individual-oriented, commercial culture that exists in the United States.

Tactically, American negotiators assume that each side will start out by presenting its proposals to the other, and that a process of give-and-take will ensue. Concerned more with practical expedients than with grand conceptual schemes, Americans are interested in getting down to discussing detail—the "nitty-gritty"—as soon as possible. They expect discussion to be businesslike and to the point; ad hominem appeals, moral suasion, and rhetorical discourse are viewed as suitable for the theater, but not for the negotiating table. As for the bargaining itself, American negotiators are typically aware of the inevitable gap between opening bid and minimal acceptable outcome, and of the desirability of leaving themselves some room for maneuver. Although they may have a fallback position ready in anticipation of maneuvering, they are unlikely to envisage an immoderate retreat. To put in an excessive opening bid would conflict with the ingrained American sense of proportion. In the negotiation to follow, they suppose, both sides will make incremental concessions until a mutually satisfactory solution is arrived at, in the nature of a reasonable compromise. Americans may be surprised to discover that not all these anticipations are shared by the other side, for they are grounded in a particular, and far from universal, approach to negotiation.

WHO GOES FIRST?

For the low-context negotiator, it seems natural for the parties in negotiation to commence the contest by setting out their opening positions as clearly as possible. The resemblance between this procedure and that of a court of law or a high school debate will not have escaped the reader: it is rooted in that adversarial style on which American law and politics are posited. However, as we have already observed, the dislike of confrontation found in interdependent, face-salient cultures (together with certain features of domestic decisionmaking) may prescribe a rather different procedure, namely, to postpone showing one's hand for as long as possible. In this case the American side is likely to find itself right away at a severe tactical disadvantage.

China and Japan are particularly prone to hold their fire in the first round of talks, though for different historical-cultural reasons. In U.S.-Japanese relations the Japanese preference for *nemawashi*, informal contacts aimed at prior understanding, has often been compounded by a lack of enthusiasm for negotiation that takes the form of passivity in the talks themselves. Partly, this is because the status quo on trade matters—imperfect American access to the Japanese market and a large trade surplus in favor of Tokyo—for long favored Japan.[1] In the strategic impediments initiative talks, for instance, which were ostensibly a two-way street aimed at reforming both countries' economies, the Japanese were resigned to their being at the receiving end of U.S. initiatives.[2] In the field of aviation, where a 1952 bilateral agreement strongly favors the United States for historical reasons, it is Japan that pressed in the mid-1990s to redress the balance, and the United States that was reluctant to move.[3] Yet here too the

Japanese were inclined to look to the United States for bright ideas. While complaining about the "unfairness" of existing arrangements, Tokyo tended to demand, quixotically, equal rights without coming up with a realistic package. The U.S. counterproposal of overall liberalization, the so-called "open skies" concept of an elimination of all government restrictions on air travel, proved a highly effective rejoinder.[4] In the 1995–96 renegotiation of the Status of Forces Agreement, which resulted from the rape of a young Japanese girl by American servicemen and local calls for closing down the Okinawa bases, the Japanese government position was depressingly familiar to its critics. In the paraphrase of a former ambassador to Thailand, it was to evade responsibility by declaring that it would "ask the U.S. Government to solve the problem."[5] William Breer suggests that the stylized pattern of Japanese passivity/American imposition reflects a broad historical trend in relations between the two countries since the time of Commodore Perry (who forcibly opened Japanese ports in 1853 to U.S. ships).

In an analysis of U.S.-Japanese bargaining, Leo Moser, a veteran diplomat and Asia specialist, observes the asynchrony that results from the partners' discordant negotiating styles:

> When the Americans state their position, the Japanese tendency is to listen quite carefully, to ask for additional details, and to say nothing at all committal. This lack of response is likely to frustrate the American side, which wants a counter-proposal put on the table "so that give-and-take can begin." To the Japanese, this approach may appear overly aggressive, embarrassing, even impolite. They may also consider it unwise to expect the two delegation leaders to make initial, clear statements of their negotiating position; wouldn't it be wiser to let them speak only after the two sides had worked out a mutually acceptable position at the working level? To Americans the Japanese response is liable to seem standoffish, dilatory, even "inscrutable."[6]

This analysis is well exemplified by the first round of the U.S.-Japanese air service negotiations of the early 1980s. Both sides sought expanded passenger and cargo access to each other's markets, beyond traffic rights, as well as the redress of certain grievances. (The American delegation to the talks was chaired by a State Department official and also included two representatives from the Department of Transportation and three from the Civil Aeronautics Board. In other words it was a fairly typical interagency team, most of whose members were not professional diplomats.) In preparation for the opening round in Honolulu in January 1981, the U.S. delegation developed a detailed set of proposals that offered substantial incentives to Japan in return for appropriate concessions. As is common in American practice, the offer did not represent an exaggerated bargaining position that could be whittled down in a subsequent haggle, but what was considered to be a fair and balanced package. In a sense, the United States had already reached a compromise—with itself.

In Honolulu, negotiations immediately settled into the mode described by Moser. With the unveiling of the American package, the Japanese delegation was able to probe away to its heart's content rather than present a proposal of its own. It was utterly predictable that the Japanese would prefer to learn as much as they could about their rival's position before embarking on the painstaking task of domestic consultation and consensus building that marks their own decisionmaking process. Moreover, they had acquired a tactical advantage, for without making a single concession of their own or even revealing any of their cards, they now knew what minimum gains they could expect from any agreement.

It was only at the second round of the talks in April that Japan tabled its own counterproposal. "It satisfied," in the censorious words of one of the American delegates, "virtually all of Japan's objectives and none of the aims of the United States." Taking umbrage, the United States rejected it as "counterproductive and self-serving." By round three in May, it had dawned on the Americans (to their annoyance) that their adversaries were going to eke out their concessions belatedly and in small amounts.[7] Unfortunately, having offered its own carrot right at the beginning, the United States had left itself minimal leverage. The opening package may have offered an equitable solution to the problem in American eyes, but it quite ignored the fundamental fact that negotiation involves an interaction between at least two parties who may not be playing by the same rules.

Chinese negotiators, like the Japanese, are slow to present their opening position in negotiations with the United States. Paul Kreisberg quotes a Chinese diplomat who explained that "China usually put its own principles forward—often publicly—but then asked the USA to open with its own views in negotiations because it often appeared the Americans preferred to do so." On commercial, legal, and technical subjects, about which the Chinese had an uncertain grasp, they would ask their Western counterparts in general to lead off. In negotiations with Third World countries, in contrast, China put its position forward first, since, the Chinese diplomat claimed, "it was better informed."[8] This account (with its significant hierarchical distinction between the West and the Third World, the powerful and the less powerful) suggests that China's opening behavior is shrewdly calculating, grounded not in the sort of inhibitions that constrain Japanese diplomats, but in a strategic view of negotiation that views it as a contest, almost like war. Making this point, Chas Freeman notes that Chinese negotiators often engage in "flanking maneuvers" intended to conceal their real objective.[9] The logic of Chinese strategy is similarly explained by another China specialist as intended "to conceal their cards while forcing the other side to reveal its hand. By letting the other side speak first, they can also point out contradictory aspects of its position and make full use of them."[10] The ingenious expedient of stating their own principles in public before sitting down at the table, then letting their opponent open the formal talks, enables the Chinese to obtain the best of both worlds: anchoring their position in the high-minded commitment of an open declaration, while leaving their hands free in the detailed closed negotiation.

In preparation for the 1978 U.S.-Chinese normalization negotiations, the Carter administration had carefully planned a "dance of the four veils" strategy, which envisaged the American delegate presenting his government's proposal on each of the major issues separately and in sequence ("seriatim" is the technical term for this approach). He would move from one item to the next only after testing "the Chinese reaction on each sensitive issue."[11] At least that is what was supposed to happen, but China had a different game plan in mind.

It is worth pausing for a point about the administrative arrangements for the talks. Leonard Woodcock, head of the U.S. Liaison Mission in Beijing and U.S. negotiator, was not a career diplomat but did have years of negotiating experience as a labor union leader. Typically, for a negotiation of such extraordinary importance, Woodcock's freedom of action—and therefore the input of personality—was strictly circumscribed. Using the White House communications system for direct contact rather than the State Department's, National Security Adviser Zbigniew Brzezinski and his staff regularly provided Woodcock "with systematic and extraordinarily detailed instructions."[12] In short, this performance was not a solo, but a negotiation meticulously orchestrated by the government apparatuses of China and the United States.

The first meeting between Ambassador Woodcock and his Chinese counterpart, Foreign Minister Huang Hua, took place on July 5, 1978. As agreed by President Carter and his principal foreign policy advisers, Woodcock proposed an agenda of four items to be tackled in turn. On July 14 China responded "by suggesting that the United States first make a comprehensive presentation on all the major issues, obviously wanting," Brzezinski remarks in his memoirs, "to smoke out the American position."[13]

Keeping strictly to his instructions, Ambassador Woodcock ignored the Chinese request and proceeded according to plan with the first item on the agenda. The Chinese side declined to respond. Sticking to his guns, Woodcock proceeded unilaterally with the agenda. Doing so did not help at all in the face of Chinese persistence; Beijing had taken the measure of its opponent. Eventually, as Woodcock himself reports, the entire U.S. position was laid out in its entirety in five meetings held from July to mid-September. Then and only then did the Chinese answer. In the words of Deputy Secretary of State Warren Christopher, they "had not responded sequentially; they responded to the overall presentation and then Vice Premier Deng came into this matter." Meanwhile, enjoying the luxury of going second, "the Chinese listened to Woodcock's presentations, finding fault with the American proposals and raising many 'nitpicking' questions, but moving very slowly and cautiously."[14]

Given the Chinese refusal to play the game by American rules, it is remarkable that Brzezinski and his team at the White House did not see fit to rethink their strategy. That they did not, but galloped on into Chinese fire, is rather reminiscent of the suicidal charge of the Light Brigade (an episode in the Crimean War, described by Lord Tennyson in a famous poem). It was magnificent, but it was not war—or give-and-take, for that matter.

ADOPTION OF A SUPPLICANT POSTURE

American assumptions of equality in negotiation may fare no better than those of reciprocity. For hierarchical cultures, as we have observed, it is natural to transfer preoccupation with status from the domestic into the international arena. And in negotiations on most issues involving the United States, the single most salient feature is the colossal preponderance of American power. It is impossible for a high-context negotiator to overlook this fact of international life, however down-to-earth and unaffected the U.S. interlocutor. Ironically, although a patronizing attitude would be deeply resented, several of the nations examined here were not adverse to turning their relative weakness vis-à-vis the United States to bargaining advantage by adopting a supplicant posture at the outset of negotiations.

The appeal to weakness has been particularly associated with Japan (and is a corollary of the passivity observed in the previous section). Many observers, including some Japanese, have noticed Japan's tendency to take on the role of supplicant in negotiations with the superpowers. In so doing, Japan is instinctively projecting onto its foreign relations the characteristic psychological orientation of dependency found throughout its society.

Amae, as it is called, is the inferior partner's expectation of the stronger party's benevolence in a hierarchical relationship. In return for protection and consideration the weaker party need offer only gratitude and a sense of indebtedness. He or she is not committed to any specific act of reciprocity. *Amae* imposes an onerous burden of lifelong responsibility and is possible only in a highly stratified society that attaches a supreme value to the fulfillment of well-defined roles and duties. It contrasts with the Judeo-Christian ethic, "Love thy neighbor as thyself," in which behavior toward others is grounded in one's personal self-esteem. Interdependent cultures reverse the causality: one's self-esteem is derived from others' approbation.

Numerous examples of the Japanese appeal to weakness, grounded in *amae*, can be detected in U.S.-Japanese relations. In the 1971 monetary crisis Japan countered pressure to revalue the yen by throwing itself on U.S. benevolence. Japan, it was argued, "is a small nation, poor in natural resources, and therefore dependent upon foreign trade."[15] In a 1977 fishing dispute, *Asahi Shinbum* appealed in an editorial for American understanding of the misery of Japanese fishermen: "We do hope that President Carter will not disappoint the Japanese, who are allied with America and have profound trust and friendly feeling toward the American people."[16] In the Nixon-Sato textile negotiations, it has been argued, the root of the damaging and drawn-out wrangle lay in a clash of cross-cultural expectations. As the weaker partner, Sato is said to have expected his powerful American patron to sympathize with the domestic difficulties he faced from the powerful Japanese textiles lobby. Nixon, on the other hand, who had been forthcoming in the Okinawa bases negotiations, had equally good reason to hope that Japan would reciprocate with "voluntary" quotas on textile exports. When both sides found their expectations disappointed, an essentially secondary disagreement escalated into a major crisis in relations.[17]

As Japan has ascended the pinnacle of economic power, the supplicant posture has become increasingly incongruous; yet it persists because of its firm psychological basis in the Japanese self-perception of vulnerability. In the trade talks that dominated the first half of the 1990s, the United States was the plaintiff, calling for the repeal of restrictive Japanese domestic commercial practices, but Japan still saw itself as the innocent victim.[18] In the talks on the Okinawa bases, which caught Tokyo between the complaints of local residents of Okinawa and the logistic needs of its U.S. military ally, the supplicant posture worked brilliantly well. Once again, as so often before, the American protector was obliged to graciously concede the needs of its Japanese dependent.

There is an element of paradox in the use of *amae* tactics outside the special case of a U.S.-Japanese negotiation. Since World War II, Japan and the United States have arguably had a sort of *amae* relationship. But in almost any other case one could mention, the necessary feature of mutual obligation, of protection in return for loyalty, is absent. Indeed, Third World powers are more likely to resent dependency than to cultivate it. Egypt and Mexico have been proud and vigorous in defending their independence against real or imagined Western encroachments. Even so, as we have already noted, on occasions of dire need the only argument that the weaker state can use may be the appeal to the *amae* responsibility of the stronger. Part of the effectiveness of the appeal, of course, is precisely the U.S. willingness, given its sense of mission in international affairs, to act as a "lender of last resort."

Glen Fisher, observing the Mexican penchant for playing the weaker partner in negotiations with the United States, was unsure whether it was a calculated tactic or a sincerely felt position.[19] Whatever the case, the situation has occurred regularly, most recently in the February 1995 peso crisis, when the Mexican request can be summed up in one word: "Help!" But this mode of behavior goes back years. In 1943 Mexico and the United States were engaged in important negotiations for sharing the waters of the great Colorado River, which, after running most of its course through American territory, enters Mexico for a short distance before reaching the Gulf of California. The construction of the Hoover Dam and U.S. irrigation projects meant that by the time the Colorado River reached the Mexican farmers of the Mexicali valley, little water was left over for their needs. The negotiation was aimed at agreeing on a guaranteed allocation.

In an unexpected démarche the U.S. ambassador was called into the Mexican foreign ministry to be greeted by a delegation including the foreign minister, the minister of agriculture, and other cabinet officers. Their message was dramatic: an unusually dry season had aggravated the water shortage, and the inhabitants of the Mexicali valley and their crops "were in immediate danger of catastrophe." The matter was of "urgent and immediate importance" and the ambassador was urged to take the matter up directly with President Roosevelt. In Ambassador Messersmith's judgment, "they were not staging a show for me." Subsequent inquiry, however, cast their claim in doubt. The day after the meeting a U.S. inspector measured more water passing into Mexican territory than its farmers could use. What had happened? The under secretary of state believed that it was a "scare tactic." Officials concerned with the Colorado River talks concluded that it was indeed so: "that certain Mexicans may be trying to induce us to set the precedent of assuring the delivery of a greater amount of water than we now contemplate allocating by treaty."[20]

Years later the problem reemerged. The 1944 treaty dividing the waters of the Colorado had fixed the quantity, but not the quality, of the water. Both sides had different assumptions on the matter. The completion in 1961 of a drainage channel in Arizona, running into the river, meant that Mexican farmers now received unusable runoff irrigation water, heavily polluted by fertilizer salts. The United States was accused of violating the 1944 treaty. In a classic gesture combining both magnanimity and patronage, Washington accepted without quibbling its responsibility for the quality of the water. (That this kind of behavior is far from axiomatic in the diplomatic realm was brought home to me by a State Department official with long service in India. Faced by a similar appeal from Bangladesh for a more generous water allocation, the government of India sent the supplicant packing. "Magnanimity," I was told, "is not a word in their vocabulary.")

From 1962 to 1972 a series of interim measures was undertaken to dilute the Colorado River's saline content. In 1972 it was decided to seek a permanent solution. When the two sides entered the formal stage of the negotiation in June 1973, Foreign Minister Emilio Rabasa of Mexico adopted a classic *amae* posture, otherwise surprising from a conventional negotiating perspective: he had no proposal to make; any solution would have to come from U.S. negotiator Herbert Brownell and his team. "They wanted help from the United States, period," Brownell remarked. They got it. Under the terms of the final agreement the American government committed itself to the unprecedented step of constructing, at enormous cost, a desalination plant to supply Mexico with water of acceptable quality.[21]

A final example of the Mexican appeal from weakness occurred in the Mexican debt crisis of 1982, setting a pattern of supplication that was to continue through one monetary crisis after another, even after NAFTA's entry into force. After Mexico had accumulated debts of approximately $80 billion during the fat years of rising oil prices, the bubble burst in 1982. In June, the Bank of America failed to syndicate a $2.5 billion loan for Mexico. On August 13, 1982, Mexico's foreign reserves stood at just $200 million while the net outflow through the central bank of Mexico was running at $100 million a day; trading in U.S. dollars was suspended. That same day Mexican finance minister Silva de Herzog flew to Washington. Like Foreign Minister Rabasa in 1973, he had no specific plan or proposal.[22] That was up to the United States.

Peter Wallison, one of the Treasury Department officials who partici-
pated in the negotiation, commented on the almost suicidal element in the
Mexican approach: unless an American rescue package was forthcoming,
Mexico would default on its massive debt with, it was believed, catastrophic
consequences for the international financial system. Ambassador Gavin
colorfully characterized the Mexican approach as follows, "We'll slash ourselves and bleed to death on your carpet." Here was *amae* as moral black-
mail. In any event, the Mexican ploy proved effective. The U.S. team (ably
led by Tim McNamar, deputy secretary of the Treasury) in a tour de force
over a hectic weekend, succeeded in putting together a rescue package
including a $2 billion loan. There was no Mexican default.[23]

The U.S.-Egyptian version of *amae* had its remarkable epitome in the
relationships President Anwar Sadat cultivated with U.S. leaders. At the
Camp David conference of September 1978, at which the framework of an
Egyptian-Israeli peace was negotiated through the good offices of the
United States, *amae* was the essence of the Egyptian president's strategy.
On the second day of the summit, Sadat disclosed to President Carter in
advance a series of concessions to be used at appropriate moments in the
negotiations.[24] This extraordinary gesture of trust makes sense only within
the context of an *amae* relationship in which the client relies on the munif-
icence of his patron. Carter got nothing like it from the ultra-low-context
Israelis, who kept him at arm's length. In the judgment of U.S. ambassador
Hermann Eilts, who was present at the talks, the end result was that Sadat
went far beyond the limit of the concessions he had intended to make. In
return for agreeing to freeze the settlements, Israel achieved a string of
concessions on the Palestinian autonomy issue.[25] Sadat's approach, which
cost Egypt dearly at Camp David, rested on the assumption that the client,
in return for his loyalty, can expect to receive special favors from the
patron. Unfortunately for Sadat, Carter, coming from a different cultural
tradition, was not inclined to confuse friendship with substance. In the
crunch he predictably leaned on the more pliable party.

Two states that have not adopted a thoroughgoing supplicant posture
are India and China, though they are not averse, in private at the negotiating table, to emphasizing their own "deserving status" and appealing to
American generosity when it suits them and when it involves no public
loss of face. ("India has to be helped," was how the chief Indian negotiator
justified an unbalanced proposal in 1995 aviation negotiations.) The contradiction between the drive for autonomy and the appeal for special treatment has already been pointed out. China and India were not ready to

compromise their independent credentials in the cases examined. Although circumstances might force them to accept help, and it was sometimes hard to resist playing up the part of the underdog, they would not acknowledge any reciprocal obligation.

In the case of China, ideology and the Cold War prevented the development of an aid relationship. Not so in the case of democratic India, which was offered, and received, U.S. assistance in diverse forms over the years. With an acute sense of national pride, India developed a unique strategy for saving face: it would accept needed assistance, but it would not say please or thank you. The style was established during the 1951 famine, when Prime Minister Jawaharlal Nehru grudgingly accepted American grain shipments. At the end of his report on a key meeting with Nehru on the subject, Ambassador Loy Henderson describes the following significant scene: "For the first time the Prime Minister talked with me about the Indian need for foodgrain. His questions indicated that he had an active interest in the matter and would like to see the proposed legislation enacted. He did not, however, express any hopes on the subject or any appreciation of the efforts on India's behalf of the United States Government."[26]

In later years the government of Prime Minister Indira Gandhi replaced absence of gratitude with what the Johnson administration perceived as deliberate ingratitude. At a time when American grain ships were unloading at Indian ports, Mrs. Gandhi went so far as to send a warm birthday greeting to Ho Chi Minh, the leader of North Vietnam, a country then at war with the United States. President Johnson's reaction was furious, and cables to the Delhi embassy (according to Ambassador Chester Bowles) "burned with comments about 'those ungrateful Indians.'" Bowles's analysis of Indian behavior was perceptive. "Indian officials," he writes, "seemed almost to be searching for ways to prove that India's integrity as a sovereign nation could never be bought with American wheat."[27] Mrs. Gandhi adopted a neo-Marxist thesis to explain why gratitude was not only inappropriate but would actually be perverse. It was India that was owed a debt by the rich Western nations, which had achieved their own success and prosperity by exploiting the "riches and labour of the colonised countries."[28]

Why was India unwilling to enter into an *amae* partnership with the United States? After all, India is no less familiar with habits of patronage and mutual obligation than Egypt, Japan, or Mexico. Indeed it is the paradigm case of the rigidly stratified society, its caste system binding its citizens in a bewildering lattice of rights and duties. Nor was the Indian experience of colonialism worse than that of Egypt or its grievance at being exploited worse than that of Mexico. Partly the answer is to be found in the unique pattern of obligations created by the Hindu ethic. *Dharma* (duty) defines two categories of recipients to whom one is under a mandatory obligation to give alms: those with a religious vocation and the lowest of the low, the untouchable and the deformed.[29] Thus persons of status most certainly do not ask for charity. Moreover, in the charitable transaction both parties are simply acting out metaphysically predetermined roles. Gratitude in these circumstances is irrelevant.[30] The other point to note is the limitations placed by caste on the giving and receiving of food. In Bernard Cohn's explanation of the phenomenon: "High status is symbolized by being able to take the rarest kinds of food from the fewest people. It is much better to give and have one's food taken than it is to receive. A Brahman theoretically can take only uncooked food from anyone of lower status than himself; hence, at a feast, a Brahman should cook his own food."[31] If one remembers that the Indian political elite are mostly high-caste Hindus (though this is changing today), it becomes possible to understand better why the request for assistance in the international sphere should be so odious. Moreover, the prospect of laboring under a burden of obligation is simply intolerable.

ASSUMING THE MORAL HIGH GROUND

A corollary of *amae* is to present oneself at the outset as the morally injured party, deserving of redress. Mostly devoid of the conventional advantages of economic and military power in negotiations with the United States, Third World states have learned that the Northern European Protestant conscience, inherited by the United States (and Canada), provides them with an effective lever of influence. From the high ground of moral superiority and self-righteous indignation, they can direct their rhetorical fire at Washington's exposed moral positions. Because the United States, like some of its other Western partners (most notably the Netherlands, Britain, and the Nordic countries), does acknowledge a vocation to act as a moral arbiter, spreading justice and aid to the developing world, such arguments find great resonance in public opinion.

India, therefore, although reluctant to play the role of supplicant, is never loath to attack supposed American moral shortcomings. American negotiators tend to be intensely irritated by Indian moralism, the assumption that India is somehow the repository of righteousness and objective truth in the world. Of course they are irritated; many Americans perceive that select role for themselves. "We are two such preachy peoples!" as a former Indian ambassador to Washington jokingly, but insightfully, put it. Confirming the point, Paul Kreisberg, who served in the Delhi embassy in both the 1950s and the 1970s, comments wittily that negotiating with Indians is intensely frustrating because it is "like negotiating with yourself"!"[32]

Another serving U.S. diplomat with long experience in India suggests that the Indian preoccupation with status makes it imperative for the Indian diplomat to establish his superiority in the negotiation at the earliest possible moment. This practice grates against the instinctive American desire to establish the equality of the interlocutors. Such a concept of equality is viewed by one's Indian counterpart as an eccentric and "unacceptable notion." Hence, at the outset of talks Indian negotiators tend to parade "a litany of all your past failures, abuses of them, sins," while India's record is presented as one of "great principle and universal approbation." Faced by this barrage, flustered American negotiators may either rebut their interlocutors' charges point by point—a fruitless exercise—or, if they have any sense, thank them for their helpful explanation and then get on with the business at hand. In parenthesis, my source noted that Japanese negotiators are utterly shocked and mortified by such offensiveness in negotiation and may even withdraw from future meetings altogether.

Perceptive Indian commentators complement this highly unusual picture by pointing out the American contribution to the "dialogue of the deaf." R. V. R. Chandrasekhara Rao writes that "self-righteous attitudes on both sides" have hindered the U.S.-Indian relationship:

> America's anti-colonial tradition, its rise to economic primacy through hard work and initiative, made the Americans tend to exhibit moral superiority. With this has gone a natural tendency to react with indignation when chinks in their moral armour are exposed. India has its own holier-than-thou mentality traceable to its consciousness of an immemorial cultural heritage and reinforced by the manifest ethical content of the Mahatma Gandhi–Nehru tradition. When rivals contend in terms of moral attitudes not only does compromise become difficult but, more important, exposure of lapses leads to a loss of credibility.[33]

Moral indignation and mutual recriminations dominated the tone of U.S.-Indian relations at various periods, including the Dulles-Nehru period of the 1950s, the Gandhi-Johnson period in the 1960s, and the Gandhi-Nixon and Gandhi-Carter periods of the 1970s. In this kind of atmosphere it was difficult to cooperate on matters of common concern. On the other hand, objective factors should not be ignored: American arms supplies to Pakistan, India's mortal enemy, exerted an invariably harmful influence on relations (although they have not affected the U.S.-Indian rapprochement since 1982).

India's dash for the moral high ground is demonstrated by its position in the 1981–82 negotiations over the question of the supply of nuclear fuel for the Tarapur nuclear facility. Under the terms of the 1963 contract to build an atomic power plant outside Bombay, the United States agreed to supply enriched uranium for the thirty-year life of the agreement. In return, India agreed to use only American-supplied fuel. Following India's "peaceful nuclear explosion" in 1974, there was an outburst of moral indignation in the United States. Demands were made for India to adhere to the 1968 Nuclear Nonproliferation Treaty (NPT). It was only with great reluctance that further uranium shipments were made. The plot thickened in 1978 when the U.S. Congress passed the Nuclear Nonproliferation Act. The administration now claimed that India was obliged to accept new restrictions on the end use of nuclear fuel. By combining, characteristically, an ethical imperative and a domestic legal requirement, the United States powerfully reinforced its negotiating position.

In 1981 the government of India decided to bring the matter to a head by cannily turning the ethical-legal argument upside down: it was the United States that was under an obligation. A delegation of Indian experts arrived in Washington determined to hold the American government to the letter of the 1963 contract: the fuel should be supplied with no added restrictions on its use. For its part the United States was caught in a bind. True, it had entered a commitment to supply nuclear fuel. But Congress absolutely required new safeguards. Negotiations, then, had acquired a moral dimension that obscured their apparently technical nature. India relished its posture of the injured party; it would not let the United States off the hook. It was not interested in the American suggestion that India turn to other suppliers, of which there was no lack. Ambassador Robert Goheen, President Carter's appointee to the Delhi embassy, felt that India sought the moral high ground in two ways: first, by insisting that the United States honor its original commitment, even though it could not under the changed circumstances; and second, by insisting that it was unfair and hypocritical to criticize India's nuclear program—specifically, to insist that India adhere to the nonproliferation treaty—before the superpowers did something about their own nuclear stockpiles. In the end, the problem was resolved not at the technical level but at the highest political level. Prime Minister Gandhi decided to turn a new leaf in relations with the United States—whether under pressure from the Indian business community or because of the Afghanistan war is a subject of conjecture. Given the political will, a simple solution was found: France would now supply the fuel.

When the Nuclear Nonproliferation Treaty came up for renewal in 1995, India struck a strikingly similar posture in the multilateral talks in New York to that taken in the 1981 bilateral negotiations. (It also seized the welcome opportunity to try to resurrect, somewhat anachronistically, the anticolonialist nonaligned movement set up in 1955, of which it was a founding member.) In the face of American demands that it come on board, though it was not a signatory of the original pact, India decided to hold the United States to the disarmament provisions of the 1968 treaty. How unjust, it thundered, taking the moral high ground once again, for states authorized under the treaty to possess nuclear weapons (Britain, China, France, Russia, and the United States) to seek to perpetuate their own monopoly while evading their ethical and legal obligations to the human race to disarm:

> The NPT is a discriminatory treaty which creates a division between nuclear haves and have-nots. The indefinite extension of the NPT perpetuates the discriminatory aspects and provides legitimacy to the nuclear arsenals of nuclear-weapons states. India's own action plan, put forward in 1988, calls for the elimination of all nuclear weapons as the only means for achieving genuine non-proliferation. India will not sign the NPT in its present form but will continue to work for achieving genuine non-proliferation through the elimination of all nuclear weapons.[34]

Ultimately, the Indian ploy was unsuccessful in thwarting an indefinite extension of the NPT in the face of an American diplomacy that called in all its debts. Nevertheless, its arguments did provide moral cover for India's refusal to sign the treaty, and for later refusing to agree to a Comprehensive Test Ban. Furthermore, the United States was seriously embarrassed by India's moral advocacy and was forced to pay a far higher political price for an agreement than it had originally bargained for.

Striking an accusatory posture is also a typical Chinese tactic. Ogura Kazuo notes its use in negotiations with Japan. To put the Japanese on the defensive, Chinese negotiators assiduously dredge up past "faults" and "errors" that have damaged relations. Demonstrating his point with a convincing list of examples, Kazuo argues that it reflects a Chinese wish "to rectify the views of the other side." China's position must not only prevail but must also be acknowledged to be morally superior.[35] Richard Solomon observes the same tactic in Sino-American negotiations. He cites a 1975 meeting of Henry Kissinger with Deng Xiaoping, when the Chinese leader repeatedly asserted that "the U.S. owes China a debt" on normalization because of the intention expressed by President Nixon in 1972 to establish diplomatic relations by the end of his second term.[36] Presumably, the intervening events in Washington between 1972 and 1975 had somehow escaped Deng's attention.

By the time of Cyrus Vance's first visit as secretary of state to China in August 1977, Deng was claiming, wishfully, that Kissinger had "agreed that the United States owed a debt to China and that normalization would be in conformity with Chinese conditions." The Chinese leader also alleged that in a December 1975 discussion President Ford had promised to normalize relations after the 1976 elections. Here, too, Deng stretched the truth, omitting to state that Ford had qualified his statement with an "if." All would depend on the working out of the Taiwan issue.[37]

China also based its opening position in the 1983 textile trade negotiations on its supposed role as the injured party. Although there had been a dramatic growth in Chinese textile exports to the United States, and unemployment in the U.S. textile industry was high, the Chinese negotiators skillfully argued that they were at a disadvantage in the larger context of Sino-American trade. They pointed to a 1981 overall trade deficit of $2.9 billion and a "textile trade deficit" of $450 million. Finally, they held that threatened protection of the U.S. textile industry would hurt China more than the status quo hurt the United States, because textiles accounted for more than one-third of their total national exports. But these arguments did not impress the hard-nosed American delegation.[38]

In contrast to seeking the moral high ground by adopting an accusatory posture, China has also shown itself skilled at using unilateral "goodwill" gestures to establish American "indebtedness." In 1955, for example, Beijing released a group of eleven American airmen on the day before the opening of the civilian repatriation talks. The release of political prisoners on the eve of negotiations, a gesture that costs China little and wins U.S. gratitude, has become a hallmark of bilateral relations. During the seminal 1969–72 period, the Chinese implemented a whole series of unsolicited concessions. These included the release of prisoners, the famous invitation to the U.S. Ping-Pong team, and the gift of panda bears. All these signals were shrewdly directed at public opinion, did not need to be reciprocated (and hence evaded possible snubs), and put China in the best possible light. They also ensured that the United States, not China, was put under a moral obligation for favors already received. Shenkar and Ronen have observed that if there is one thing that disturbs Chinese negotiators, it is to be placed under a burden of moral indebtedness. A debt "must eventually be repaid, perhaps at a higher cost."[39] Better by far that one's bargaining partner be beholden.

A further advantage of the unilateral gesture on the eve of negotiations is that it disarms criticism, while at the same time avoiding the impression of bowing to pressure. A concession given freely and without any direct connection to demands made at the negotiating table is arguably not a concession per se, and thereby entails no loss of face. On the eve of intellectual property rights talks in 1996, called under the threat of U.S. trade sanctions because of Chinese nonimplementation of an agreement reached the previous year to protect U.S. copyright holders, China launched a high-profile crackdown on unauthorized compact disc producers. "The move again shows the Chinese government's firm stand on protection of intellectual property rights and fighting copyright piracy," unctuously—and disarmingly—claimed a spokesman with China's Press and Publication Administration.[40]

A moralistic tone can be frequently detected in U.S.-Mexican negotiations. Doris Meisner, at the time an official with the U.S.-Mexican Commission on Migration, recalled that every meeting started off with a litany of Mexican grievances at U.S. conduct over the years. This recitation was extremely unpleasant for the American delegation. "I really just cringed . . . it bothered me a great deal . . . being berated like that." It never occurred to the American delegates to defend their country's record or, conversely, to point out the shortcomings in Mexico's conduct toward the United States over the years. And even if it had, Meisner admitted that they lacked detailed historical knowledge upon which to draw. Another issue frequently raised by the Mexican delegation and calculated to create defensiveness on the American side concerned the "violation of the rights of Mexican nationals" by agents of the U.S. Immigration and Naturalization Service.[41]

A similar story was related by Timothy Bennett, deputy assistant trade representative for Mexico from 1985 to 1988. In 1986 a U.S. delegation went to Mexico to discuss Mexico's accession to the General Agreement on Tariffs and Trade. The delegation was flabbergasted by the Mexican opening statement, which ran through Mexican grudges against the United States going back to the nineteenth century. Bennett's reaction was that it was all a ploy "to set us up . . . put a guilt complex on us."[42]

The most notorious example of Mexican hectoring came during President Carter's February 1979 visit to Mexico City, at a time of deadlock in negotiations over the supply of Mexican gas to the United States. In his public opening remarks President José López Portillo of Mexico launched an extraordinary assault on his astonished guest. "Among permanent, not casual, neighbors," López Portillo lectured, "surprise moves and sudden deceit or abuse are poisonous fruits that sooner or later have a reverse effect. Consequently, we must take a long-range view of ourselves. No injustice can prevail without affronting decency and dignity. It is difficult, particularly among neighbors, to maintain cordial and mutually advantageous relations in an atmosphere of mistrust or open hostility." How this broadside was supposed to promote trust and amity was left unclear.[43] In private, López Portillo was even more offensive. A member of Carter's entourage described the Mexican leader as using "stiff, harsh language, blaming the United States for everything that had gone wrong since the beginning of man." The U.S. president, who was eager "to find practical solutions to bilateral problems, found the Mexican's accusatory monologues unwarranted and irritating."[44]

PRINCIPLES BEFORE DETAIL?

At the opening stage of talks negotiators must decide how to present their case in the most convincing and tactically advantageous light. Edmund Glenn, a former State Department interpreter (and a source of inspiration for researchers in the field of intercultural communication), argued from practical experience that culture and language were formative in the choice of approach. Three basic styles of persuasion, he believed, can be observed. One, the "factual-inductive," draws conclusions on the basis of factual evidence; eschewing grand philosophical debate, it plunges straight into discussion of concrete detail. This style is in the Anglo-Saxon, pragmatic tradition of the common law, which has had such a formative influence on philosophy, science, and politics. The second, the "axiomatic-deductive" style, argues from general principles to particular applications; it seeks a principled underpinning for every practical derivation. It is usually associated with the Roman law tradition and other axiomatic systems. The third, the "affective intuitive" style, makes its pitch on the grounds of emotion, aiming not at the head of the audience but at its heart.[45] Elements of the two latter styles have already been observed in the appeals to weakness, moral indebtedness, and friendship of high-context negotiators. In this section we shall examine the tendency of some (but not all) of these same negotiators to appeal to general principles before turning to particular cases, and consider the impact of this tendency on negotiations with representatives of the Anglo-Saxon school.

From the evidence of this study it is clear that American negotiators do rely overwhelmingly on the "factual-inductive" approach. This style is the one used by the State Department and by other domestic agencies to prepare their negotiating briefs. It is also consonant with the legal training that so many American public officials have received. Finally, and perhaps most important, concrete specificity is the form invariably required by the Congress of the United States. Imprecision in legal documents is anathema to the nation's legislators. Vague treaty commitments fly in the face of all their instincts, and an accord not couched in appropriate language is given short shrift.

The appeal to principle, however, is utterly characteristic of the Chinese negotiating style. Writers on the subject are unanimous on this point. At the first stage of negotiations Chinese negotiators tend to avoid detail and instead seek to reach agreement on broad, apparently philosophical principles that are to govern any ensuing contract. "A Chinese official," Richard Solomon concludes, "can be expected to initiate a negotiation either by pressing his foreign counterpart to agree to certain general principles, or by invoking past agreements of a general nature with the foreigner's predecessors which he is expected to accept and abide by."[46] Only when there has been a meeting of minds on the principles governing the negotiation does the Chinese official wish to move to specifics. This style is almost the exact opposite of the American approach, in the view of Lucian Pye. Americans assume, he suggests, "that progress in negotiations is usually best facilitated by adhering to concrete and specific details, avoiding debates about generalities, which can easily become entangled in political or philosophical differences." However, Pye warns that it would be a serious error for American negotiators to concede seemingly vague general principles on the grounds that they are "up in the air," without specific application. Later in the negotiation their Chinese counterparts will present them with a philosophical promissory note, to be repaid in practical coin.[47]

According to Pye, the U.S. propensity for concrete discussions and the Chinese attachment to general principles seriously hindered any improvement in relations in the 1950s and 1960s. He cites just such disabling dissonance in the Korean truce talks and the drawn-out ambassadorial talks. The U.S. strategy of proposing limited agreements on concrete issues such as the exchange of journalists collided with the Chinese insistence on general principles implying the abandonment of Taiwan. Such conditions were quite unacceptable to the United States. A renewed attempt under President Kennedy to improve relations fell foul of the same problem.[48]

Pye's argument is certainly borne out by the evidence of the abortive talks held between the two sides on the Taiwan question in 1958. The Chinese position was that any agreement should rest on a general renunciation of the use of force. Because this demand entailed recognition of the Beijing government by Washington, it was quite out of the question at the time. Secretary of State John Foster Dulles suggested that it would be constructive to move away from arguing over issues of abstract principle to the pressing, practical problems involved in the mechanics of a cessation of hostilities. But a cease-fire was "totally impermissible" in the opinion of the People's Republic of China. A secure cease-fire without an overall renunciation of force would leave the U.S. right to engage in "individual or collective self-defense" in the Taiwan area intact, while depriving China of its right to resort to force to liberate Taiwan.[49]

It was not until 1972 that Beijing and Washington put their joint signatures to an agreement, the Shanghai communiqué, establishing the framework of their relationship. This document, a radical departure in its form from established U.S. diplomatic practice, entailed in effect American adoption of the Chinese reliance on general principles. (The international circumstances were very different from those of 1958, of course.) It stated, inter alia, the agreement of the two sides

> that countries, regardless of their social systems, should conduct their relations on the principles of respect for the sovereignty and territorial integrity of all states, non-aggression against other states, non-interference in the internal affairs of other states, equality and mutual benefit, and peaceful coexistence. International disputes should be settled on this basis, without resorting to the use or threat of force. The United States and the People's Republic of China are prepared to apply these principles to their mutual relations.[50]

How was it possible for the United States to transcend its familiar insistence on specificity in both the conduct and the outcome of negotiations? The answer seems to be in the acceptance by National Security Adviser Henry Kissinger, the principal negotiator in all these contacts, of the need to adopt the Chinese approach at this time if the two sides were to get anywhere. At his first meeting with Zhou Enlai in July 1971, Kissinger eschewed the "conventional wisdom," which would have "counseled the removal of specific causes of tension." One of those problems, Taiwan, "permitted no rapid solution, while the others were too trivial to provide the basis of an enduring relationship. The answer was to discuss fundamentals . . . Precisely because there was little practical business to be done, the element of confidence had to emerge from conceptual discussions. Zhou and I spent hours together essentially giving shape to intangibles of mutual understanding."[51]

It is hard to escape the thought that the conceptual, rather than empirical, approach came easier to Kissinger—Harvard intellectual, nuclear strategist, and student of Metternich and Talleyrand—than it would have to the average State Department official. Kissinger was also well prepared, then, when confronted by Egypt's penchant for general principles. This preference had confused Americans in the past. President Johnson was puzzled when the only message delivered him from President Nasser on the occasion of a visit by Vice President Sadat in 1966 was the enigmatic desire to be understood. Egypt wanted neither wheat nor aid. "What we want, and we think it is the key to everything, is understanding."[52] Nasser surely meant that it was useless for the two countries to address details without broader agreement on the basic nature of the relationship: Was Egyptian nonalignment between the superpowers to be tolerated? Was the relationship to be one of mutual respect? Were Egyptian concerns and Israeli concerns to be given equal weight?

Henry Kissinger was first confronted by Egypt's tendency to anchor agreements in general principles before the 1973 war. In February 1973 he met with President Sadat's adviser Hafez Ismail in New York. Ismail proposed that the two sides work to achieve "an agreement on fundamental principles ('heads of agreement')." He did not clearly explain what he meant by that proposal, although he did insist on one absolute precondition for Egypt's joining a negotiating process with Israel: Israel's prior agreement to return to its 1967 borders with all its neighbors.[53] After the 1973 Arab-Israeli war, Kissinger entered into direct negotiations with President Sadat for a disengagement agreement to separate the armies of Israel and Egypt in the Sinai. Sadat's first move in the talks was to take Kissinger to one side, away from the experts, and tell him, "We first have to agree, you and I, on the principles on which they will work." Having reached a broad understanding on purposes in a remarkably short time, Sadat left it to his military experts to translate "the general agreement to practical form."[54]

With the Shanghai communiqué under its belt, and with some insight now into Sadat's work methods, the Nixon administration agreed to formulate the basis of its relationship with Egypt in terms of a general text. Under the heading "Principles of Relations and Cooperation Between Egypt and the United States," the two states set themselves a whole series of "tasks" to occupy them in the years ahead. Here was broadbrush diplomacy with a vengeance. They would "intensify consultations at all levels," "continue their active cooperation and their energetic pursuit of peace in the Middle East," "develop their mutual relations in a spirit of esteem, respect and mutual advantage," and so on, in an ambitious agenda of cooperative endeavors.[55] It was bold, it was sweeping—and it was very un-American. U.S. diplomacy, Ambassador Eilts acknowledges, tends to prefer more specific agreements. He himself was uncomfortable with the open-ended commitments that the United States had signed. The promise, for instance, that "the United States will make the maximum feasible contribution, in accordance with Congressional authorization, to Egypt's economic development," was liable to create unfulfillable expectations.[56]

In the consultations between the Egyptian and American governments both before and after President Sadat's November 1977 trip to Jerusalem, the aim was also "to produce some prior understanding on basic principles, some frame of reference." Once this understanding had been achieved, Egyptian-Israeli negotiations would concentrate on working out the details.[57] The search for such a framework continued through 1977 and 1978 and was eventually realized in the Camp David Accords of September 1978. It is clear that, despite its usual bent, American diplomacy, as in the China case, had successfully accommodated itself to the deductive approach favored by its interlocutor. Also noteworthy is the fact that in both cases broad philosophical foundations for the new relationship had first to be laid before detailed cooperation could get under way.

In the NAFTA negotiations between Mexico and the United States, Charles Roh noted, Mexican officials were at first inclined to address problems in the Latin tradition of broad general principles. In contrast, U.S. negotiators were typically preoccupied with "micro writing" the agreement, believing it in everybody's interest to spell out the parties' rights and obligations in exhaustive detail in order to avoid misunderstandings later. They were also aware that a treaty that left something to the imagination would simply get tied up in Congress.[58] The solution lay in a mature Mexican willingness to address problems in a pragmatic spirit. Moreover, it could be argued that what made the accord possible in the first place was a mutual prior understanding on the economic foundations of the new partnership: the virtues of free trade.

An ability to negotiate in a spirit of "principled pragmatism" underpins other notable U.S.-Mexican negotiating successes, starting with the Chamizal boundary negotiations. Ambassador Manuel Tello, the Mexican delegate, did not conceal his conviction that it was all a matter of principle. But Ambassador Thomas Mann grasped "that the psychological line of the boundary was far more important than the actual physical line." In other words, once the United States conceded the 1911 award in principle, Mexico would be flexible in practice.[59] And so it proved. Mexico had no interest in actually demarcating a boundary running through the center of an El Paso school. This distinction between the ideal and the achievable underpinned the final agreement. Of the 437.18 acres estimated to have been awarded to Mexico in 1911, the government of Mexico agreed to accept 71.18 acres from an area of El Paso slightly downstream from the Chamizal zone.

In the 1979 U.S.-Mexican gas talks the ultimate solution hinged on a similar distinction. The apparently straightforward focus of the talks was the price to be paid Mexico for the supply of natural gas. But energy, as noted, is an emotive subject for the Mexicans, and the danger that they would be accused of selling out their patrimony to the United States was foremost in the minds of Mexican negotiators. Their opening position, therefore, was to insist on pegging the price of their gas to the heat equivalent of number-two fuel oil delivered in New York harbor—a roughly comparable energy source. The attraction of this proposal to Mexico was that the United States would not be acquiring an unfair bargain and exploiting the Mexican people. Unfortunately, the offer was unacceptable to the Carter administration (and particularly to Secretary of Energy James Schlesinger), which proposed to pay U.S. domestic suppliers only two-thirds that price.

The first sessions of talks were unproductive. Julius Katz, the joint leader of the U.S. delegation, recalls the Mexicans appealing to many principles, including justice and equity. The Americans proposed an alternative pricing formula, but with no success. The Mexicans, terrified of appearing to have sold out, "clung like bulldogs" to their position. Price, as another American official realized, had become "a matter of national honor." On August 3 Ambassador Lucey met with President López Portillo, at Katz's urging, to determine whether there was any genuine interest in an agreement. Portillo is reported to have said that his problem was "not with prices but with principles."[60] Lucey took this statement to mean that the Mexican president was signaling acceptance of the current American offer, but it turned out that López Portillo actually intended just the opposite.

The key to the negotiation proved to be a switch in the American approach, away from discussing pricing formulas based on some energy equivalent to discussing specific prices. As long as the negotiations were conducted at a theoretical level no progress was made: the delegations were transfixed by principled disagreement. It was only when the "carpet trading" started that convergence became possible. Katz had been tipped off by Díaz Serrano, director general of PEMEX (Petroleos Mexicanos, the Mexican national oil conglomerate), that this was the way to go: "This is just like buying a used car." In Katz's opinion there was a true ambivalence in the Mexican position between insistence on honor and willingness to haggle. But in the final analysis the Mexicans were ready to climb down from the high tree of principle in order to cut a deal, as long as it could be justified before public opinion.[61]

India and Japan more resemble the United States in their avoidance of a deductive style of presentation. India has been influenced by long acquaintance with case law and the British preference for specific applications; Japan, in accordance with the *awase* style, places "emphasis on the special circumstances that distinguish each concrete case and work to make general principles inapplicable."[62] So we may conclude that the axiomatic approach is not to be considered an invariant component of high-context negotiation.

The contrast between egalitarian and hierarchical cultural expectations was one theme of this chapter. Another was the contradiction between low- and high-context approaches to compromise. Americans tend naturally to assume a give-and-take model of negotiation in which reciprocal concession leads to eventual compromise. This model may, however, be confronted by a quite different one, which does not take reciprocity or compromise for granted but is quite happy to demand one-sided concessions in payment of a supposed moral debt or as the duty of the stronger party.

It was observed that the U.S. delegation's premature disclosure of its position might result in serious disadvantage in the face of a less confiding opponent. Finally, the pragmatic American preference for treating specifics was found to run up against a high-context leaning to achieve agreement first on axioms and philosophical principles. One way to reconcile this contradiction is to combine the two: to agree on practical steps under a canopy of general principles that meet the other side's psychological needs.

7

On Tactics and Players

Middle Game I

The concept of a middle game in negotiation is admittedly an artificial one. There is not much, for instance, in Japanese or Chinese behavior to distinguish this stage from the preceding one. Japanese reticence, first detected in the opening phase, may simply continue in a holding pattern that looks a lot like temporizing and stalling, with a few minor concessions thrown in, to ward off predictable American pressure in the end game. Chinese negotiators may persist throughout in an attritional, probing mode until a critical point is reached, when, having determined their partner's absolute bottom line, they jump straight to their final offer. Nevertheless, the distinction is still useful. For one thing, it permits an orderly presentation of the evidence for the working of cross-cultural dissonance. In the long haul between the inception and the termination of the negotiation, differences in the use of language and contrasting understanding of such key concepts as time, authority, and negotiation itself come into focus.

But the main justification for the distinction is that the baseline culture for this investigation—that of the United States—does suppose a separate function for the intermediate stage of talks. American negotiators tend to assume that a certain process of give-and-take, governed by identifiable rules of the game, is appropriate in the period between the presentation of one's opening proposal and the final, intense resolution of the contest. The middle game is also seen as the stage when, in an atmosphere of greater confidence and openness than that prevailing at the outset, it becomes possible to probe behind opening positions to discover where the real and possibly unstated problems lie.

What, then, are American expectations for the middle game? To answer this question let us ponder the resonances of the American-English term "negotiate." The word itself, a moment's reflection reveals, is synonymous with a willingness to give up something, make a concession, in order to arrive at a compromise, "somewhere in the middle," that meets the needs of both parties. Thus to say "let's negotiate this" or "this is negotiable" implies a willingness to give and take. Almost everything in American life is negotiable, including the outcome of litigation, which in most cases does not reach adjudication but is usually settled, even in criminal cases, by a negotiation between plaintiff and defendant known as plea bargaining. (To legal systems with a more absolutist sense of justice, this is an incomprehensible idea.) "Concession" and "compromise," on the whole, have acquired either neutral or positive meanings. Obviously, concessions may be wise or foolish, favored or deplored, depending on circumstances; but they are not usually thought to be inherently illegitimate. Quite the reverse: to make a concession in order to reach a desired agreement is fully justified behavior. If anything, expressions like "I'm willing to concede that point" have connotations of open-mindedness and generosity.

It should be noted that in other languages the connotations of "negotiate," "concede," and "compromise" are not necessarily positive, just as in eighteenth-century English—reflecting the way of life of an honor-based, high-context society—they had the derogatory sense of a shameful act. Traces of this are still found in expressions such as to compromise one's virtue or integrity. There is significantly no indigenous word in Arabic, the language of the high-context, shame culture par excellence, for "compromise." *Tanazol* means concession by one of the parties alone and therefore implies retreat, abandonment of a right. To avoid this negative, shameful connotation and reflect the reality of negotiation with cultures that do have the concept of compromise, new terms have had to be introduced. *Khaleena nitjaham* means "let's reach a common understanding." *Musawama* implies mutual concession, the process of reaching a fair or "middle solution," *hal wassat*. If we assume that language reflects and directs behavior, it follows that in negotiation among Arabs concessions, to be acceptable, must be reciprocal or mutually contingent; this is a key point. In these circumstances, they are not thought of as "concessions" in the old negative sense, but as coordinated actions in the search for a settlement. Talks involving synchronized concessions, in which no one loses face, are subtly different from talks involving sequential concessions in which one party may well gain at the expense of its rival. In situations in which disputes over high principle, as opposed to trade, are involved, this state of joint and therefore honorable contingency may be very hard to reach through direct negotiations, because sequential concessions are fraught with the risk of shame. A desirable outcome of mutual, face-saving concession may sometimes be attainable only through the good offices of a third-party mediator, with rivals insulated from each other.

The most intuitively plausible model of the middle game, the heart of the negotiation, for Americans is the one known as "concession-convergence," according to which the parties start out from different positions and approach each other in a series of concessions until they arrive at a compromise. In its crudest version, concession-convergence portrays negotiators as inching toward each other incrementally along a continuum. This notion more or less corresponds to Americans' day-to-day experience of bargaining over a car or a house, or negotiating the terms of a contract. A more sophisticated version of the model, intended better to capture the essence of international negotiation, has participants not inching but "jumping," and not haggling over a deal, but engaged in a "joint search" for a "formula."[1] In practice this version is less radical than it appears at first sight, because a joint search under conditions of perceived competition necessarily implies concessions offered and received. Moreover, although the term "formula" has the advantage of emphasizing the conceptual dimension rather than the quantitative dimension of international problems, it is still expected that the contending positions of the parties will be reconciled through a compromise.

BIDDING

Perceptions of competition in the United States are deeply influenced by two dominant and complementary families of metaphors: one associated with sport and the other with the marketplace. The sporting metaphor encapsulates values of team play, rule-governed conduct, chivalry, tough endeavor, and discipline. A sporting contest is fascinating and suggestive because superior virtue (in its original Greek sense of skill at one's job) receives its just reward. Complementing the idealized metaphor of the sporting competition, however, is the equally powerful metaphor of the market. If sport generally precludes negotiation, persuasive argument, and give-and-take, the market rests on negotiation. If sporting outcomes are deserved, in the market, in the words of the Charles Karass advertisement, "You don't get what you deserve, you get what you negotiate!" For Americans, negotiation in the marketplace, just like sport, produces benevolent—peaceful and socially efficient—outcomes. In principle, as noted, few areas of American life exclude negotiation: democracy, not just as a theory of government but the way the United States settles its public affairs in practice, rests on negotiation. Ironically, although it is accepted that almost everything important is negotiable—open to adjustment and accommodation by a process of communicated bids—from wage contracts, via laws, to prison sentences, the prices of day-to-day commodities bought in the shops are not negotiable. Ordinary Americans, therefore, are not always comfortable with bargaining and have come to rely on a special class of people for major negotiations: lawyers. This has had a critical impact on the American negotiating style, which to outsiders appears highly legalistic.

High-context negotiators do not necessarily share American assumptions about the universal virtues of the give-and-take of negotiation. At this point readers may object—from their experience of holidays in Cairo, Hong Kong, or Guadalajara—that lively bargaining is hardly alien to those places. Indeed, Americans rarely better the locals in a haggle. But in contrast to the United States, which is a society based on contract and grounded in commerce, communally minded cultures do not view the market as ubiquitous. Some spheres of life are considered totally inappropriate for marketlike behavior. To clarify the matter it will be helpful to adopt a distinction between two paradigmatic types of negotiation observed by William Quandt in the Middle East.[2]

One is the *suq* (Arab market) model. Bargaining is preceded by elaborate ritual, much drinking of coffee or tea, and the exchange of social courtesies in order to establish a personal relationship. The bidding itself starts off with the seller asking a price that is much higher than he expects to receive. The buyer, in turn, is expected to make an offer that will also leave him considerable leeway for adjustment. After haggling for some time— and patience and imperturbability are of the essence—the bids of the parties will progressively converge until they arrive at an agreed figure. When they do shake hands on the deal, both sides must feel that they have gained something. An unhappy customer will not come back. This is the model that is familiar to the tourist from the bazaars and markets of the non-European world.

But not everybody is expected to haggle, nor is everything a fit object of haggling. There is a time and a place for it. One of the peculiarities of the etiquette of bargaining is that it shifts with the social status of the bar-gainer. "Men of honor and prestige in the Middle East do not bargain," argues Lebanese anthropologist Fuad Khuri, "even when they realize that the goods they have bought have been overpriced. This is because bargain-ing, like pennypinching, does not go with prestige."[3]

A similar proviso is attached to the scope of haggling. Business transac-tions obviously provide a suitable occasion for the activity. Matters con-cerning the honor of the group most certainly do not. Here a quite different mode of operation takes effect, involving the resort to mediation, gestures of conciliation, and face saving. Quandt refers to this pattern of behavior (not very aptly) as the *bedouin* model. Although he makes his distinction with particular respect to Egypt, it can also be seen to hold for all the face-salient, high-context societies examined here. Whenever a problem arises touching on the "sacred" values of sovereignty and identity, the "pro-fane" give-and-take mode, which has its quintessential expression in the marketplace, must be discarded or concealed.

As could be predicted, in transactions involving prices and quantities the *suq* model was generally applicable in the cases examined. Bidding followed predictable lines where quantifiable issues were at stake in questions such as trade negotiations with China and Japan, the 1942–43 talks with Mexico over distribution of the waters of the Colorado River, the 1953 thorium nitrate purchase from India, and negotiations between the U.S. Department of Defense and the Egyptian War Ministry over the cost of using Egyptian range facilities. The 1995–96 U.S.-Chinese intellectual property rights talks, which introduced complex issues of international and domestic law, trade, compliance, and supervision, ended as a straightforward haggle over the entry of foreign movie and music companies into the Chinese market and the number of pirate compact disk factories the Chinese government would close. In the end Chinese negotiators announced to the U.S. dele-gation that they had closed two factories in addition to thirteen already shut down in 1996, a sweetener clearly prepared in advance to be thrown into the pot at the last moment, in the best tradition of the *suq*.[4]

It would be worth investigating further examples of this mode (and comparison with cases where Western negotiators bargained with each other might also be of interest), but the pattern is clear. Skill at haggling is mostly a function of experience since the rules and stratagems are simple: know the competition, start high (or low, as the case may be), bargain stubbornly, be prepared to walk away. In the intellectual property rights case mentioned above, the talks were doomed to succeed, because U.S.

negotiators, in the final analysis, were not prepared to leave Beijing without an accord. The threatened imposition of U.S. trade sanctions on China was not credible. The haggling skills of U.S. negotiators in more favorable conditions cannot be determined on the basis of a limited sample. My impression is that trade negotiators have learned to haggle better than technical experts, although many Americans, brought up on the single price system, are unhappy with the exaggerated posturing and the uncertainty of the *suq*. American friends whom I have accompanied to the *suq* in the old city of Jerusalem sometimes inject an ethical tone into their disapproval of haggling: "It seems so mean-minded to deprive these poor people of a few dollars." But in cities like Teheran, where literally everything is for sale in the bazaar, it would be considered very strange indeed to see something immoral or shameful in bargaining.

The validity of Khuri's observation that "carpet trading" is not engaged in by notables or in matters of honor is also borne out. Kissinger observes that Zhou Enlai "never bargained to score petty points. I soon found that the best way to deal with him was to present a reasonable position, explain it meticulously, and then stick to it." At one point in the negotiations over the 1972 Shanghai communiqué Zhou assured Kissinger: "You do not have to trade; all you have to do is to convince me why our language is embarrassing."[5]

Kissinger had a similar experience in dealing with Anwar Sadat. The Egyptian president, Kissinger writes in his memoirs, "generally did not haggle; like Zhou Enlai . . . he started with his real position and rarely moved from it." In the January 1974 disengagement talks, Kissinger asked the Egyptian leader how many battalions of troops he wanted in the limited force zone (separating the two armies). Sadat wanted "as near ten as possible" and settled for eight, which was as high as the Israelis would go. The Israeli negotiators had pressed Kissinger to try for a lower figure with Sadat before finally agreeing, but Kissinger declined. "I thought I knew my man; it would backfire if we started haggling."[6]

Between the extremes of the *suq* and *bedouin* models—"carpet trading" and an austere refusal to bargain at all on matters of honor or high principle—there is what we may call "normal" diplomatic bargaining for the reconciliation of contending positions, the search for a common view of a situation. Much international negotiation falls into this third category, which may contain elements of both prototypes. This mix is doubly confusing, for one can never be absolutely certain which mode is prevailing at a given time. Nor is it certain that the non-Westerners themselves, given the psychological difficulties they sometimes have in dealing with the United States, always know.

The most salient cross-cultural antinomy in the middle phase is a disagreement between high-context and low-context negotiators on the competing claims of fairness (and its corollary, generosity) and power (and its corollary, greed). For Americans, thinking in mercantile terms, compromise is an inherently desirable outcome in most cases. Compromise, by sharing out benefit, creates equilibrium, mutual satisfaction. One-sided advantage, it is assumed, creates imbalance and is therefore unstable. It is strange for non-Americans to be faced by negotiators representing the greatest commercial and military power on earth and yet deliberately aiming at an equitable outcome. As far as non-Americans are concerned, there is no inherent virtue in compromise for its own sake; if one has the upper hand in a negotiation one will seek to capitalize on that fact unsentimentally and greedily.

Faced by opponents who adopt tough opening positions that they are ready to modify only slowly and grudgingly (if at all), Americans generally redouble their effort to find a "reasonable compromise." Creative flexibility is the order of the day. Patience and the willingness to postpone gratification are not traits that automatically garner reward in American public life. Rather than digging in their heels for the long haul, Americans energetically cast around for a new and innovative idea to break the deadlock. If one proposal has failed to produce results it is to be rejected for another one, more generous and attractive to one's partner. The search for compromise results in a negotiation with oneself. In a domestic negotiation against a rival playing by the same rules the search for compromise is a recipe for joint gain; against a determined opponent with other assumptions it puts Americans at a tactical disadvantage.

It is here that Glen Fisher detects the principal difference between American and Mexican approaches to negotiation: whereas American negotiators "are among the most enthusiastic proponents of compromise," Mexicans perceive no inherent virtue in accommodating their adversaries.[7] In practical terms this difference implies that Mexican negotiators maintain their positions more tenaciously than do their American counterparts. One American diplomat, with experience of dealing with the Mexican government on drug-related issues, felt that the "lion's share" of concessions was invariably made by the American side. "We gave in 75 percent of the time, the Mexicans 25 percent of the time."

Of course, it could be argued that the United States is in an inherently weaker position on the narcotics issue because it is more eager for cooperation.

However, Timothy Bennett, who dealt with trade issues, observed the same phenomenon. His explanation was that American negotiators are generally more anxious for agreements because "they are always in a hurry" and basically "problem solving oriented." In other words, they place a high value on resolving an issue quickly. Their catchphrase might be, "Some solution is better than no solution." An interagency team—Ambassador Newsom's "drop-in delegation"—would be put together, parachuted into Mexico City, and try to get down to the job at once. Having clarified the points at issue, they would seek a solution and move on to tomorrow's problem. Impatience (and, we might add, mixed cross-cultural expertise) led to a willingness to concede more than they should have in order to get a deal. With a more leisurely view of time, the Mexican delegation had an advantageous position from the outset.[8]

American willingness to concede, however, would not be important were it not confronted by a much greater tenacity on the part of the Mexicans. Adolfo Aguilar accounted for the stubbornness of Mexican negotiators in negotiations with the United States by referring to the burden of history and his compatriots' consciousness of the tremendous difference in size and power between the two countries. They are obliged to exercise great caution in making concessions because any agreement with the United States "carries a high risk of surrendering important national interests."[9]

The confrontation of these contrasting styles is exemplified by the negotiation of the 1957 U.S.-Mexican air transport agreement. Having dragged on through several inconclusive rounds over more than a decade, negotiations resumed in May 1955. Ambassador White, the chief U.S. negotiator, became almost distraught with the intransigence of his Mexican counterpart, Minister of Communications Buchanan. In a meeting with President Ruiz Cortines of Mexico in March 1956, White complained bitterly about his treatment:

> Buchanan had been a stumbling block for a long time. I said that Buchanan had stated, among other things, that all the concessions have been made on the Mexican side. But this is just not borne out by the facts. The facts are that we have made countless concessions over the years, each one of which has been accepted by the Mexicans and then they have gone on to make further demands and to raise fictitious issues . . . When we permitted CMA in 1947 unlimited flights between Mexico City and Los Angeles it was on the understanding that it would lead to a bilateral agreement and so far it hasn't and, similarly, in 1951 when we permitted Aerovias Guest to fly from

Mexico City to Miami we were given the same assurance but we still have no bilateral agreement. I said that Buchanan had tried these tactics again several times.[10]

White's intercession with Cortines did not alter the situation one whit. Clearly the problem was not Buchanan the individual. Only when the United States resorted in September 1956 to the ultimate threat to terminate all services by Mexican airlines into the United States was Mexico finally convinced that it had extracted every last possible concession.

The final agreement was highly favorable from the Mexicans' point of view. As they had demanded, it was done as an exchange of notes, not in the form of the standard U.S. air transport agreement (which was attached as an appendix). The contract was for one year only, not, as the United States had requested, of indefinite duration. On the most important point— whether there would be a division of traffic (to protect the weaker Mexican airlines) or free competition, as the United States had long insisted—the agreement substantially met Mexican concerns: Mexico was given exclusive rights on three routes, whereas on three others the parties would run only one airline each; that is, there would be some competition, but it would be strictly limited.[11]

In a laboratory study it was found that Indians—like Mexicans—are more competitive bargainers and are prepared to bargain longer than Americans.[12] These differences were displayed in the 1953 thorium nitrate affair. After India, a U.S. aid recipient, had supplied thorium nitrate (a prohibited commodity under the U.S. Battle Act) to the People's Republic of China, the U.S. government insisted on a formal Indian commitment "not to do it again." Otherwise the aid program would have to be canceled. As far as India was concerned, the U.S. demand was unacceptable and flew in the face of the untrammeled exercise of Indian sovereignty—a matter of national honor on which no concession was possible. Nehru preferred no aid to aid with strings.

The initial American proposal came on August 13 in the shape of a detailed legal document, which, it was suggested, should form the basis of an exchange of notes. In the proposed document the U.S. government would recognize the Indian right to trade with whom it pleased, while the government of India would equally accept the American right to grant or withhold financial assistance to India if strategic materials were sold to enemies of the United States. Accordingly the Indian government would agree to desist from future shipments of restricted items. This proposal was

turned down by Under Secretary Sir Naravana Raghavan Pillai at the
Indian foreign ministry on the grounds that Prime Minister Nehru "might
make a rash decision if confronted with the draft, leaving no room for
negotiation."[13]

Accordingly the United States shifted its position. On September 18
Ambassador George Allen proposed a simplified oral statement meeting
U.S. concerns. He wished to be assured that although the government of
India did not accept the Battle Act as binding, it (a) had "no intent" to ship
listed commodities to prohibited destinations and (b) would inform the
ambassador of "any change in the situation." Although Pillai did not reject
this form of commitment in principle, he did object to its specific content
—a fine distinction. "He urged that we not press GOI [the Government of
India] too strongly on this issue in order not to weaken his hand and the
hands of other GOI officials genuinely working for a solution of this matter."
By now, Allen was eager to get the issue out of the way and had concluded
that no general declaration or commitment would be forthcoming.[14]

And so it continued. The U.S. government balked at the alternative of
cutting off aid and decided to solve the problem in another way—by purchasing the total Indian production of thorium nitrate. On January 16,
1954, Secretary of State Dulles pronounced himself content with the
"thorough airing" the problem of restricted commodities had received. In
this situation, he concluded, the United States might well attain its objective by putting the matter squarely in the hands of the Indian government
with the implication that it had a "moral responsibility" to control the
export of Battle Act items.[15] And there the matter rested. It had been a
counterproductive exercise and an inelegant withdrawal.

Of all the cultures discussed here, the Japanese has been the most
closely scrutinized in recent years. Experts are in general agreement that
few societies find give-and-take more distasteful. Instead of step-by-step
concession, Thayer and Weiss observe, Japanese negotiators "call for consideration of their situation and reiterate their initial position." They "may
have little leeway to do otherwise, because of the difficulty they have had
in reaching consensus within their own ranks."[16] Leo Moser adds that they
are likely to be unresponsive to "trial balloons" and suggestions for compromise, much to the surprise of Americans. Americans "may then see their
Japanese counterparts as simply unwilling to compromise or as uninter-
ested in keeping the negotiation process alive."[17]

Apparent Japanese immobility in the middle game has indeed been a
recurrent and disconcerting feature of U.S.-Japanese negotiations. In the

1970 textile negotiations Japanese Foreign Ministry officials were unable to get representatives of their own textile industry to agree to a modification of a formula that had proved quite unacceptable to the Nixon administration. Rather than appear empty-handed at the resumed talks, Japanese negotiators presented a "position paper" that was in fact no more than a summary of the current state of internal Japanese consultations. U.S. negotiator Peter Flanigan was "taken aback" and "expressed extreme unhappiness with the failure of the Japanese government to take a clear stance." Nor was this case an isolated one; the Japanese persistently failed to come up with counterproposals.[18]

The chemistry of U.S.-Japanese negotiations has changed, in certain respects, remarkably little over time. In 1994 as in 1970 Japanese paralysis produced American frustration. Talks to open the Japanese market to foreign-made medical equipment and telecommunication technology had deadlocked over the question of establishing objective criteria to measure progress. They resumed in Washington in July 1994 with U.S. hopes that a solution was in sight. U.S. negotiators were then astonished to discover that the Japanese position had not changed in the slightest. A senior official angrily denounced the Japanese for instigating the latest round of talks on the basis of false expectations, commenting: "They came here with nothing. It's unbelievable. No one's in charge. They don't negotiate at all, and the only thing they react to is pressure."[19]

From an American time perspective, the Japanese make concessions "slowly and grudgingly," in the words of Michael Blaker. Initial positions are abandoned only after painful soul-searching and the prolonged evolution of a new domestic consensus.[20] This pattern certainly held up in the 1981 air service negotiations. It also characterized the 1985–86 semiconductor negotiations over U.S. allegations that the Japanese were dumping microchips on the American market. The U.S. position was that a major trade dispute would be triggered unless Japanese industry cut overcapacity, raised semiconductor prices (which were artificially low), and permitted improved U.S. access to the Japanese market. At informal meetings in July 1985, Japanese trade officials agreed to encourage increased purchases of U.S. microchips but declined to alter prices. While preparations for an antidumping suit went ahead, the United States demanded more far-reaching concessions. On August 23 there were further talks on the subject, but little progress was made because the Japanese side would not move from its earlier stance. It was not until November that the Japanese made an improved (but still unsatisfactory) offer on both prices and access. Although it was "turned down flat" by the United States, the same proposal was offered in different forms and at different levels several times in November and early December with only minor changes in language. On the last occasion before the administration's filing of its antidumping case U.S. trade representative Clayton Yeutter was asked to receive a top Japanese Ministry of Trade and Industry official at a 6:00 A.M. pre-breakfast meeting, only to hear the same old tune. When negotiations resumed in January 1986, Japan, in typical fashion, repeated its previous proposal without modification.[21]

Different notions of time are clearly also a prominent factor in the frustration that seems such a frequent accompaniment of U.S.-Japanese negotiation. "We're too fast, they're too slow," mused former senator and veteran ambassador to Tokyo (1977–89) Mike Mansfield. "We have to slow down, they have to quicken up."[22] All too often the two sides find their rates of concession utterly unsynchronized. Of course, the frustration cuts both ways. Whereas Americans find Japanese negotiators painfully deliberate, the Japanese view American negotiators as alarmingly precipitous. Haste, one observer has remarked, evokes "a sense of confusion and chaos" in Japanese minds. Their instinctive response is to dig in their heels.[23] In the semiconductor affair, U.S. Department of Commerce initiation of the antidumping suit in the middle of talks shocked Japanese officials, conditioned by domestic practices to expect a protracted process of consultation and negotiation.[24]

In the case of the People's Republic of China, the intermediate stage between the opening moves of a negotiation, when initial proposals are put on the table, and the end game, when the final terms of the agreement are hammered out, is recognized to possess unusual features. Richard Solomon argues that the Chinese do not view negotiation "as a highly technical process of haggling over details in which the two sides initially table maximum positions and then seek to move to a point of convergence through incremental compromises. Indeed, they disparage haggling and can show remarkable flexibility in making concrete arrangements once they have decided it is in their interest to conclude an agreement."[25] It has been suggested by some scholars that the Chinese are not comfortable with the concept of reciprocal bidding—mutual and serial concessions—because of a culturally derived reluctance to incur an obligation to anyone from outside their primary kinship group.[26]

Thus, rather than engage in a protracted exchange of bids, the Chinese prefer to spend the middle game in a meticulous and patient probing of the firmness of their opponent's position in order to gauge the real nature of its bottom line. Having established to their own satisfaction their opponent's absolutely irreducible minimum, they then jump to a final position intended to reconcile contending principles. This philosophy of negotiation clearly flies in the face of many American assumptions, for example, that one's opening position must have some "give" in it, that concessions are made and reciprocated at discrete intervals throughout the middle game, and that the outcome will be a compromise somewhere in the middle. To a rival negotiator mainly concerned with discovering the American bottom line, flexibility, by indicating the softness of the U.S. position, may impede and not facilitate agreement. If U.S. negotiators wanted to help their Chinese interlocutors, Chas Freeman argued, the very best thing they could do was to make their irreducible position crystal clear. To do this might require a tough display of resolution; walking out or setting ultimatums did not build mutual confidence but might be effective in communicating a bottom line. Only when Chinese officials could convince their superiors that the outer limits of U.S. tolerance had been reached would an agreement become possible: "If the consequences aren't Armageddon, they can't carry the situation internally!"[27] ·

In his study of U.S.-Chinese negotiating in the ambassadorial talks of the 1950s and 1960s, Kenneth Young warns that "Americans tend to put too much material between what can be conceded away and what cannot be given up under any circumstances."[28] Despite some experience—and considerable study—of negotiating with the People's Republic of China, precisely this approach was taken by the Carter administration in the 1977–78 normalization talks. Secretary of State Cyrus Vance acknowledges that he intended to start out with "a maximum position" on the Taiwan issue: U.S. government personnel would have to remain on Taiwan after normalization (Beijing would not tolerate an official presence, only a nonofficial presence through an ostensibly private organization). "I did not expect the Chinese to accept our proposal, but I felt it wise to make it, even though we might eventually have to abandon it." Confusing matters even further, Vance then made, alongside this "soft" position, a major unreciprocated concession at his first meeting with Foreign Minister Huang Hua of China: the U.S. defense treaty with Taiwan would "lapse" and the withdrawal of military forces and installations from the island be completed. When, the following day, Huang Hua reiterated the Chinese position and noted that normalization would be further delayed, Vance hastened to add that the U.S. position was merely "a starting point for discussion."[29]

Playing their hand closer to the chest, the Chinese kept back one crucial trump from the final normalization agreement. Three years later they used it to extract yet more U.S. concessions in a quite separate game.

In the 1955 talks for the repatriation of American citizens kept in China against their will, the same characteristic pattern of early, unreciprocated concession by the United States is found. At the second session of the talks on August 2, Chinese delegate Wang seized the initiative and put forward a series of demands, among which he called on the United States to supply a list of names of Chinese who had been issued exit visas and proposed that third-party countries take charge of both the American and the Chinese nationals. At the next session on August 4, Ambassador Alexis Johnson spent the whole time responding to the Chinese position and handed Wang the requested list of seventy-six names. Far from thanking him, Wang "expressed dissatisfaction" and demanded a complete list of names of Chinese nationals in the United States. Other unreciprocated U.S. concessions followed in subsequent sessions, including the major one of agreeing to third-party representation.[30]

By August 23 the negotiation had stuck on the Chinese refusal to agree to release all Americans at once. In an appeal to Wang's sense of fair play, Ambassador Johnson implicitly admitted the failure of his approach. Johnson "carefully outlined [the] successive concessions we had made to obtain agreement and repeatedly stressed 'we could go no further.'" He poignantly added, "'We did not even have a definite promise, much less [the] performance we expected.'" Wang continued to fight tenaciously to avoid an explicit commitment. On September 6 there was a final battle over how to characterize the exercise by expatriates of their right to return home. Johnson made a stand on including the word "now." Wang refused point-blank, insisting on the (vague) term "expeditious." Johnson admitted that "although I used to [the] maximum my very strong negotiating position [I] was entirely unable to shake him."[31] Reasoned persuasion, it transpired, was not enough against patient tenacity.

Even at this late stage Johnson still had one final card to play. The agenda of the talks, agreed to on August 1, contained two items: the civilian repatriation issue and "other practical matters at issue between the two sides" (implying the U.S. economic blockade of China and the confrontation over Taiwan). It was this second item that the Chinese were really interested in, not the handful of unfortunate American civilians. Item one was simply the entry price for item two. However, Wang never revealed his interest by the merest hint and ignored Johnson's statement that he would not proceed to anything else until item one was settled.[32] Deciding that an imperfect agreement was better than no agreement, the United States conceded the Chinese position. This concession was a damaging comedown hardly calculated to help U.S. credibility. In simultaneous "agreed announcements" issued on September 10 the "right to return" was acknowledged, but there was no explicit determination of when.[33] The U.S. State Department was to regret this omission for years afterward. In the final analysis, Wang had played his cards adeptly, concealing his real objective, putting Johnson on the defensive from the outset, shrewdly exploiting U.S. impatience and willingness to compromise, even if this meant leaving U.S. citizens in Chinese hands.

It cannot be too much emphasized how surprising and disorienting it is for U.S. negotiators to be faced by an interlocutor who does not accept the "self-evident" convention that concessions are to be reciprocated. This implies that deliberate violation of the rule gains tactical advantage. To conclude this section, it is worth demonstrating how China resorted in the very recent past, in unfavorable conditions, to just this tactic with similar effect to that of twenty-five years before. In September 1989 Secretary of State James Baker met at the United Nations with Foreign Minister Qian Qichen.[34] In this negotiation China was in a difficult position, facing international ostracism, the repression of human rights in China having produced a domestic outcry in the United States and severe disapproval throughout the Western world. Baker's aim in the conversation was to salvage as much as possible of the U.S.-Chinese relationship in the aftermath of the June 4 bloodbath in Tiananmen Square. Qian, like Wang, adopted the aphorism that "the best defense is a good offense."

From the outset Secretary Baker displayed a cross-cultural insensitivity that could only be counterproductive to his aim of improving relations. "There's a perception developing in the United States that China is closing the *Open Door*," Baker said, apparently oblivious to the painful historical connotations that his words would have for any Chinese patriot. (The "Open Door" was the turn-of-the-century U.S. policy, enunciated by Secretary of State John Hay, compelling China to open up, on an equal basis, to trade with the Western imperialist countries. It sparked off the 1900 Boxer Rebellion which, in turn, drew in Western military intervention in Beijing.) "Anything you can do to preserve the Open Door will be helpful," Baker continued, hinting at the desirability of easing the repression. "We are not the ones who want to close it," Qian retorted. "Our door is open. But an open door requires two sides."

Looking back on the meeting, Baker explains that the task facing him was to tread a fine line between nudging Qian "toward a preferred course without embarrassing [him] in the process." Accordingly, Baker acknowledged the domestic problems facing the Chinese government, while suggesting it might still consider lifting martial law and lessening anti-American propaganda. This would help the U.S. administration with its own public opinion.

At this point in the conversation Baker put in his bid. In the classic tradition of American negotiating he proffered, without overt conditionality, what he believed to be an open-handed concession. President Bush, he told Qian, had decided—though not yet announced publicly—to allow U.S. contractors to resume work upgrading the avionics of Chinese F-8 jet fighters. Baker knew that the military relationship was vitally important to China; Western technology was the key to transforming the Chinese army into a modern force. "Given such a generous gesture," Baker said, "a reciprocal gesture seemed in order."

Qian was having none of it. From his perspective, putting business in the way of the American aircraft industry was no one-sided concession to China. He pocketed the offer, unsurprisingly leaving the impression that he was the one doing the United States a favor. His government, he complained, "was extremely annoyed by continuing pressure from the G-7 nations." Directly referring to the historical confrontation between China and the West that Baker had himself thoughtlessly mentioned, Qian bitterly observed that "not since the 1900 Boxer Rebellion . . . had Chinese sovereignty been treated with such disdain." This "unjust attitude" would not be tolerated. "If this continues day after day we could not avoid hurting the feelings of the Chinese people and damaging Sino-American relations."

Ruefully, Baker notes that Qian "had no compunction about asking for American concessions while simultaneously ignoring my request for 'visible and positive Chinese steps' to allay congressional and public anger with Beijing." So, far from reciprocating Baker's "generous gesture," the Chinese foreign minister pressed for the resumption of suspended World Bank loans, the renewal of bilateral science and technology agreements, and the sale of communications satellites. Baker justifies the one-sided administration approach on the grounds that "goodwill begets goodwill." Later in 1989 further "generous gestures" followed: the dispatch of U.S. envoys to Beijing, the lifting of a ban on Export-Import Bank loans to U.S. firms doing business with China, and the sale of communications satellites. Finally, in January 1990 martial law was lifted in Beijing and Tiananmen

Square reopened to the public. These, Baker hints, were the payoff for U.S. concessions. To the outsider the deal looks very lopsided indeed, the U.S. paying in hard currency for internal Chinese measures that would have had to be taken sooner or later in China's own interest anyway. Here was a relationship both sides wished to preserve; but Qian's hard-nosed negotiating approach and Baker's inept handling of the situation ensured that China received the better end of the deal.

HABITS OF AUTHORITY

The crucial influence of culture on political norms and conduct should have been clear at least since the publication in 1940 of Fortes and Evans-Pritchard's classic anthropological study, *African Political Systems*. For reasons of academic parochialism, however, political scientists largely ignored the insights of anthropology. The "political culture" school did, admittedly, use the term "culture," but in a narrow, specialized sense, and it was more concerned with the study of national institutions and attitudes than with investigating the organic link between political behavior and culture as it is understood by anthropologists. Only in recent years have political scientists begun to realize, alongside their colleagues in management studies, that behavior in both public and private organizations is simply one facet of the overall culture.[35] The logical conclusion is that intercultural communication problems can affect international relationships involving foreign ministries, departments of commerce, and defense ministries just as much as business corporations.

In any negotiation the actual interaction between the delegations represents the tip of the iceberg of internal governmental consultation and decisionmaking. Negotiators are not free agents but representatives of departments and interests, and at one remove, of wider communities. This has several important implications. First, it means that not everything that happens in a negotiation is the product of a deliberate process of rational decisionmaking or the confused encounter of subterranean, cultural currents. Electoral expediency, political necessity, and public mood can set powerful limits on a negotiation. Second, it implies that negotiators are obliged to make continual judgments—whether consciously or not is immaterial—about one another's political and administrative processes. How constrained are one's opposite numbers by domestic political factors? Do they have the discretion to make binding decisions? If they do not, who does? Are decisions made on the basis of some conception of the national interest, or are they influenced by sectorial and even private considerations? Whom, in short, do one's counterparts speak for?

National bureaucratic operating procedures and traditions are of the essence here. Any tendency to project one's own culture-bound expectations onto others is bound to confuse and complicate the issue. An important question is the latitude allowed by a government to its negotiating team. Compared with ultra-low-context countries like Israel, American negotiators are not allowed much leeway. Ambassador David Newsom notes that

> on sensitive political matters (Cuba for example) US negotiators are on a very short leash. Not only must the political problems of the White House be considered, but so must congressional sensitivities. Often many other agencies are involved—keeping a wary eye on the State Department. The US, also, is the only country I know of in which its diplomats cannot say at the end of a session, "I can agree and sign on behalf of my government." If a treaty is involved, it must have Senate ratification. If an aid budget is involved, it must have congressional authorization and appropriation. If a simply executive agreement is involved, it must, under the Case amendment, be submitted for congressional review.[36]

Despite these major restrictions, American negotiators still have more discretion, relatively speaking, than their high-context partners. Obviously, all negotiators work to a brief and must follow their instructions more or less closely. But built into the instructions U.S. envoys receive is the tacit understanding that they leave some scope for creative interpretation, especially when something is not explicitly precluded.[37] Mike Smith, deputy U.S. trade representative (1979–88), indicated that American trade negotiators had far more latitude than their Japanese counterparts, for example. Although the latter were "exquisitely well prepared," they were lacking all flexibility at the negotiating table: they "couldn't go to the bathroom without Tokyo's permission."[38] Gerard Bowers, who negotiated a 1992 memorandum of understanding with Mexico on behalf of USAID noted that "the Mexican negotiator did not operate with as much freedom" as he did personally.[39] Charles Roh expanded on this, observing that in general Americans were on a longer leash, and had "more authority at lower levels." Mexicans were more centralized and disciplined, would not exceed their instructions, and avoided the sort of hypothetical question that can be so helpful in a negotiation ("If we agree to so-and-so, how would you react?").[40] Egyptians, Chinese, and Indians all display, to an even more marked extent, the strict limits placed by rigid, bureaucratic hierarchies on individual initiative. This goes a long way to account for the slow rate at which negotiations usually proceed with these countries. Before a decision can be made, a file has to wend its way up through the hierarchy, its progress dependent on successive layers of consent. This implies that the claim that one's interlocutor does not have the authority to discuss certain matters, however frustrating, is likely to be well founded.

The United States and its non-Western partners have quite different habits of authority—and political traditions—that may interact to affect the chemistry of negotiation. Dissonance may arise not from any misunderstanding but from the encounter between incompatible administrative procedures that officials are powerless to alter. This has more to do with culturally grounded assumptions and customs than meets the eye because, behind the formal constitutional facades, lie habits of governance that are deeply rooted in the respective national cultures. The origins of Chinese, Egyptian, and Japanese bureaucratic procedures are lost in antiquity. Collectivistic societies tend to be paternalistic and hierarchical, and they take the relationship of dominating father and compliant children as their paradigm of leadership. In the individualistic culture of the United States, power is divided and dispersed precisely to avoid the emergence of an absolute and centralized authority, viewed with deep suspicion as a threat to individual liberties. Whereas it would be hard for Egyptian or Mexican officials to question a presidential decision directly, American officials would usually feel it their duty to make their views known, hardly seeing such an action as a challenge to duly constituted authority.

The American system of checks and balances—of rivalry between executive and legislature, and of the supremacy of due process of law—can be particularly confusing for those used to more paternalistic habits. That the American president should be hemmed in by rival sources of power and unable to make decisions without question or appeal is indeed puzzling. Nasser believed that Lyndon Johnson could "do anything" he liked when he became president of the United States.[41] With the renewal of diplomatic relations between Cairo and Washington in 1974, the Egyptian government received firsthand instruction from Secretary of State Kissinger on such matters as the power of the Congress to block appropriations, and the divergent views of the State Department, the Department of Defense, and the Treasury. Nevertheless, despite this growing insight, the Egyptian government still tended to underestimate the limits on presidential power.[42] Even at the height of the Watergate crisis, Foreign Minister Fahmy believed that Nixon's "authority was strongly felt by everybody . . . it was clear that he ran the show single-handedly on behalf of the United States." (This view would not be universally shared.) When facing a delegation led by Kissinger, Fahmy projected this same perception of omnipotence onto the secretary of state.[43] Later, Fahmy was deeply disillusioned when Carter admitted that he "could not simply impose his own views" on Congress and public opinion.[44] Unfamiliarity with truly representative government, and the possibility that factors external to the bureaucracy might have an input into decisionmaking, inclined Fahmy to exaggerate his American interlocutors' freedom of action.

To this day, twenty-five years after the Nixon visit to Beijing, American pluralism remains opaque to many Chinese observers. "Our concepts of 'checks and balances' and 'separation of powers' were utterly alien to them and to their experience with government," former secretary of state George Shultz writes. "Skepticism about Western concepts came easily from a people who assumed the superiority of their ancient culture. Many of the welter of problems between our two countries stemmed from this gap in perceptions."[45] This insight was brought home to Senator John Glenn on a trip to Beijing at a particularly tense moment in U.S.-Chinese relations. A high government official criticized the U.S. Congress for causing trouble and for letting Chinese politics be drawn into the U.S. domestic political debate. "As though we could prevent it if we wanted," wryly commented Glenn.[46] It is doubtful whether the Chinese ambassador to the United States would be ignorant of this elementary fact of American political life, but to many Beijing-based officials Washington is terra incognita.

It is strange to find that Mexicans, too, despite their proximity to the United States and long experience, overestimate U.S. presidential authority. They assume, Alan Riding comments, "that not only the executive branch but Congress, the judiciary, the state governments and even municipal authorities in the United States are all subservient to the President."[47] Because the many agencies that deal with Mexican-related issues in the vast Washington bureaucracy do so in a relatively autonomous (and all too often uncoordinated) manner, the impression is given of either extraordinary deviousness or confusion over priorities.

A graphic illustration of Mexico's misperception of U.S. presidential authority came in 1977, during talks concerning the supply of Mexican gas to the United States. The initial round of negotiations was conducted between PEMEX (Petroleos Mexicanos) and a consortium of U.S. oil companies and crystallized into a memorandum of intent signed in August 1977. Because of opposition to the deal in the Congress and from Secretary of Energy Schlesinger, the original agreement eventually fell through. The Mexicans had been warned by U.S. officials that any agreement was subject to ratification by federal regulatory agencies as early as April of the same year, but they failed to fathom the administrative process. Accustomed to the dominant role of the chief executive in their own country, they assumed (in the words of a key U.S. official) "that Carter could wave a magic wand and the deal would go through."[48]

Since the signing of NAFTA it is doubtful whether this kind of naïveté is common in Mexican government circles. Moreover, if they are in doubt they now do what any domestic U.S. interest does: hire a Washington law firm or public relations outfit to represent their interests and find a way through the political maze of the nation's capital.

The converse of an American president's hampered exercise of power is the ability of a non-Western (but not Japanese!) leader to make clear-cut decisions. There were many examples of this phenomenon in the cases examined: Indira Gandhi's decision in 1982 to cut through the thicket of debate and agree to settle the nuclear fuel issue; Sadat's extraordinary virtuoso performance in the peace process with Israel mediated by the United States; the on-again, off-again decisionmaking of President López Portillo of Mexico in the gas talks and 1982 debt negotiations.

Dominating leadership has its advantages and disadvantages. In putting together the anti-Iraqi coalition in the run-up to the 1991 Gulf War, President Bush and Secretary of State Baker found it convenient and expeditious to deal with their foreign counterparts at the highest level. In November 1990 Baker flew to twelve countries, and was able to receive commitments on the spot that in other circumstances would have taken much longer.[49] Unfortunately, in most circumstances, this kind of direct personal diplomacy is simply not feasible. In 1996 U.S. military commanders in Saudi Arabia were given the runaround for months by their Saudi counterparts when they asked for an improvement in security surrounding buildings in Dahran housing U.S. military personnel. On June 25, 1996, a terrorist bomb killed nineteen Americans; had requested security measures been agreed to, these casualties might not have occurred. Baker's comment, from his own experience, was that the Saudi authorities would have cooperated with U.S. requests had they been conveyed by top-level officials.[50] Although doubtless true, it is impractical within an alliance relationship facing day-to-day challenges to pass every stymied request up the hierarchy. Not only would this be more, not less, time-consuming, but bypassing one's opposite number in the host hierarchy would likely create resentment and complicate, rather than simplify, matters. Failure to manage would quickly result in the replacement of the U.S. officials or officers unable to fend for themselves by others more willing to take responsibility. The U.S. general was right to assume that he had to solve this problem on his own, should he wish to keep his job. The Dahran controversy encapsulates the difficulty of dealing with highly hierarchical systems.

Paradoxically, there is an opposite problem in dealing with highly centralized governments: the risk of underestimating the power of bureaucracy. On matters that do not come to the personal attention of the chief executive—that is, most things—the bureaucracy still plays the dominant role. A 1988 study of Indian bureaucratic morality by two Indian academics strikingly exemplifies the incongruence of American and high-context (but, again, not Japanese) administrative procedures and norms, external features notwithstanding. The authors' point of departure is their insistence that "an understanding of the Indian bureaucracy must include its symbolic relationship with the Indian culture." Officials are bound to conform to "culture-bound" behavior or risk "social disapproval." Despite the formative British influence on the Indian civil service, formal patterns are overridden by informal practices. Rigid hierarchy, "mutual suspicion," and an authoritarianism "destructive of any team spirit" are the norm. The evasion of responsibility is rife. "When confronted with a difficult decision, the Indian bureaucrat seldom makes any attempt to tackle the problem with initiative and imagination. Instead, he will refer the matter to another department to make a series of unnecessary references to subordinates to gain time."[51]

Foreign Service officers with experience of Delhi strongly corroborate this portrait. Indian officials are described as being eager to shuffle responsibility onto someone else and reluctant to exercise personal judgment or make decisions. They are more likely to find reasons for inaction than for action, and they are very subservient to their ranking superiors. An experienced State Department official observed that the caution of the Indian bureaucrat had a very direct impact on negotiations: all successful negotiations, he argued, have a momentum of their own. But there was inevitably a point when the engaged officials, having arrived at an agreement to their own satisfaction, had to be prepared to sell it to their superiors. Indian negotiators were reluctant to do so.

Another State Department official, who served for four years in a senior position in the Delhi embassy, observed that Indian negotiators thought of two things: (a) how they were perceived by their superiors and (b) how the public would react. The higher the negotiators ranked in the bureaucracy, the greater their sensitivity to these points. Point b was more important even than point a. If officials felt that they could not defend a position before public opinion—parliament and the press—they would subvert it, whatever the wishes of their minister. But if they felt that a position was defensible and had a directive from on high, then they were likely to be cooperative. By and large, then, the Indian bureaucrat was "exceptionally cautious" and "unwilling to expose himself." He found little difficulty in slowing things down or sabotaging the process altogether.

Influenced by opposing interests, local officials negotiating with Pepsi Cola to set up an Indian subsidiary were able to drag the negotiation out for years. A senior USAID official bemoaned prolonged Indian procrastination in a negotiation in the mid-1990s over funding for a program to help prevent the spread of HIV-AIDS in Tamil-Nadu. A solution was eventually found, but progress through the bureaucratic maze was glacial. USAID projects to help control Indian population growth have been particularly problematic. One plan to spend $47 million on marketing contraceptives ran aground in 1991 after seven years of fruitless negotiation: $17 million already spent was wasted because U.S. and Indian officials failed to agree on a method of administering the funds. In another similar case, a $325 million USAID program to help curb the high birthrate (5.4 children per woman on average) in Uttar Pradesh mired for two years *after the agreement had been signed* in "political squabbles, bureaucratic red tape, and anti-American sentiment." The idea was to make a variety of birth control options available at the level of the villages—of which there are thirty thousand throughout the state—but years were spent negotiating how the program was to be organized and who would be on the state board responsible for administering it. To make a long story short, the local non-governmental organizations (NGOs) chosen to operate the village schemes did not trust the bureaucrats whom the Indian government nominated for the board, while the government would not allow the NGOs to operate independently of tight government control.[52]

There is no consensus on the utility of establishing contact with officials at a high level in the Indian hierarchy. One view is that doing so might facilitate a negotiation in the sense that high-level approval will filter down and favorably influence the negotiators directly involved. On the other hand, a minister might give apparent consent to an idea and promise to intervene, but nothing would follow. "You get this kind of runaround for months on end," a foreign service officer remarked. It is significant that N. Ram, an Indian, decries precisely the practice of bypassing the appropriate official. He notes that in the nuclear fuel talks the Indians strongly resented the penchant of the leader of the U.S. delegation, Assistant Secretary of State James Malone, for going over the head of his opposite number—an atomic energy expert—to discuss the issues privately or informally with the Indian External Affairs Ministry official. Malone's perception that his diplomatic colleague might be more receptive was misguided. "The approach did not seem to enhance confidence in the U.S. negotiating position."[53] Highly "sensitive to the rank of the person negotiating with them," Paul Kreisberg adds, senior Indian officials also resent having to negotiate with someone of a lower status.[54]

Many of the features of the Indian bureaucracy are reproduced in Egypt. USAID in particular has faced problems of bureaucratic obstruction. Negotiating in Cairo can be a nightmare for American diplomats, for they find themselves entangled in congeries of disorganized, inefficient, and overlapping ministries. Officials are unwilling to accept responsibility and are, on the whole, unfamiliar with Western concepts of planning and administration. America's aid program in Egypt has been hindered by these factors from the beginning. Once Congress had voted Egypt an aggregate sum of $250 million (in December 1974), the U.S. embassy in Cairo then had to negotiate with the various ministries on how this money was to be spent. The experience was chastening—and typical. The Ministry of Development demonstrated an inability to plan properly or to determine its priorities, the minister simply presenting the embassy with wish lists. When Ambassador Eilts turned to the prime minister for guidance, he was told, "You decide." Short ministerial incumbency was an added complication. On agricultural matters, talks began with one minister and continued with another, who put in a new and fanciful request for, of all things, an agricultural museum.[55]

The General Motors negotiation provides a classic case study in the problems of dealing with the Egyptian bureaucracy. General Motors, which already had a truck plant in Egypt and was pleased with the productivity of Egyptian workers, entered into talks with the Egyptian government in 1984 to set up an automobile spare parts industry. A deal would have been of great mutual benefit. The Egyptian plant would have provided spares for the large home market and would have been well placed to export to Europe, Saudi Arabia, and the Persian Gulf. It would have provided thousands of jobs, both saved and earned foreign currency, and provided the nucleus for the development of ancillary industries. What should have been a six-month negotiation dragged out for years. In the first place, a cautious President Mubarak declined to give a lead but left the matter in the hands of the manifold ministries and interests involved. A senior diplomat described him as "the ultimate creator of consensus in this ultimate bureaucratic system."

Many other bureaucratic obstacles hindered progress. A bureaucracy embedded in the socialist, statist dogmas of the Nasserist period found the General Motors wish to build upon private enterprise deeply distasteful. Officials, sometimes benefiting financially from vested interests, proved obstructive. Procrastination was the order of the day. Negotiations were not always conducted in a spirit of candor. In the end the deal fell through over the refusal of the Egyptian customs agency to grant General Motors exemptions from import duties. "It could not," explained a senior Egyptian official with unconscious irony, "allow for any exceptions."

During the 1990–91 Gulf crisis and war, when Egypt and the United States were allies against Iraq, the Egyptian government at first required a separate note requesting individual permission for every flight of a U.S. aircraft through Egyptian airspace. Clearly this was an extraordinarily cumbersome procedure. A senior U.S. official was proud of the embassy's success in working out an arrangement whereby one request note was used for multiple flights. Small mercies!

Chinese and Japanese bureaucracies present rather different and special features compared with those of Egypt and India. Collectivism and hierarchy have taken a different turn in the Far East. Dealing with the Chinese, Henry Kissinger has written, is like being "engaged in one endless conversation with an organism that recalled everything, seemingly motivated by a single intelligence." Each remark by a Chinese official appeared as part of a purposeful overall design.[56] Other American negotiators have talked of an "unfolding dialogue" as they moved rung by rung up the ladder of the Chinese hierarchy. By keeping interlocutors at arm's length at first, and only gradually permitting them access to the higher echelons of the bureaucracy, the Chinese are able to assess at leisure their negotiating position and reserve the denouement for the appropriate moment.

Since the Nixon-Kissinger period the United States has obviously gained considerable direct experience of doing business with the People's Republic of China. The very peculiarity of the Chinese system in Western eyes has alerted the State Department to the need to modify work methods in dealing with Beijing. Cyrus Vance, secretary of state under Carter, indicates that he was well aware of the pitfalls of jet-age diplomacy. In the 1978 normalization talks it was decided to have a resident negotiator in Beijing, not a special envoy. "The Chinese decision-making process," he observes, "is a methodical, careful one, which requires extensive consultations among the leadership after each proposal. Trips by senior American officials, bathed in the glare of publicity, would not have left the Chinese enough time to go through the difficult process of adjusting their positions."[57]

Such insight into Chinese decisionmaking has not always been matched by equal appreciation of Japanese requirements. A cause of difficulty in U.S.-Japanese negotiations has been the American tendency to underrate the essentially consensual style of Japanese decisionmaking. Due allowance has not always been made for the very limited ability of Japan's political leadership to impose its views on the bureaucracy. In the Japanese system of government, as has been frequently pointed out, initiatives originate from below and not from above. Through the painstaking process of decision-making known as *ringisei*, a draft *(ringisho)* circulates among all concerned middle-ranking officials to be appraised and discussed. By the time the document reaches the highest echelon, it represents a consensus of opinion that is highly resistant to modification. Leaders, seen as being above the detailed day-to-day management of affairs and playing a largely moral and representative role, are expected to have absolute confidence in subordinates and to approve the document without change.[58]

Japanese ministers, therefore, do not perform an intrusive, initiatory executive function, as in the American tradition. Former Foreign Service officer Thomas P. Rohlen comments that Japanese managers are simply not as busy as their American counterparts but adopt a calmer and more detached attitude. "When I worked in the State Department," Rohlen observes, "the Secretary of State was very much involved with daily events. He was not sitting back watching how the State Department worked. Kissinger hired others to do that for him."[59]

In negotiation after negotiation American decisionmakers have been disappointed by the failure of Japanese leaders to fulfill American expectations. In 1955 Foreign Minister Shigemitsu of Japan was obliged, at the insistence of Secretary of State John Foster Dulles, to sign a joint communiqué committing Japan to a greater contribution to regional defense. But the Japanese government was actually interested at the time in a revision of the lopsided 1951 security treaty, and in the face of domestic necessities Shigemitsu was forced to retreat from the commitment contained in the Washington communiqué.[60] Again in 1969 Prime Minister Sato was browbeaten at his summit with President Nixon into endorsing a formula on textile imports that went well beyond the limits of the Japanese domestic consensus. Back home, lower-level Japanese officials rejected the agreement reached by their own prime minister. Unable to deliver on his assurances, Sato was embarrassed, and the Nixon administration was outraged. Extraordinarily enough, the same pattern repeated itself a few months later. What Sato accepted in Washington was repudiated by his negotiators in Tokyo.[61] American misapprehension about the working of the Japanese system caused distress again in 1987 during negotiations to improve access to Japanese construction projects for U.S. firms. At a Reagan-Nakasone summit, American officials believed that the Japanese prime minister had promised to open the door to public works projects. When detailed negotiations resumed at the level of experts, Japanese officials were perceived to have reneged on Nakasone's summit "pledge."[62]

A shared tendency to intercultural dissonance can be seen in these examples. Used to dealing with leaders who lead, American statesmen found it natural to meet with their Japanese counterparts at a critical juncture in the negotiations in order to break the deadlock at the highest level. They overlooked the possibility that the locus of practical authority lay elsewhere, that Japanese decisionmaking procedures could not be bypassed, and that the personal pledge of a minister (with the best possible intentions) might not be redeemable. For their part, Japanese ministers preferred to take the line of least resistance, feigning agreement, rather than lose face by admitting that they could not meet American anticipations.

Time is of the essence in the intermediate stage of a negotiation. Initial proposals have already been submitted, and the outer bounds of the negotiation have been staked out. What everyone now wants to know is the opponent's bottom line. If the negotiation is perceived, in the proactive, cooperative American tradition, as the "joint search for a solution," then it will be natural for U.S. negotiators to reveal progressively more of their position, come up with innovative options, and suggest the basis for a compromise. However, this "you win, I win" approach entails hidden assumptions about trust, the reciprocity of concessions, and the desirability of moving forward expeditiously. Sometimes these expectations are justified. In the Gulf War, Egypt and the United States were allies; the NAFTA negotiations between Mexico, the United States, and Canada were about filling in the (albeit immensely complicated and contentious) details when the overspanning architecture of the future partnership was understood; in the 1996 U.S.-Japanese talks on the Okinawa bases the two sides were indeed faced with a shared problem. In many other cases, though, "win-win" assumptions are not mutual. In the intellectual property rights talks with China and the endless negotiations to open up the Japanese domestic market, the United States was as much competitor as partner. In these circumstances power factors outweigh trust, precipitous concessions may be unreciprocated, domestic politics weighs heavily, and eagerness for progress may shade into counterproductive impatience. Too much flexibility may delay progress by generating exaggerated expectations of further concessions. Alternatively, agreements may be reached that are in effect premature and require painstaking further clarification and negotiation before they can be implemented. Time "saved" in the middle game may then be frustratingly spent in an implementation phase of "postnegotiation negotiations." Against an intractable opponent or when far-reaching trust is unjustified, flexibility and the temptation to generate new initiatives are better avoided for a more conservative, cautious approach. Imagination is not always a virtue in international negotiation.

8

Sounds, Signals, Silence

Middle Game II

The single most characteristic feature of the American negotiating style from the perspective of a high-context observer is its low-context legalism. Even if U.S. negotiators are not lawyers by training, their approach will be lawyerly: they view themselves as playing a fiduciary role, that is, conscientiously and objectively representing the interests of their client to the best of their ability without injecting their own personal bias into the equation. Within this tradition one may as easily represent the defendant as the plaintiff, since one's role and the rights of one's client are paramount, not some concept of absolute truth. Indeed, "truth" emerges from the exposition of rival versions of the facts before a jury, an approach that places a particular onus on persuasion through the convincing presentation of evidence. Emotion may conceivably be manipulated for histrionic purposes on occasion to convey an impression of conviction or annoyance, but would usually be considered out of place or even bad form. Great emphasis is placed on procedure, the due process of law, even at the expense of substance; this has a far-reaching influence on the conduct of negotiation, which is perceived as a highly structured activity governed by strict, albeit implicit rules of procedure.

As the lawyerly negotiator understands it, the objective of the entire negotiating exercise is the drawing up of a detailed, binding contract that will withstand legal scrutiny by other lawyers working in the government.

It is natural to work from the outset with written texts, paying particular attention to language, appealing to precedent and past agreement, honing down phrases in a painstaking and sometimes nitpicking exercise in joint draftsmanship. Grandiloquent principles or absolutist norms are of no interest, because the point of a written contract in the United States is rarely to propagate ambiguity but rather to produce clear operational commitments that will provide an exhaustive linguistic blueprint for defined action. Although, notoriously, domestic law and international law involve entirely different principles of enforcement, the propensity of the American negotiator is, following domestic practice, to draft contracts that envisage legal remedies in the event of possible infringement by the parties. Resort to the courts or binding arbitration may be an option for multinational corporations like Enron. But when international negotiation is being conducted on behalf of sovereign entities not subject on the whole and certainly not well disposed to each other's legal procedures, excessive legalism often injects a dogmatic and incongruous element into a fundamentally political arrangement.

Persuasive arguments

In the legalistic negotiating tradition, a central role is reserved, accordingly, for the exercise of forensic persuasion, arguments suitable to a court of law or a debate. Civilized people of goodwill, it is firmly believed, are amenable to reason and should try to persuade one another according to legitimate rules of discourse. Like legal advocates, negotiators are expected to make a logical case for their point of view, appealing to certain acceptable criteria of "evidence" such as the facts of the situation, mutual interest, foreseeable consequences, equity, and especially points of law, existing rights, and relevant precedents. The hope is that one's interlocutor will be convinced by the rigor of one's arguments; if not, a compromise form of words will emerge from the interplay of opposing arguments that is satisfactory to both sides. In the problem-solving, *erabi* paradigm, therefore, logic is seen as the vehicle of progress. Otherwise, negotiation would be reduced to a crude contest of power, a distasteful prospect to be avoided if possible.

The protocol of any negotiation involving an American official, senior or junior, would exemplify the profile sketched out here, whether the protagonist was William Rogers, Cyrus Vance, James Baker, or Warren Christopher. To give a single example: On June 10, 1989, a week after the Tiananmen Square massacre, Secretary of State Baker met Chinese ambassador Han Xu at the State Department. The immediate issue under discussion was the fate of Fang Lizhi, an critic of the Beijing government who had sought refuge in the U.S. embassy shortly after the shooting started. President Bush had granted Fang temporary asylum to the annoyance of the Chinese. Here is Baker's presentation in brief: "We understand how important this issue is to your leadership, but I must stress that it is also a matter of importance for President Bush." Baker added that the President was "open to any suggestion" Beijing had on how to resolve the matter "in a manner that respects both our interests." Sanctuary in a third country was a "reasonable compromise," but the United States would not allow Fang and his wife forced out of the embassy.[1] Note Baker's judicious tone—a lawyer to the fingertips, cool, objective, rational, pragmatic, persuasive.

Forensic argument is a particular feature of Anglo-Saxon civilization. Indeed it is rooted in a long history of parliamentary government, the rule of law, and domestic stability. Outside the English-speaking world these conditions have hardly held over the long term. Thus, though it may seem obvious that negotiators should seek to persuade each other in a rational manner, a moment's reflection from a cross-cultural perspective serves to caution one that nothing should be taken for granted. Different cultures, Edmund Glenn warns, reason in different ways—some inductively, some deductively, some emotionally. Japanese writer Abe Yoshio goes so far as to argue that his compatriots eschew logic altogether, intuiting a conclusion with no intervening steps. He contrasts the Western employment of "logical thinking to convince the other person" with the reluctance of the Japanese to attempt to persuade their interlocutors, "even if they are certain they are correct." In these circumstances dialogue performs no purpose in negotiation: "No matter how much one negotiates there is no concrete result, no agreement on the basis of a thorough statement from both sides as to where their differences lie."[2]

The Japanese generally view debate as unwelcome, a threat to communal harmony. In a study comparing American and Japanese subjects, a wide, cross-cultural gap was found in attitudes toward the notion of due process. Explicitly accounting for the difference in terms of the individualism-collectivism dichotomy, Roger Benjamin concluded that the "adversarial, bargaining style of conflict resolution" chosen by Americans was not congenial to the Japanese. The Japanese expected the parties to a dispute simply "to do the 'right' thing," in other words, to conform to behavior determined by the pattern of obligation implicit in the relationship.[3] This idea is difficult to comprehend for someone not brought up in the Confucian tradition, with its intricate lattice of roles and duties.

In the middle phase of negotiations a distinction may become apparent between the lawyerly claims employed by U.S. negotiators and the more diffuse, personal arguments employed by their high-context counterparts. Interdependent cultures, lacking the Anglo-Saxon legal tradition and declining to isolate a problem from its interpersonal or intergroup context, are less impressed than their American interlocutors by forensic or instrumental considerations. (I hasten to add that many negotiations, where a clear cooperative basis for agreement exists, are likely to be conducted in a businesslike manner without the distorting effect of alternative traditions of rhetoric. Cultural differences tend to be salient precisely when the existence of overlapping interests is not self-evident, but has to be established through mutually intelligible dialogue.)

In the 1995 U.S.-Indian civil aviation talks, both sides knew that the negotiation would end up as a straightforward barter in which one basket of items would be traded against another. Nevertheless, each side played from what it intuitively felt to be its strongest suit. The American delegation typically decided to base its case (inter alia, for on-flight ["fifth freedom"] privileges from Delhi to Hong Kong) on its existing rights under a 1954 treaty. The Indian side was unimpressed, shrewdly hinting that if its wishes were not met (for on-flight rights from Delhi, via London, to Chicago) it would abrogate the 1954 treaty, something the Americans were not overjoyed to hear. In other words, the appeal to law in this instance was revealed for what it was: a weak argument that was trumped by the Indian rejoinder. Not that the Indian case had any more inherent merit, appealing equally lamely to India's "developing status" and the purported U.S. obligation "to help India because it was poor."[4]

According to Abe Yoshio, the Japanese see no inherent virtue in persuasion; either you get it or you do not. In an international negotiation, however, they will obviously marshal as good an argument as they can in their favor. In the 1993–95 series of U.S. trade negotiations, in which American negotiators attempted to obtain quantifiable benchmarks of access for U.S. products to the Japanese market (the most important of which were automobiles and spare parts), the Japanese used jujitsu tactics to reverse the force of an ostensibly strong U.S. claim. When the United States based its case for market opening, conventionally enough, on an appeal to the free trade principles of the General Agreement on Tariffs and Trade, the Japanese stood this argument on its head, leaving American negotiators in some discomfort. "How could measurable targets be defended on free trade principles," Japanese officials self-righteously opined, "when they were intended to produce managed trade by guaranteeing market share?"[5] There was an answer to this—benchmarks had been dreamed up because of Japanese nontariff barriers on imports—but the Japanese case had the virtue of plausibility and was defensible publicly.

When at a loss for a good argument, though, the Japanese may make use of any old claim, as if to emphasize that the defense of their core interests requires no logical justification. Deputy U.S. trade representative Mike Smith recalls wryly that Japanese beef quotas were explained on the grounds that "Japanese intestines are different from American ones."[6] Years later Japan defended its quotas on rice imports, a particularly sensitive issue for a historic rice culture, which wanted to protect its marginal farmers growing rice at a cost several times that of other international producers, with the argument that "American rice is neither cheap nor particularly tasty," and that Japanese consumers were not interested in purchasing it.[7] Of course, the obvious rejoinder was, "At least give them the choice!" But the issue was not who could win the debate, but how atavistic, emotive Japanese attachments could be loosened.

Like the Japanese, Chinese negotiators are quite prepared to eschew a reasoned exposition of their case and make do with weak arguments when they lack stronger ones. Arguably, the abandonment of logic strengthens rather than weakens their hand against U.S. negotiators by presenting an elusive target not vulnerable to conventional counterarguments based on facts and legal claims. Franklin Lavin, who served at the U.S. Department of Commerce from 1991 to 1993 as deputy assistant secretary for East Asia and the Pacific, describes the futility of the U.S. attempt in market access talks with China "to shape a convergence of interests by explaining the benefits the Chinese would receive from a more open trading system." The American approach was eminently reasonable, suggesting phased-in reforms for different sectors of the Chinese economy to minimize dislocation, offering "symbolic concessions to provide the illusion of reciprocity," patiently and politely rebutting inaccurate allegations. The delegation was particularly "well-versed on all the facts of U.S. trade policy, international regulations and the history of U.S.-China commercial relations."[8]

Sadly, "none of the U.S. arguments ever 'worked.' The Chinese never conceded one point in the debate. No U.S. statistic, no citation of international law, no familiarity with international trade or commercial practice mattered in the end . . . Even if U.S. arguments worked as exercises of logic, they could not work as exercises of negotiation." For the American delegation, negotiations were a study in frustration. China's "case," to the extent that it mattered—which it did not—was self-contradictory, repetitious, unasham-edly self-serving. "Talks sometimes took on the air of theater in which the Chinese lines were all scripted. The Chinese were not actually negotiating anything, at least not as Americans understand the term." Lavin's final com-ment is significant: for the Chinese words were simply obstructive devices to wear down the American side in a war of attrition. Lavin concludes that "negotiations to the Chinese are a calculation of interest and power, and they can only progress once your partner moves beyond mere talk."[9]

Such cynicism would be inappropriate if applied to contemporary nego-tiations with Egypt, India, Japan, and Mexico, and very much reflects the sorry state of the U.S.-Chinese relationship since 1989. In these other cases, though, ad hominem arguments may be on occasion more effective than dry legalisms. A major asset for high-context partners is their ability not to marshal an irrefutable argument, but to apply the personal touch in one's dealings, appealing to an affinity that transcends the immediate busi-ness transaction. Before it is possible to engage in a frank and productive exchange with the members of high-context cultures, one must gain their confidence and trust. The implication is that a good negotiator will possess outstanding social skills as well as technical competence. There is a caveat here: Good personal relations are a necessary but not sufficient condition for doing business. Between states and companies, without a confluence of interests not even friendship can help.

"So much is personal" in dealing with Mexicans, I was told by an old State Department hand. It all boiled down to "me and you," not "my gov-ernment and your government," and so friendship and personal rapport had to be carefully cultivated. (Indeed, the Mexicans sometimes overstepped the bounds of propriety in their wish to ensure a favorable atmosphere between negotiators.) Before business could be done, one had to know one's partner reasonably well. Long lunches, sometimes even more than formal negotiating sessions, were the occasion for progress. Joseph Friedkin, who served for many years on the U.S.-Mexican Boundary and Water Com-mission, recalls that in the Chamizal negotiations the commission met for-mally only "when we sat down to sign something." Most of their work was "very informal, usually two on two or one on one."[10] Herbert Brownell, chief U.S. negotiator to the Colorado River salinity talks, made his decisive breakthrough on a walk with Foreign Minister Emilio Rabasa (reminiscent of the famous Paul Nitze "walk in the woods" accord with Soviet arms control negotiator Vladimir Semyonov). Fortunately, the two men enjoyed good personal relations.[11]

Ellsworth Bunker, one of the most experienced American roving ambassadors-at-large and negotiators in the postwar era, mediated an agreement between Egypt and Saudi Arabia in 1963. Among the techniques of negotiation that he found most effective in working with Arabs, John Badeau (ambassador to Egypt at the time) recalled, was the use of a "personal as opposed to official argumentative presentation." Whether as a result of intuition or sound briefing, Bunker grasped the strongly personal element in inter-Arab rivalries. As a *wasta* (broker or middleman) passing between the disputants, he knew that the person-to-person element was of the essence. He would say to Nasser, "'I've got to have something in my hand to go back with. You can give me this,' rather than arguing on the higher level of disembodied Egyptian-U.S. interests. He could do this charmingly, but very, very firmly."[12]

It does seem that the quality of the personal relationship at the highest executive level has also had substantive implications. President Kennedy, for instance, appreciated that it was helpful to maintain a personal correspondence with President Nasser. His letters were businesslike and straightforward, but they were carefully drafted to contain a warm, personal element. In addition to regular notes, Kennedy made a point of keeping Nasser informed through other channels of anything that might impinge on their relations. By notifying Nasser in advance of the sale of Hawk anti-aircraft missiles to Israel, for instance, Kennedy managed to soften the blow. On other occasions the Egyptian president had been angered by less. U.S.-Egyptian relations greatly improved during this period.[13] In contrast, Nasser developed an antipathy for President Johnson. Although they never met, Nasser studied Kennedy's successor carefully in word and picture. An undignified photograph showing Johnson displaying his famous operation scar in public shocked Egyptians as unbefitting the leader of a great nation. Then President Johnson abandoned the practice of writing personally to the Egyptian leader. Whether this action was the cause or the effect of a deterioration in state-to-state ties is a moot point. It had the practical effect of closing a useful channel of communication when it was most needed—in the Middle East crisis of May-June 1967.[14]

President Johnson did at first achieve a striking personal rapport with Prime Minister Indira Gandhi of India, however. In January 1966 Gandhi visited the United States for eleven days. Behaving toward her with "Texan chivalry," Johnson addressed her as "little lady." Strange as it may seem, Mrs. Gandhi blossomed at this display of flirtatiousness and attention. The trip was productive politically, and the two sides succeeded in putting together a package of reforms of the Indian economy to be accompanied by U.S. assistance.[15] American officials had long realized the need to cultivate personal ties with the proud and sensitive Indian leaders, ever since an unsuccessful visit by Jawaharlal Nehru—Gandhi's father—to the United States in October 1949, marked by disappointing meetings with President Truman and Secretary of State Acheson.[16] Chester Bowles (ambassador to India, 1951–53 and 1963–69) determined to cultivate Nehru and as wide a circle of Indians as possible on arrival, succeeded superlatively, and became one of the most popular U.S. ambassadors ever to serve in Delhi.[17]

President Eisenhower reached the conclusion that Nehru was "often more swayed by personality than logical argument. He seems to be intensely personal in his whole approach." Accordingly, he suggested that Secretary of State Dulles "urge our new Ambassador there to do everything possible to win the personal confidence and friendship of Nehru."[18] Ironically, Eisenhower's vice president, Richard Nixon, established a very poor personal relationship with Gandhi, who viewed him, in the words of a State Department official, as a "slippery, untrustworthy" customer. They met in 1969 when Nixon visited India, and in November 1971 on the eve of the India-Pakistan war. Their mutual dislike was palpable. Nixon loathed what he perceived as Gandhi's condescending and self-righteous manner. Gandhi clearly found no common language with this personally least engaging of presidents.

The reluctance to say no

The contrasting uses of language by Americans and their high-context negotiating partners have provided grounds for misunderstanding, though this should not be overstated; much of the time the parties do understand each other. In the straightforward style of American culture, language has primarily the instrumental function of transmitting information. For the members of face-salient societies, however, it performs the important additional role of social lubricant, easing and harmonizing personal relations. High-context individuals are unable to subordinate the personal impact of a message to its semantic accuracy. A painful and disruptive truth is no virtue to those who tend to view actions, verbal and nonverbal, through the prism of social consequences.

A striking feature of communal-minded, high-context speakers consistently remarked upon by American diplomats is their dislike of the negative; a direct contradiction is invariably avoided. President Clinton personally complained to President Boris Yeltsin of Russia that the Japanese often said yes to the United States when they really meant no. The Japanese are well aware of this trait, and certainly Minister of International Trade and Industry Hashimoto made a point of bluntly rejecting U.S. proposals in 1995 automobile talks, yet it is an ingrained manner of speech not easily evaded. One episode in particular has entered the annals of intercultural misunderstanding. On Prime Minister Sato's 1969 trip to Washington, President Nixon insisted that Japan exercise export restraint. Mr. Sato's classic reply, delivered with a heavenward glance, was *"Zensho shimasu."* Literally translated as "I will do my best," the expression really means "No way." Nixon naturally understood it to mean that he had his guest's agreement. When there was no practical follow-up, he denounced Sato as a liar. (An almost identical misunderstanding occurred between Margaret Thatcher and Takeshta Noburu in 1988, when the Japanese prime minister promised that he would take a "personal interest" in solving the problem of high duties on British whisky entering Japan. On returning home, however, Takeshta denied that he had given his "personal commitment," and Thatcher was disappointed.)[19]

Unlike Americans, who expect yes or no answers, Japanese are quite happy with the gray areas. "They hate 'no,' and they hate 'yes,'" as an American official put it.[20] Expressions such as *taihen muzukashii* ("very difficult") are quite translucent ways of saying no, but without the unpleasantness the Japanese associate with a blunt rejection.[21] Masao Kunihiro, a Japanese anthropologist, goes so far as to pick out this feature "as the most important characteristic of the Japanese language and the cognitive behavior of the Japanese people." The reluctance to say yes or no, to agree or disagree, is rooted, he argues, in a deep-seated aversion to either-or, dichotomous thinking. The Japanese instinct, unlike that of Westerners, is not to categorize or differentiate, but to combine and reconcile. He points to this factor as a powerful "source of gaps in intercultural communication."[22]

The first lesson to learn in Egypt, one eminent diplomat remarked, is that "Egyptians hate to turn you down; they never say no." Another foreign service officer with long service in Mexico City noted that the Mexican habit was "not to say no, just never to say yes." In other words, a negotiation might continue indefinitely and indeterminately. How, then, was one to know whether consent was genuine or feigned? If one's antennae were sufficiently attuned to accompanying verbal and nonverbal signals, it might be possible to read between the lines. Otherwise, the true message became clear only in retrospect. If nothing happened, then one had been the victim of the "social affirmative."

An amusing instance of Egyptian politeness being mistaken for agreement occurred at the beginning of presidential envoy Robert Anderson's secret mission to try to mediate between Nasser and Prime Minister Ben Gurion of Israel in January 1956. Anderson presented his proposals in a strong Texan drawl and was encouraged by Nasser's nodding and smiling in apparent agreement. After Anderson returned to his hotel, his colleague Kermit Roosevelt stayed behind for a few minutes at Nasser's request. "What," Nasser wanted to know, "was Mr. Anderson talking about?" Neither he nor his vice president had understood a word. Roosevelt rushed off to intercept an upbeat cable Anderson was dictating for Secretary Dulles.

Because persistence (not taking no for an answer) is a fairly familiar American trait, the Egyptians' reluctance to disappoint their interlocutor may set the scene for mutual disappointment and frustration. William Quandt argues that drawn-out negotiations of this kind are a sure "sign that the Egyptian side is not ready for a deal but does not want to bear the onus for breaking off negotiations."[23]

This inconclusive pattern of behavior has repeated itself on several occasions in the past. One negotiation that dragged on for almost a decade concerned the passage of nuclear-powered warships of the U.S. Sixth Fleet through the Suez Canal. The Egyptian government was genuinely sensitive to the environmental risks, real or imagined, of nuclear power and of its possible effect on navigation through the canal. Ambassador Eilts first raised the issue in the mid-1970s with Sadat, who sent him on to Defense Minister Gamasy. The latter noted in turn that his authority did not extend to running the waterway and shuffled him off onto the bureaucracy. Egyptian procrastination continued for an extended period without the U.S. Defense Department grasping that its interlocutors wished to let the matter drop. Eventually, some years later, President Mubarak was persuaded to agree, and in 1984 a nuclear-powered warship went through the canal for the first time. But it was a Pyrrhic victory. When National Security Adviser John Poindexter tactlessly leaked news of the ship's passage, the agreement, which Egypt had entered into reluctantly and against its better judgment, was immediately called off by the embarrassed Egyptians.[24]

Much the same pattern was repeated in negotiations initiated by the Department of Defense for a privileges and immunities agreement to cover the naval and military medical research unit staff in Cairo. Defense Minister Kamal Hassan Ali gave his good-humored assent, although in fact Egyptians resented American personnel being granted extraterritorial status in a manner all too reminiscent of the hated capitulations. (Incidentally, the

unit had already functioned for years without such an agreement, so here
was a case of excessive American eagerness to dot the i's and cross the t's.)[25]
Yet another example of Defense Department legalism and rigidity was the
case of the ill-fated negotiations for an American facility at Ras Banas on the
Gulf of Suez. Inherited by a reluctant Mubarak from Sadat, the negotiations ran into insuperable difficulties. Unwilling to meet American conditions
and unhappy about the prospect of a base reminiscent of the Soviet (and
before that the British) experience, the Egyptian government was caught
in a bind. Although agreement was out of the question, Egypt was loath to
offend the United States by a blunt refusal. Negotiations might have continued indefinitely had the American side not forced the issue.[26]

For high-context individuals it is always easier to agree than to disagree.
Confronted by a persistent and undesirable request, they find the "social affirmative" the best way out of an uncomfortable situation. In a cross-cultural
encounter, therefore, the responsibility for misunderstanding may not just be
theirs but also that of their obtuse interlocutor, who has failed to draw the
correct conclusions from the hesitancy and unenthusiastic nature of the reply.

Not even a sophisticated and cosmopolitan ambassador like John Kenneth Galbraith was immune to this solecism. The occasion was the first
days of the 1962 Sino-Indian border war. The State Department (looking
ahead to the postwar period and a possible resolution of the Kashmir dispute) decided that it would be helpful if Nehru requested, through U.S.
good offices, Pakistani assurances of nonintervention. Galbraith describes in
painful detail his insensitive importuning of the Indian prime minister.

Nehru, whose forces were being pushed back by seemingly irresistible
Chinese pressure, appeared (according to Galbraith's own account) frail,
old, and desperately tired. Galbraith asked him if the United States could
inform Ayub Khan, the Pakistani leader, that India would welcome Pakistani
assurances. Nehru replied lukewarmly that "he would have no objection to
our saying so." This was not good enough for the ambassador. Galbraith
then "moved in very hard." Would Nehru say that he would warmly accept
such assurances? Looking "a little stunned"—as well he might—Nehru
consented, adding that such a gesture might be helpful for the future. Galbraith resolved to press home his advantage. Could Nehru assure him that
he would respond to such assurances? Yes, "on some appropriate occasion
he would," Nehru responded with telltale discomfort. Galbraith moved in for
the kill. "This was a time for generosity and [the Indian prime minister]
should be immediately forthcoming." Pressed to the wall, Nehru agreed.[27]
It was a ruthless performance by Galbraith, and an empty triumph. Of

course Nehru, under extreme duress, had no choice but to give his unwilling consent. To beg a favor of Pakistan, a sectarian state that in Indian eyes stood for the antithesis of everything secular India represented, was excruciating. It was a bad beginning to a doomed mediation.

Mexican negotiators display the same inhibitions on the expression of a blunt refusal. The three days of talks in 1969 that preceded Operation Intercept, the largest drug enforcement effort ever launched on the U.S.-Mexican border, were marked by Mexican disenchantment with American proposals. Mexico had not been consulted in the formulation of those proposals and yet was being required to comply with far-reaching measures that were likely to be extremely disruptive. It was impossible in a single round of negotiations to secure the far-reaching cooperation and coordination required to make the operation a success.

Unable to express their wholehearted consent, yet unwilling to reject American proposals out of hand, the Mexicans predictably opted for polite and emollient expressions of goodwill and encouragement. They agreed to nothing concrete. At the conclusion of the conference the two delegations jointly declared their firm resolve to use all available resources "to strengthen further the cooperative efforts" against drug manufacture and shipping. This essentially vacuous formula was apparently sufficient to convince U.S. attorney general Kleindienst that he had obtained the support of the Mexican government for his plan and that he could look forward to its cooperation in a drive against the sources of marijuana. Both judgments proved utterly ill founded.[28]

DIRECTNESS VERSUS INDIRECTNESS

To the dislike of confrontation and contradiction, high-context cultures add a related, characteristic propensity for indirect and understated formulations. Both patterns of behavior have a similar underlying motive: the wish to avoid an abrupt and abrasive presentation, to maintain harmony, to save the face of the interlocutor. Meaning is better imparted by nuances that permit a dignified retreat. Moreover, relatively homogeneous, traditional societies are able to take much more for granted in their discourse than highly mobile, socially fluid cultures like that of the United States. The Japanese particularly take pride in their familial skill at reading between the lines, at intuiting the intention behind an elliptical hint. They even have a term for it: *haragei*—communicating from the belly, that is, reading the other's mind, or talking around an issue until a consensus emerges.

In view of the American preference for straight talking, however, Americans may take subtlety and opacity for evasiveness and insincerity. Clearly, to do so is to judge from a culture-bound perspective. Protecting the feelings of one's interlocutor and relying on shared meanings are very far from a lack of frankness, let alone deliberate falsehood. At this point the reader may object that surely no U.S. officials worth their salt could be misled by circumlocution? And non-American diplomats surely realize by now that Americans need things spelled out? No, for all their experience, many diplomats on both sides of the cultural divide have fallen into the trap of assuming that members of other cultures always mean what they appear to say.

On the eve of the departure of Prime Minister Sato of Japan for a crucial summit with President Nixon in 1970, Sato released the following remarkable statement to the press: "Since Mr. Nixon and I are old friends, the negotiations will be three parts talk and seven parts *haragei*." Nothing could have been more natural for Japan's prime minister than to assume that he could have a heart-to-heart talk with the leader of his country's closest ally, a man he considered a personal friend.[29] Sadly, his faith in their personal chemistry was misplaced. Nixon declined to intuit Sato's domestic difficulties and insisted he agree to an explicit five-point proposal as the basis for a settlement. Equally, Sato had overlooked Nixon's own domestic problems. Similarly, in more recent construction industry talks the Japanese Ministry of Foreign Affairs was accused of communicating in such a circumspect fashion that the American side had real difficulty in ascertaining its true position.[30]

Egyptian articulations have also sometimes been a source of puzzlement. In December 1968, during the interregnum between the Johnson and Nixon administrations, Secretary of State Dean Rusk presented a seven-point proposal to Foreign Minister Riad of Egypt at the United Nations. He had been encouraged to do so by Ashraf Ghorbal, head of the Egyptian interests section in Washington. After some delay, the Egyptian response came back from Cairo. It turned out to be "legalistic, nit-picking." The State Department viewed this less than enthusiastic reply as a rejection. "When somebody accepts something, they give you a clear answer," is Richard Parker's commonsense explanation of this judgment. But is American common sense the same as Egyptian? Ashraf Ghorbal insisted that it was "not a rejection, an acceptance."[31] Was it so, or was an embarrassed Ghorbal defending his earlier advocacy? Even today it is hard to penetrate the double layer of obscurity. The likeliest conclusion is that the Egyptian foreign ministry was reluctant to commit itself on the eve of Nixon's inauguration, yet was equally loath to rule out a rather helpful American initiative. In the event, the proposal died of neglect.[32]

On the eve of Sadat's November 1977 Jerusalem visit, which so surprised the Carter administration, American diplomacy quite failed to grasp the Egyptian president's position and intentions. As William Quandt points out, "From their very first meeting Sadat had indicated his skepticism about [the] Geneva [international conference] as a forum for actual negotiations." But Sadat's repeated, albeit elliptical, hints fell on deaf ears. In August he told Secretary Vance that "there was no rush with respect to Geneva. It could be later in the year or 'whenever we are really ready.'" Foreign Minister Fahmy repeated precisely this formulation— "Egypt was not in a hurry for Geneva"—in September.[33] Sadat wanted substantive talks with Israel before Geneva—without a Syrian veto, Soviet interference, and the complicating presence of the PLO. On October 1 Sadat made a final, unsuccessful effort to convey his views to Carter, urging "a phase of preparatory talks before going on to Geneva to complete the details."[34]

As a result of continued administration support for reconvening the Geneva conference, Sadat became convinced of the need to travel directly to Jerusalem. As we now know, the Sadat visit paved the way for an Egyptian-Israeli peace. At the time, however, it astonished the U.S. government. Harold Saunders, a central figure in the negotiations, acknowledges that he and his colleagues had failed to perceive Sadat's unhappiness. Why, Saunders wondered, did Fahmy not come out and tell his American counterparts that Sadat was not interested in Geneva? Perhaps, he mused, they did not hear Sadat because his message was not put in "a clear-cut Anglo-Saxon form."[35] Quite.

At the same time the State Department was overlooking Sadat's understated rejection of Geneva, the Egyptians were having an equally hard time because they overinterpreted Carter's straightforward statements. Fahmy describes the mistaken impression he received from some remarks made by the U.S. president at a meeting of the American and Egyptian delegations in September 1977. Carter's candor was a far cry from the devious, conspiratorial world of Middle Eastern discourse. Carter was commenting on Syrian and Palestinian objections to PLO representatives joining a Jordanian delegation in possible Arab-Israeli peace talks. Oblivious to the effect he was having on his listeners, Carter dismissed the issue in a few words. "Mr. Fahmy, I would like to know the Egyptian positions; you should not worry about the Syrian or Palestinian positions, let me handle this myself."

In typical Middle Eastern style, Fahmy erected an entire edifice of conjecture and suspicion on this seemingly trivial remark. He was stunned by Carter's words, because they implied that the United States had contacts with both Syria and the PLO, that Carter knew something about their positions unknown to the Egyptian government, and that he was "hiding important information from Egypt." The implications were staggering. "If this was really true, Egypt was no longer the leader in the peace process." After checking out the whole story, Fahmy concluded that Carter's remark was simply baseless "bravado." Although the episode is most revealing about Egyptian mistrust, it serves as a reminder of the need for precision in diplomatic exchanges with high-context individuals.[36]

Nehru's habit of understatement posed in its time an equal conundrum for U.S. diplomats. A classic failure of understanding occurred in February 1954. In what was to be a watershed in U.S.-Indian relations, the Eisenhower administration had decided to grant military aid to Pakistan. This moment was bitter for Nehru and the Indian government, and it marked a stunning diplomatic defeat. In the Indian worldview, Pakistan was the "enemy of the race," its arming by the United States a most alarming development. Before the public announcement of the deal, Ambassador Allen had been instructed to deliver a personal letter from President Eisenhower and to make clear that the American decision was not directed against India. It was hoped that friendly relations between the two countries would in no way be impaired. If the aid were misused for aggression against India, the United States would take action both through and outside the United Nations to thwart it. An Indian request for military aid would also be sympathetically considered.

Nehru carefully read the letter and the text of the forthcoming announcement. When he had finished, "he smiled, studied his cigarette for a few moments, then said in a pleasant and almost confidential tone, 'I have never at any moment, since the subject arose two or three months ago, had any thought whatsoever that the U.S. Government, and least of all President Eisenhower, wished to do any damage to India.'" After expressing appreciation for the letter, Nehru proceeded to a judicious and calm explanation of his concerns. "What disturbed him was not American motives but the possible consequences of this action." He spoke of "small groups of extremists among the Indian Muslims who did not conceal their pleasure over Pakistan aid because they hoped it might lead to a renewal of Muslim domination of India." Communal violence in India and increased tension between India and Pakistan might follow. Moreover, although the present government of Mohammed Ali in Pakistan was moderate, its political organization was weak, and some successor might depart on a reckless adventure.

For all the dignity and restraint of his manner, Nehru was in fact revealing his innermost fears. The American decision was a nightmare come true. Nehru had publicly expressed his opposition to military aid for Pakistan, and the Indian government had officially protested such a move. But Allen completely missed the true meaning of Nehru's words. The ambassador commented on how "surprisingly pleasant" the conversation had been and how Nehru had "made a conscious effort to be agreeable." In an extraordinary misjudgment, both of Nehru's reaction and of his policy of nonalignment, Allen concluded that Nehru "showed no adverse reaction to the President's offer to consider sympathetically any Indian request for military aid, and it is possible that he was rather pleased." The ambassador hoped that discussion on this subject would diminish after a few days. "I do not anticipate any serious public demonstrations."[37]

In fact, the Indian reaction was vehement. Particularly offensive to India were the patronizing offer of military aid and the assurances that the deal was in no way directed against India—but that if necessary the United States would thwart any aggression. As a historian of U.S.-Indian relations has pointed out, Indians complain about the 1954 episode to this day. "It may have done more to complicate Indo-American relations than any other single development."[38]

Except, perhaps, for one other: the disastrous 1971 meeting between President Nixon and Prime Minister Gandhi. It was, Kissinger admits, "a dialogue of the deaf." Describing their encounter in all its unpleasantness, Kissinger is convinced, however, that the breakdown and prolonged dislocation in U.S.-Indian relations following the unexpected Indian invasion of East Pakistan was not the result of a subjective failure of understanding but of a traditional clash of irreconcilable interests. The two leaders, he claims, understood each other only too well.[39]

From the accounts of the principals themselves, however, it is doubtful they did. In fact, their mutual failure of understanding is uncannily reminiscent of Nixon's unfortunate 1969 meeting with Prime Minister Sato of Japan. Nixon received the impression that the Indian prime minister had given him some kind of implicit assurance that her country would not attack Pakistan. "India has never wished the destruction of Pakistan or its permanent crippling," he quotes her as saying. "Above all, India seeks the restoration of stability. We want to eliminate chaos at all costs."[40] Gandhi tells a very different version. In her opinion, Nixon failed to grasp just how unbearable the situation was to India. "I told him, without mincing words, that we couldn't go on with ten million refugees on our backs, we couldn't tolerate the fuse of such an explosive situation any longer." Other European leaders with whom she had spoken had understood, said Indira Gandhi to her interviewer, "but not Mr. Nixon."[41]

For an American diplomat, to turn from Indian understatement to Chinese indirection is to enter a new realm of semantic opacity. A sense of the dense and allusive Chinese communicatory style can be obtained from almost any account of diplomatic contact with China—not that U.S. officials always grasped what the Chinese were getting at. Secretary of State James Baker, for instance, suggested to the Chinese that the two Koreas, North and South, should be brought into the United Nations. Their reaction was "an interesting comment, but it won't work this year." The words "this year" might—or might not—be significant. Were they the diplomatic equivalent of "not today, thank you," or "not this year, but next year"? It turned out, as was correctly surmised, that they meant the latter, and in 1991 North and South Korea were admitted to the United Nations after China withheld its veto. On another occasion the United States pressed China to allow a dissident to leave the country. Contacts continued for months and the issue weighed painfully on relations. One day an American diplomat was told by his Chinese interlocutor that "Barkis is willing." A puzzling remark, it turned out on subsequent investigation to be a reference to a character in Charles Dickens's classic *David Copperfield.* Barkis asks David to pass on a message to Peggotty hinting at his wish to marry. In other words, the Chinese were signaling their agreement to the deal, wrapping the concession in a witty veneer of civilized accomplishment.

The well-documented account of an alert participant can be found in the pages of Kissinger's diplomatic memoirs. His description of the 1971–72 negotiations that resulted in the momentous Shanghai communiqué is particularly enlightening. The first example to consider is Chinese prime minister Zhou Enlai's treatment of the Vietnam issue. (At the time, Kissinger was engaged in the Paris talks with a North Vietnamese delegation led by Le Duc Tho aimed at ending the Vietnam War.) Zhou conveyed the Chinese position on the Vietnam issue in the course of three separate meetings. This kind of rolling dialogue, in which the message is gradually unfolded over a period of time, is characteristic of Chinese diplomacy. On July 9, 1971, during Kissinger's first trip to Beijing, Zhou listened to his guest's account of the Paris talks but professed ignorance of them. As

Kissinger appreciated, "it was a good device to avoid being pressed to take a position." It also hinted that Vietnam was not high on the list of Chinese concerns.[42]

A further revelation of the Chinese position came in nonverbal form on Kissinger's second trip to Beijing. On October 23, the U.S. diplomat was taken for an ostentatious public appearance at the Summer Palace. Tea was served on a boat on the lake in plain view of hundreds of Chinese spectators. Thus China conveyed messages that it was willing to commit itself in public to a profound shift in foreign policy, that it considered its American guests acceptable, and that it insisted that the U.S.-Chinese relationship was to be no hole-and-corner affair. The Vietnamese dimension of the occasion was not made clear to Kissinger until afterward. Among the spectators of the tea party, as Zhou later mentioned in an apologetic aside, was a North Vietnamese journalist taking photographs. Kissinger notes in passing that he "suspected" that Zhou was interested in North Vietnam getting the message of the incipient Sino-American relationship. But if an observer for Hanoi was on the spot, it was not by accident. The Chinese carefully orchestrate these occasions. Zhou was surely signaling to North Vietnam—and ensuring that Washington grasped—that China would not permit North Vietnam to hinder a rapprochement with the United States.[43]

The final veil was removed during President Nixon's historic visit to China in February 1972. Zhou's treatment of the Vietnam issue, according to Kissinger, was a "masterpiece of indirection." He expressed "sympathy" for North Vietnam but explained Chinese support for that country on the basis of a historical debt rather than congruent national interests. The implication was that the U.S. connection, based on the perception of a common foe (the Soviet Union), was paramount. States do not go to the wall for historical debts. Zhou, as in July, declined to express his view on the Paris talks. Then, in a crucial but elliptical remark, he reiterated that "differences between China and the United States would be settled peacefully." This statement was interpreted by the U.S. delegation to mean that China would not intervene militarily in the war. The Vietnam issue was treated "largely in the context of long-term Soviet aspirations in Southeast Asia."[44] The covert message underlying the whole extended exchange was that China was effectively dissociating itself from its supposed North Vietnamese ally—a far-reaching development indeed. That actuality was confirmed before long.

The archetypal example of the Chinese conversational style is found in the famous Nixon-Mao meeting of February 21, 1972. The encounter was

characterized by bantering and seemingly evanescent philosophical remarks by the Chinese leader, but later it could be seen to have laid down
definitive guidelines for the new Sino-American relationship. Looking
back, Kissinger refers to the "many-layered designs of Mao's conversation,"
comparing it to the "courtyards in the Forbidden City, each leading to a
deeper recess distinguished from the others only by slight changes of proportion, with ultimate meaning residing in a totality that only long reflection can grasp."

On the question of trade, for instance, Mao conveyed his decision in the
form of an explanation of Chinese slowness in responding to the Nixon
administration's easing of export controls during the previous two years.
China, he said, had been "bureaucratic" in insisting that the solution of
major issues precede the resolution of smaller issues like trade and people-
to-people exchanges. "Later on I saw you were right, and we played table
tennis." In this disarming, understated way Mao gave his green light to
progress on those matters at the summit. Other views were thrown out
seemingly offhandedly, to avoid loss of face if the Nixon visit failed. Taiwan
was placed on a subsidiary level as a relatively minor internal Chinese dispute. Banter and passing historical references hinted that the Chinese
would solve the problem among themselves in their own good time.

In a discussion of Chinese security concerns, Mao made his point by
omission: the threat of American or Chinese aggression, he opined, was
"relatively small . . . You want to withdraw some of your troops back on
your soil; ours do not go abroad." By a process of elimination, it was the
threat from the Soviet Union that was to be feared. At the same time he had
in a few words ("ours do not go abroad") touched on a whole list of American preoccupations. Anticipating Zhou, he eliminated the U.S. nightmare
of Chinese intervention in the Vietnam War. He was also disclaiming any
Chinese wish to challenge vital American interests in Japan and South
Korea. But what of the ideological struggle? Mao disposed of the ringing
anti-American slogans that had marked his rule with equal facility. Laughing
uproariously, he dismissed them as the "sound [of] a lot of big cannons."[45]
In sixty-five minutes, half of which were taken up by interpretation, Mao
succeeded in providing a set of signposts for his American guests and the
Chinese bureaucracy. Again and again, in the week of intensive negotiations that followed the Nixon-Mao meeting, Chinese officials would
return to Mao's words. References that were originally obscure were later
seen as significant. The dialogue, Kissinger sums up, had been conducted
on the Chinese part "with extraordinary indirection and subtlety."

Nonverbal communication

Nonverbal communication embraces a vast area of human behavior, including facial expression, gestures, body contact, movement, use of space, costume, ceremony, and so on. Like language, it is a universal phenomenon with a great range of local variants. A gesture of approval in the United States may be taken for a very rude sign in Egypt. A smile in Japan may mask embarrassment rather than indicate enjoyment. Even when the act or expression itself—the frown, the gift—is common, rules of legitimate display may differ. What is an appropriate moment for tears in Egypt is one for self-restraint in the United States. An act of hospitality in Mexico City may be seen as a bribe in Washington. Many studies have documented this cross-cultural diversity.[46]

Actual misunderstanding—whether based on ignorance or misinterpretation—aside, the main difficulty for low-context individuals may simply be to appreciate the emphasis placed by their high-context counterparts on the nonverbal dimension of communication. Whereas the burden of meaning in low-context cultures is transmitted through the medium of words, high-context cultures are particularly sensitive to sign and symbol. The tendency of Foreign Minister Fahmy of Egypt to read more into American articulations than was justified has been noted. His memoirs also provide remarkable testimony of his attentiveness to American body language. In all his accounts of meetings with U.S. officials, Fahmy describes their facial expressions and the emotions he read there. He provides meticulous detail about just when Nixon smiled or Kissinger lost his cool. The state of mind of his interlocutors was obviously of major importance to the Egyptian diplomat.

Although Egyptians do not make shows of anger, they have no inhibitions about exhibiting seemly (that is, socially acceptable) emotion in public. There is no shame attached to extreme expressions of grief or joy in the Arab world. On the contrary, Egyptians wear their emotions on their sleeves as a sign of social solidarity. To remain impassive while others grieve would be egoism of the worst sort. Fahmy's tendency to project this very Egyptian trait onto Americans is evident. He describes an indicative incident during the 1973 disengagement talks (immediately following the Yom Kippur War) in which Chief of Staff Gamasy, hearing that he would be permitted to retain only limited Egyptian forces on the East Bank of the Suez Canal, began to weep before the company of Egyptian and U.S. officials. "From the look on the faces of the American delegation," Fahmy writes, "one could easily see they too were upset by the injustice inflicted upon Egypt." It is easier to believe, and more likely, the Americans were disconcerted to see a senior army officer shedding tears in public. Egyptian and U.S. delegations met again in April 1974 in Alexandria. Secretary of State Kissinger had given President Sadat certain assurances about future U.S. arms supplies to Egypt. Fahmy was incredulous and detected the same reaction on the other side. "I watched the expressions on the faces of [Kissinger's] American colleagues; they were shocked and unbelieving."[47]

The United States—founded in the Age of Reason, rigorously de-marcating Church from State, and passionate in its belief in progress—has relegated ritual to the sidelines of public life. The national shrines and inaugural events that make up the so-called civil religion of the United States are a pale version of the pomp and circumstance that mark more traditional societies. Even private life is increasingly bereft of those intricate rites of passage that communities evolve to proclaim and sanctify the ages and stages of human growth. High-context cultures, steeped in tradition and placing crucial emphasis on the individual's standing in the group, reserve a central role for ceremony. Religious and civic activity alike revolve around ritual events and celebratory occasions, rich in costume and rite, dramatizing key events in the history and life of the society. Ceremony, in fact, is a key mechanism of group identity and cohesion.

High-context cultures, therefore, display acute awareness of the subtle messages about rank and reputation reflected and communicated in the fine detail of ritual and choreography. Of course, American officials strictly observe the rules and regulations of diplomatic etiquette, but it is doubtful whether they impute to it quite this seriousness. Protocol is required so that meetings between government leaders can take place "with a minimum of misunderstanding."[48] Although it may be fun, it is mostly just a means to an end. "Protocol and striped pants," President Truman once wrote, "give me a pain in the neck."[49] Non-Western societies are not only skillful at manipulating protocol and ceremonial for political purposes, they are also prone to cherish subtle political symbolism as almost an end in itself.

Here lies fertile ground for confusion. In the early days of U.S.-Chinese contacts under President Nixon, the dense and allusive richness of Chinese political choreography was sometimes overlooked. For instance, U.S. observers entirely missed the most significant Chinese signal of reconcili-ation of all in the 1970–71 period. On October 1, 1970, Edgar Snow, the American journalist and author of sympathetic books on the Chinese rev-olution, was invited to stand next to Chairman Mao on top of the Gate of

Heavenly Peace. This unprecedented gesture associated the Great Helms-man with the unfolding process of détente. Ruefully noting U.S. oversight, Kissinger concludes: "Excessive subtlety had produced a failure of com-munication."[50] The Chinese doubtless did not regard the gesture as partic-ularly subtle.

Since its introduction to Chinese symbolic politics, U.S. diplomacy has become more familiar with this mode of communication. Alexander Haig, chief of staff in the Nixon White House, was conscious of the need for alertness during his stint as secretary of state from 1981 to 1982. Visiting Beijing in 1981, he was received by Deng Xiaoping in the Fujian Room of the Great Hall of the People. (Fujian is the province of China situated across from Taiwan.) Haig was unsure whether this was "happenstance or a subtle reminder." His hesitancy was unwarranted. Ten years before, Henry Kissinger had also been received by Zhou Enlai in that same room. But it was, Kissinger confesses, "a subtlety which—like the Snow inter-view—unfortunately was lost on me since I did not then know the name of the room nor to my shame would have recognized its significance. There is some advantage in invincible obtuseness (Chou was obliged to point all of this out on a subsequent visit when we met in another room)."[51]

The significance of meeting in the Fujian Room should therefore have entered the institutional memory of the State Department and been explained to Secretary Haig. The United States (his hosts were saying) might temporarily support the Taiwan government but, situated thousands of miles away, would eventually loosen its attachment. For the People's Republic of China the link with Taiwan was not a political expedient but an immutable geographical and cultural bond that must eventually be con-summated in reunification.

For years U.S. support of the Nationalist Chinese cause had been a painful thorn in the side of Beijing. During the Carter presidency impor-tant progress had been made in resolving the issue, but in the Reagan era it threatened to reemerge. Running for office in 1980, Ronald Reagan, to Beijing's alarm, had expressed strong support for Taiwan. Chinese displea-sure with this possible regression in U.S. policy was marked in various ways. During the election campaign vice presidential candidate George Bush, although a former ambassador to the People's Republic of China, was received with "reserve bordering on coldness." Now Haig was being made to understand that China had not abandoned its claim to Taiwan. At the airport the secretary of state was seen off by the vice foreign minister, not the foreign minister as protocol required. Haig understood that this

slight indicated Chinese displeasure at President Reagan's remarks at a
news conference that day that the Taiwan Relations Act (which formalized
U.S. commitments to Taiwan's security) would be carried out as the law of
the land.[52]

The consistent American tendency to "obtuseness" (Kissinger's term) on
symbolic matters was confirmed by U.S. behavior during the ill-fated and
indeed counterproductive attempt by the Clinton administration in 1994
to link renewal of China's most-favored-nation (MFN) status to concessions on human rights issues. Angrily rejected by Beijing as interference in
internal affairs, the Clinton administration was eventually obliged, with
serious harm to American credibility, to separate human rights from trade
and extend MFN status unconditionally. The low point of the negotiation
occurred in March 1994 during a visit by Secretary of State Warren
Christopher to China that produced meager results in terms of human
rights, was politically damaging to the president, and was a diplomatic
embarrassment. During the visit Christopher received the full cold shoulder treatment: reception at airport by deputy foreign minister with per-
functory handshake, no pomp, and no public words of welcome; no five-
star banquet; detention of activists during visit; cancellation of a joint
news conference.[53]

It was realized, too late, that Christopher should not have exposed himself to this rebuff by going through with the visit. Signals of what he could
expect had been broadcast verbally and nonverbally on the eve of his
arrival. Assistant Secretary of State John Shattuck had visited Beijing at
the end of February to prepare the ground for Christopher. To the anger of
the Chinese, Shattuck held a meeting in the public setting of the coffee
garden of the China World Hotel with prominent democracy activist Wei
Jingsheng.[54] Shattuck clearly reasoned that a public meeting would be
more dignified than a suspicious private encounter. As far as the Chinese
were concerned, the very openness of the conversation lent it the air of a
staged provocation intended to shame the authorities. Calling Wei a "criminal on parole," they charged Shattuck with breaking Chinese law. A few
days later, Wei and other democracy campaigners were detained. The purpose of the detentions, a pro-Chinese communist newspaper published in
Hong Kong explained, was "to convey a message" to the United States and
the U.S. secretary of state, who was scheduled to arrive in Beijing for a visit
on March 11: "Do not take China for a weak country which can easily be
bullied; do not take for granted that China will kowtow to the United
States on the human rights issue in order to retain its MFN trading

status."[55] Of course, a foreign ministry spokesperson denied that there was any connection between the arrests and the Christopher visit;[56] indeed, the deniability of nonverbal messages is precisely their advantage. But if this signal was not clear enough, the Chinese suggested that the secretary of state postpone his trip because "it coincided with the opening of the National People's Congress."[57] The detention of Wei, then, was the writing on the wall for the United States. To the end, U.S. officials expressed the hope that Chinese conduct was pure posturing and that the leadership would eventually agree to a deal.[58]

On the whole, the U.S. is a most hospitable host for visiting dignitaries. Yet occasionally low-context insensitivity is reflected in maladroit protocol, whether at home or abroad. Presidential staffs tend to be more attuned to domestic political considerations, public relations, and security require-ments than to foreign sensibilities. Matters are not helped by congressional and popular skepticism. Diplomats, it is popularly felt, should be hard-nosed operators, not bleeding hearts. U.S.-Indian relations were damaged in 1964 when an invitation to Prime Minister Shastri was abruptly with-drawn by President Johnson. There was no diplomatic reason for the cancel-lation; never very enthusiastic about protocol and its niceties, the president had simply decided that his calendar was too crowded. Plans for the visit were in full swing at the time. Worse, the announcement was first made in a news broadcast, with no prior warning to the Delhi embassy permitting it to soften the blow. Ambassador Bowles lamented that Shastri, an inse-cure and sensitive man, had been "rudely and publicly embarrassed." As a result, the government of India was deeply angered.[59]

In 1974 a presidential advance party, preparing for a visit by President Nixon to Cairo, was guilty of gross breaches of courtesy. The arrival of an advance party of several hundred people overwhelmed and disconcerted local officials. The arrogant behavior of the U.S. contingent in a host coun-try was indefensible. The Cairo Hilton was evacuated of all guests; Egyp-tian arrangements were "sloughed aside"; Secret Service officers refused Egyptian transportation for the president and insisted that their own armored vehicle be brought in. When the Egyptians put their foot down on that demand, Nixon personally overrode the wishes of his security men.[60]

In 1969, in a similar incident in Delhi, Indian objections were overrid-den when Nixon's staff threatened that, if the Indians insisted on their own vehicle, the American president would not be allowed to stay at the Indian presidential residence. On this earlier occasion, Gandhi conceded the point. She is supposed to have remarked, "If he's killed, it's his car!" On a visit by President Carter to Mexico City in 1979 one White House staffer, oblivious to Mexican feelings about the "lost provinces," had the bright idea that a "Texas barbecue" would be an appropriate event at which to entertain Mexican guests. Fortunately, the embassy overruled the suggestion.[61]

At the level of body language, the most noteworthy feature of Chinese, Indian, and Japanese behavior is their unusual (to Westerners' eyes) capacity for self-restraint and impassivity. These are enviable assets to bring to the negotiating table, where they deprive U.S. negotiators of highly desirable information about the interlocutors' true feelings. Imperturbable negotiators are able to conceal their eagerness for agreement, their interest in a particular concession, and any pressures to settle to which they might be subject.

Kissinger recalls seeing Zhou Enlai lose his massive composure on only one occasion. The Chinese prime minister epitomized the Confucian ideal of the cultivated person who strives to maintain perfect self-control, regardless of circumstances.[62] Secretary of State Baker, too, admired the ability of Chinese ambassador Han Xu to remain "completely composed" amid the emotional and diplomatic turmoil of the Tiananmen debacle. The corollary of self-control, though, is inscrutability, and Baker ruefully notes that secret envoys sent to Beijing shortly after the massacre learned little from their impassive hosts.[63]

To the Confucian concept of virtue as dignified poise and mastery of one's emotions, Japanese culture has added a remarkable aesthetic of silence, summed up in the Zen Buddhist aphorism that "Words are of no use." At negotiating sessions Japanese place great stress on clearheaded attentiveness rather than loquacity. Americans describe their astonishment at observing Japanese officials sitting in on meetings with their eyes closed.[64] Secretary Shultz found that "at meetings the Japanese are generally silent. They have ideas, but they don't say much." The Japanese are themselves aware that they come across as "inscrutable" to the outside world and bemoan their lack of facility in intercultural communication.[65] Mitsuru Inuta has also written on his countrymen's tendency to disguise their real intentions beneath an agreeable, smiling appearance *(tatemae)*.[66]

U.S. trade representative Mickey Kantor, probably as low-context a negotiator as Washington has ever fielded, had difficulty intuiting the message beneath the mask. During a visit to Tokyo in February 1994 to press the Japanese to agree to numerical targets to increase its imports of American goods, Kantor was clearly told, according to a Japanese negotiator, that Japan most certainly would not back down. However, Kantor heard things differently, reporting that his interlocutor, Foreign Minister Tsutomu Hata, *was silent on that issue.* He thought that this might hint at an opening. Other officials wondered whether Hata was simply trying to avoid an unpleasant confrontation.[67] The correct answer was the latter, as subsequently became obvious. Whereas the Western rule is that silence implies consent, no such convention exists in Japan. In a negotiation, the reverse is usually true.

An experienced U.S. negotiator emphasized the Indians' facility at masking their emotions. Like good poker players they were able, in his experience, to avoid "tipping their hand." He explained this ability by a combination of two factors: a sense, derived from the British, that to do so would be bad form; and conformity to the Hindu tradition of abjuring desire. Nehru's impassivity certainly misled U.S. diplomats on several occasions. Allen's failure in 1954 to detect Nehru's true reaction to the U.S.-Pakistani arms deal has already been described. Galbraith was also repeatedly led astray throughout the ill-fated Anglo-American attempt to mediate the Kashmir dispute. For instance, at one point Galbraith was instructed to try to sell the idea of partition to Nehru. "Nehru's face did not brighten perceptibly this evening when I brought up the idea," Galbraith writes, "but he did not throw me out." The ambassador quite wrongly concluded that the Indians did not "entirely rule out giving the Pakistanis some position in the [Kashmir] valley."[68] At this time India doubtless felt that it had no choice but to play along with the initiative. But the last thing the Indians had on their minds was transferring territory to their sworn enemies.

Nehru was also famous for his silences, which were always disconcerting to the more loquacious Americans. During the period of deterioration in U.S.-Indian relations that followed the 1971 Indo-Pakistani war, India decided to close American libraries that had been set up in the provinces at the instigation of Chester Bowles. When the State Department sought in its files the documentary basis of the establishment of the libraries, it discovered that none existed. The agreement had simply derived from a conversation between Ambassador Bowles and the prime minister. Bowles had suggested the matter to Nehru, and Nehru, without uttering a word, had given a brief inclination of the head.[69] Galbraith, Nixon, and Shultz were highly disconcerted by long pauses in discussions with Indian leaders.[70] They were better equipped to handle arguments than to intuit feelings. Nothing could better illustrate the gap between results-oriented and relationship-oriented views of negotiation.

In the middle phase of negotiations there is much evidence to corroborate the antitheses suggested by my theoretical framework. A clear picture emerges of opposing and sometimes incompatible negotiating models. The fact that episodes of dissonance are exceptional does not render them any less consequential. The ill-advised March 1994 Christopher visit to Beijing was a blunder that damaged U.S. interests. On the one hand, the United States, in the adversarial, can-do tradition, is confirmed as predominantly short term and results oriented, placing emphasis on concession and compromise, incremental convergence, and the techniques of forensic argument. On the other hand, high-context subjects, in the consensual, face-salient tradition, are predominantly relationship oriented, eschewing bargaining on issues of high principle, not viewing compromise as an end in itself, minimizing techniques of confrontation and advocacy, and reflecting more hierarchical modes of government.

As far as communication is concerned, the low-context–high-context dichotomy is often justified. American negotiators have inherited a legalistic modus operandi that ascribes peculiar weight to the written word. Literal meanings and plain speaking are emphasized, and the opportunity to hammer out disagreement in open debate is welcomed. In contrast, non-Western negotiators possess less faith in the powers of the written word and are more inclined to value the spoken word as an instrument of social affect. Sensitive to questions of face and to the disruptive consequences an unguarded utterance may have for communal harmony, they display a preference for emollient rather than abrasive face-to-face language, avoid harsh contradiction, and opt for a more allusive style of speech. Nonverbal cues acquire analogous importance as devices to express social solidarity; when necessary, they are kept under tight control lest offense be given inadvertently. By extension, particular weight is attached to symbolic politics. In all, the confrontation of communicatory styles provides ample opportunity for misunderstanding in the prelude to the crucial end game.

9

Under Pressure

End Game I

The final phase of a negotiation can be characterized in various ways. Zartman and Berman see it as occurring when negotiators cross from the formula stage of general principles to the elaboration of a detailed agreement. Before that can happen there is a "turning point of seriousness."[1] In general, we can agree that the end game is that decisive stage of a negotiation reached after substantial progress has been achieved and obstacles overcome, and at which the agreement is hammered into final form. It is very far from a trouble-free part of the negotiating process, and indeed some of the most intractable problems may arise at this point, as negotiators balance the benefits and drawbacks of the emerging deal. Nevertheless, if they have reached this far in the talks, the assumption is that they have invested considerable assets in the whole process and are committed to completing the task.

As this critical point is reached, low- and high-context philosophies of negotiation face off for a final settling of accounts. Unnecessary or premature concessions tilt the balance of advantage to one's opponent. What has been given away cannot be recalled. For one last time contrasting assumptions confront each other. Conceptions of time are crucial at this stage. Americans, viewing time as a wasting asset, are more likely to feel the pressure of approaching deadlines. Decisions have to be made about the form of the agreement, raising questions about the nature, scope, and finality of contracts: Americans, after all, spring from a tradition that seeks to regulate by contract certain relations that other cultures leave to ties of sentiment and obligation. The issue of face looms large: the accord must be presented in such a way that contrasting needs for intangible, and not merely material, gratification can be reconciled. Final obstacles must be overcome in a manner that does not jeopardize what has already been achieved and, indeed, wider policy goals.

BREAKING THE DEADLOCK

Some negotiations go relatively smoothly. Many lock into immobility. Druckman and his colleagues see impasses as resulting from "a lack of synchronization between the delegations: in preferences or objectives, in activities, in negotiating rhetoric."[2] Deadlocks go beyond brief standoffs and involve more protracted periods of paralysis. Usually arising from a basic disagreement over major points under discussion, they threaten the success of the entire operation. However, deadlocks should not necessarily be viewed in a totally negative light. Certainly, failure to untangle them will terminate the negotiation; on the other hand, their resolution clears away major impediments, boosts the morale of negotiators, and strengthens the psychological commitment of the parties to a successful outcome. Paradoxically, crises may actually be functional in a negotiation. They oblige the parties to confront the unpleasant reality that the desirable and the attainable may not coincide. Negotiators must make the hard choice: address the needs of the other side and surmount the difficulty or fail. Crisis and a clash of wills may also be cathartic and help to build a bond between the parties. Negotiation is not a study in harmony.

Breaking deadlocks, then, is one of the key tests facing negotiators. It can be done in a number of ways: Procedural solutions work by bypassing obstacles, raising the level of talks to generate political momentum, or changing the framework of negotiation in some other way. Bridging mechanisms may facilitate agreement by providing transitional arrangements or periods of protracted implementation. Where appropriate, technical solutions may leave everybody satisfied by genuinely enlarging the cake to be divided. Failing that, compromises are intended to distribute benefits more or less equitably and, as noted, are particularly favored by U.S. negotiators. Finally, but without necessarily precluding any of the above, deadlock may be broken by the exercise of coercive power—threats of punishment intended to shift the other side's assessment of the costs and advantages of agreement on the terms offered, as opposed to a continuation of the status quo.

How well does coercion work in negotiations between high- and low-context cultures? There is no easy answer to this difficult and important question, except to say that it depends on circumstances and issues, that unmasked pressure may be counterproductive, and that if it can be used credibly—and preferably discreetly—it may produce short-term benefits, but only at the expense of longer-term resentment and damage to the overall relationship.

As one might suspect in dealing with high-context, face-salient societies that place such emphasis on group harmony and the avoidance of unpleasantness, personal confrontation is not the acceptable form of behavior that it is in societies founded on the adversarial approach. According to David Newsom, "brashness is not only offensive, but it leads to a loss of respect for the negotiator who cannot seem to control himself/herself. This does not rule out occasional calculated outbursts for theatrical purposes."[3]

In dealing with the Egyptian government, Ambassador Eilts insisted, "table thumping" was quite out of the question.[4] U.S. trade representative Mickey Kantor (1993–96), who used angry body language and sharp comments in his dealings with Japanese negotiators, in the courtroom tradition of the staged tantrum, discovered that such tactics were ineffective, indeed counterproductive. If anything, they undermined trust and alienated the domestic Japanese constituencies that would have to be recruited were Kantor to prize open Japanese markets to newcomers.[5] Former ambassador to Mexico John Jova (1974–77) stressed the need to avoid confrontation. He always tried to "get the message across in a softer, more indirect way." Above all, one had to avoid "humiliating them," giving the appearance that the Mexicans were "taking orders from Washington." He believed that public criticism of the Mexican government was "fatal."[6]

One of Jova's successors, John Gavin, deliberately ignored this caveat and found his effectiveness in Mexico City curtailed, and some pressure created for his removal. Appearing before a Senate subcommittee in 1986, Gavin strongly defended his outspoken style. The Mexican "dread of [U.S.] intervention" should not deter the pursuit of "a frank, an open, and a respectful dialogue." His view was well received by critics of Mexico in the Senate. Senator Pete Wilson (R-Calif.), for instance, thought that the time for undue sensitivity on the part of the United States was "really past if we are going to deal with the monumental problems that are afflicting both nations . . . the United States cannot engage in politeness." Why Mexico should be more responsive to strident criticism was not explained. State Department professionals learned long ago that rhetoric—"Mexico bashing"—might be popular back home but was not calculated to elicit Mexican cooperation. "Denunciation is counterproductive," points out William D. Rogers, a former assistant secretary of state for inter-American relations. "Quiet diplomacy, a sense of our long and troubled history together, a sensitivity to the very special psychology of our coexistence, these are the essence of the relationship."[7]

Corroborating Rogers's view, Christopher Dickey of the *Washington Post* observed among Mexicans an "almost oriental obsession with saving face." He concluded that "the fastest way to reach a dead end in any kind of negotiation is to force an issue." According to Dickey, the difficulties faced by the United States in the 1979 gas talks were largely a result of the pugnacious approach adopted by the U.S. Department of Energy.[8] It is quite true that Mexican negotiators found Secretary Schlesinger abrupt and arrogant. By all accounts he behaved in a rude and offhand manner. He later became a special target of their displeasure. There was, however, a substantive and not simply subjective disagreement, namely, the secretary's view that the Mexican asking price was far too high. In the end, the price achieved by the United States was better in real terms after Schlesinger's brutal veto than it would have been otherwise. Although his manner may have offended the Mexicans, and was not particularly helpful, it did not distract them from a rational calculation of where their interests lay.

Hectoring apart, the United States clearly has substantial, tangible assets to bring to bear in a negotiation, especially with countries dependent on American goodwill in the form of investments and trade. There is no question that potential loss is a consideration that high-context negotiators are bound to take into account irrespective of culturally grounded needs. As markets have opened up, however, the balance of advantage has become less clear-cut. Today, U.S. consumers are accustomed to enjoying lower-cost foreign products, and American corporations have massively diversified their operations abroad. Neither is happy about jeopardizing those benefits.

In the past, the attempt to condition American help—whether financial aid, military assistance, or food relief—on the beneficiary's compliant behavior was often surprisingly unsuccessful. Egypt's point blank refusal to have any truck with Western alliance schemes in the 1950s has already been mentioned. If the supply of American arms was to be contingent on foreign policy concessions, Nasser preferred to turn to the Soviet Union. Failure to recognize the futility of crude pressure in dealing with Egypt (or India for that matter) in conditions of superpower competition was to cost the United States dearly.

After the announcement of the so-called Czech arms deal between Egypt and the Soviet Union in September 1955, paid for by the mortgaging of the Egyptian cotton crop, Secretary of State Dulles concluded that Egypt was unlikely to be left with sufficient foreign exchange to service loans then under negotiation with the World Bank to build a dam at Aswan. He was also determined to give the Egyptians a short, sharp lesson for their association with the Soviet Union. In a dramatic gesture, Dulles baldly informed the Egyptian ambassador of the rejection of the loan application. The Egyptians were humiliated and infuriated. Far from becoming more compliant with American wishes, Nasser was even more alienated from the Western world and driven deeper into the Soviet camp. Within twenty-four hours of Dulles's snub he decided to nationalize the Suez Canal.[9]

Later attempts by the United States, particularly the Congress, to use food aid as explicit levers of influence were also a resounding failure. To some senators it appeared self-evident that because Egypt was receiving one-third of all its grain from the United States it should be compliant with American wishes, for example, on the need to make peace with Israel. But as Ambassador John Badeau argues, Egyptians would not concede a deeply felt principle "for greed or for money." The mere suspicion, he writes, that food was being used for political ends robbed it "of much of its diplomatic usefulness."[10] In the mid-1960s, following a series of unpleasant incidents in U.S.-Egyptian relations, Ambassador Lucius Battle informed the Egyptian minister of provision that he thought the time was inappropriate to press President Johnson about the supply of wheat (under the Public Law 480 program). The message reached Nasser in garbled form, although its purport was clear enough. In a speech that day at Port Said, Nasser launched a vitriolic personal attack on President Johnson: "The American Ambassador," he stormed, "says that our behavior is not acceptable. Well let us tell them that those who do not accept our behavior can go and drink . . . from the sea . . . we are not going to accept gangsterism by cowboys."[11]

Much the same pattern can be found in U.S.-Indian relations in the 1950s and 1960s. The 1951 negotiations for a loan with which to purchase two million tons of American wheat after the failure of the monsoon rains were conducted under the shadow of congressional demands for an Indian quid pro quo in the area of foreign policy. It appeared to Nehru that the United States was "taking advantage of India's food shortage to drive a hard bargain."[12] He certainly was not going to abandon nonalignment in return for food. If used with tact, aid can create goodwill; mishandled, it may only feed resentment.

A state cannot be forced by the threat to withhold aid to abandon a cherished principle. Sadly, this lesson has had to be repeatedly relearned. It was again demonstrated in the aftermath of the 1962 Sino-Indian border war. Initially, the United States gained enormous credit in India for coming so promptly to its assistance at a difficult time. The temptation to capitalize on this fund of goodwill to achieve other foreign policy goals proved irresistible for the Kennedy administration and particularly its envoy, Ambassador John Kenneth Galbraith. In cooperation with the United Kingdom, the United States began a process of mediation between India and Pakistan to resolve the Kashmir dispute. Overriding the doubts of Undersecretary of State Chester Bowles, Galbraith unwisely seized on India's acute need for military supplies to force concessions on it. In a letter to President Kennedy, Galbraith outlined how pressure was to be judiciously exercised, "We are urging the importance of a settlement as a prime goal of Indian foreign policy, for that makes our military aid both possible and effective."[13]

In the immediate aftermath of the war, Nehru was content to play along with the mediation initiative, unwilling to antagonize the United States and Britain while continued Western support and military supplies were needed. Given Nehru's views on Pakistan and Kashmir there was no chance that he would agree to meaningful concessions. The talks dragged on. Finally, Galbraith decided to confront Nehru. "If I did not press hard," he writes in his diary, "the failure would be blamed on me . . . So I made the best of a bad situation and tried too hard." He saw Nehru on two occasions to bring his "careful buildup of persuasion here in India to a climax." Nehru turned him down flat both times and the initiative petered out.[14] Unfortunately, the end result was the loss of most of the capital that the United States had acquired for helping out during the emergency. Gratitude was converted into resentment. The Indians concluded that the United States had taken advantage of their moment of weakness to force on them an unacceptable course of action.

On trade matters the picture is rather different. On the road to the deregulation and liberalization of international trade, pressure tactics of various kinds on the part of U.S. administrations have become common. The experience of recent years, particularly in dealing with China and Japan, suggests the hypothesis that pressure is effective in breaking a deadlock if it (a) is completely credible; (b) is exercised on a matter removed from connotations of high sovereign principle; (c) is appropriate and proportionate; (d) clearly tips the balance of advantage away from immobility to arriving at a settlement; and (e) helps the other side convince its own superiors and domestic interests of the desirability of a resolution.

In commercial negotiations conducted with China in the 1990s, agreement has repeatedly been reached at the very last minute before a deadline for the imposition of trade sanctions was to come into effect. For instance, in January 1994 Mickey Kantor announced that the United States would cut Chinese fabric imports to the United States by over $1 billion in retaliation for Beijing's refusal to halt the illegal shipment of textiles. Within a short time China complied with the American demand.[15] Chas Freeman explains Chinese responsiveness to this kind of pressure in terms of its preoccupation with raw calculations of power and interest. Until pushed up against a bottom line by a tough—even "outrageous"—interlocutor, Chinese negotiators would not be able to persuade their principals and recalcitrant special interests of the need to compromise. "If the consequences aren't Armageddon they can't carry the situation internally," he argued. Hence, pressure tactics such as walking out and setting deadlines might be effective, though not calculated to build mutual confidence.[16]

The accuracy of Freeman's analysis is borne out by the 1995 intellectual property rights agreement. In December 1994 U.S. diplomats Deborah Lehr and Lee Sands confronted a situation in Beijing that had become familiar to China experts: a deadlock that could be expected to persist to the very last minute, when Chinese negotiators would settle "as late as possible for as little as possible." This strategy often worked with U.S. negotiators under political pressure to settle or on a tight schedule. This time Sands and Lehr decided to play China at its own game, cutting off deadlocked talks a day early and heading off home, even missing a high-level banquet. China responded with threats of a trade war and invective in the press against lead negotiator Sands. When Washington stuck to its guns, and refused to be drawn into a public debate, the Chinese realized that they had struck bedrock; there was no more give in the American position and Sands was playing from a strong hand: Washington had well-documented evidence of Chinese copyright abuse; garnered support back home, especially in the business community; presented clear proposals on ways China could enforce its own existing laws; and was under no pressure to come up with a quick fix. The deadlock breaker was the credible threat of punishment under the Special 301 provision of U.S. trade law. This allows Washington to impose sanctions commensurate with damage done to American producers by illicit trade practices in another country. Another unspoken incentive was the Chinese wish to be admitted into the new World Trade Organization.[17]

"That was the turning point," Sands recalls of his December 1994 walkout. On the delegation's return to Beijing in February 1995 it found a compliant Chinese interlocutor ready to agree to many American demands. Key advances in the talks were made away from the negotiating table in quiet, one-on-one, nonconfrontational conversations during smoking breaks. In chapter 11, though, we shall see that Sands's prediction at the time that "in China negotiations never really end" was amply borne out in a frustrating "post end game" of Chinese noncompliance with agreements reached.[18]

Success in 1995 stood in marked and significant contrast with the U.S. failure in 1994 to extract human rights concessions under threatened nonrenewal of China's most-favored-nation (MFN) status. In this case the conditions for agreement were spelled out in March 1993 at the highest level by President Clinton in a public statement and an executive order. For over a year talks continued at various levels until, in the face of utter Chinese obduracy and exceptional damage to wider relations, President Clinton was obliged, humiliatingly and damagingly, to climb down. On May 26, 1994, he announced the unconditional renewal of China's MFN status and permanently delinked trade from human rights, thereby admitting that the strategy had been ill-conceived from the outset. A series of errors underlay this abortive exercise of pressure: First and foremost, the sensitive topic of human rights was the worst-possible grounds for a face-off, since China flatly rejected the U.S. *locus standi* (right to intervene) on the issue, and was convinced any concession would undermine the stability of the regime. Burt Levin, a former U.S. ambassador to Korea and Taiwan, commented that "there are some things all the toughness in the world won't change overnight. Anyone who takes the lesson [that] we should hit hard on human rights is barking up the wrong tree."[19] Second, within the framework of China's succession struggle, no contender for power could appear to be weak by submitting to publicly trumpeted U.S. coercion. In these circumstances, not only could U.S. negotiators not recruit domestic Chinese allies, but solidly united Beijing behind resistance to demands.[20] Third, as time passed it became increasingly clear that the United States itself was deeply divided on the issue, with the Commerce, Defense, and State Departments concerned that their agendas were being harmed, and business deeply unhappy about Chinese threats of retaliation. These fears were skillfully played upon by Chinese propaganda, with counterthreats of spoiling tactics at the United Nations and sanctions against *American* exports, with a purported loss of two hundred thousand U.S. jobs. By May 1994 Washington was ready to throw in the towel, finally realizing how inherently incredible and counterproductive pressure had become: revoking China's MFN status was "increasingly viewed as the economic equivalent of dropping an atom bomb: too devastating to contemplate."[21]

During the Bush and then Clinton administrations a new word entered the vocabulary of U.S.-Japanese relations: *gaiatsu*, meaning external pressure forcing the Japanese to adopt policies really in their own domestic interest. *Gaiatsu* came to be seen as a kind of "magic bullet" for dealing with Japanese procrastination. It worked as follows: First, the United States trade representative, under industry and congressional pressure, would complain about an unfair Japanese trade practice, usually a restriction on the access of an American product to the Japanese market. The Japanese Ministry of Trade and Industry, constrained by powerful domestic interests of its own, would prevaricate with a variety of arguments, either denying that a problem existed or claiming that it lacked the influence to alter the existing state of affairs. The United States, in an atmosphere of political outrage and thinly disguised ill-feeling toward Japan, would then turn on the heat, escalating its rhetoric and threatening to impose various sanctions. Japan would go on the defensive and fight a determined and protracted rear-guard action to the accompaniment of bitter complaints of U.S. brutality, capitulating at the very last moment under extreme duress. The beauty of *gaiatsu*, it was claimed, was that it provided the Japanese government with a face-saving pretext for taking action required anyway in the interests of consumers but precluded by bureaucratic constraints.[22] An appeal to *force majeure* might also be useful for Japanese producers who would be provided with a pretext for switching from local to foreign suppliers, something normally very difficult within Japan's relationship-based business culture. Nor did Japanese commentators deny it: "It's shameful really, that we need *gaiatsu* to improve our lifestyle," commented Atsushi Kuse, an analyst of U.S.-Japanese relations, "but the fact is, we need this pressure to make changes in our society."[23]

The single greatest achievement for *gaiatsu* was the March 1994 accord allowing Motorola to compete on an equal basis with Japanese companies in providing cellular phone services in the region from Tokyo to Nagoya. The original negotiation arose from the U.S. claim that the Japanese company IDO was in violation of a 1989 agreement obliging it to permit "comparable market access" to U.S. companies by building a system compatible with the North American standard. Having failed to make progress using

conventional methods, the U.S. trade representative set in motion proceedings under the Special 301 trade provision to designate Japan an
"unfair" trader, subject to punitive retaliation. With five days to go before
Washington was to publish a list of likely targets for sanctions, Japan capit-
ulated and consented to unprecedented and far-reaching measures to open
up its market, including specification of the number of base stations, relays,
and radio frequencies to be made available to Motorola, and even agreed to
back low-interest loans and encourage investment in Motorola's system by
IDO.[24] The cellular phone triumph—which resulted in a sales boom for
Motorola products in Japan because of their price and technological edge
—was hailed as an exemplary U.S.-Japanese negotiation. Eric Gan, a telecommunications analyst with Goldman Sachs (Japan), went so far as to
claim that "sanctions are one of the only ways to open the market."[25] However, the major point surely was that *gaiatsu* had succeeded for the best
possible reason: it had persuaded Japan to accept an accord that was to the
mutual benefit of both sides but had been obstructed by special interests.
The lesson of Motorola was *not* that Japan could always be bludgeoned
into agreeing to something likely to be to its detriment.

A much more nuanced picture emerged from negotiations launched
under the so-called Framework Agreement concluded in July 1993 between President Clinton and Prime Minister Hosokawa for opening up
five priority Japanese markets: automobiles and auto parts, insurance, flat
glass, medical equipment, and telecommunications. Talks conformed to
the familiar pattern of procrastination, deadlock, American pressure, and
nemawashi—informal Japanese feelers to dismantle the impasse. Results
for *gaiatsu*, though, were decidedly mixed in this case. An October 1994
agreement was reached involving substantial last-minute Japanese concessions in four of the five areas, at the end of a marathon twenty-hour final
session of talks. Had the negotiation not been productive, U.S. officials let
it be known, a long list of sanctions would have been imposed on Tokyo,
including action under Special 301 and the barring of Japanese companies
from bidding on certain federal government contracts. The flat-glass accord
was favorable to the United States and committed Japan to opening up its
market and promoting greater use of types of glass in which U.S. companies had the lead. In the medical and telecommunications equipment
area, Japan agreed to open up government purchases to foreign manufac-
turers, and accepted, under duress, a U.S. plan to gauge Japanese "progress."
Elsewhere, in the really lucrative insurance and automobile markets, the
Japanese were less forthcoming. They did agree to reform their insurance

regulatory system, but it subsequently transpired that the agreement was hopelessly vague and permitted endless evasion. In the major area of dissension, motor vehicles and auto parts, there was little progress.[26] Increasingly acrimonious talks, conducted under a Damocles sword of threatened U.S. sanctions, continued into the summer of 1995, when Mickey Kantor declared victory and went home. He completely failed to extract Japanese consent to the numerical targets for automobile purchases that the United States had for so long insisted upon. Tokyo refused to repeat the traumatic experience of the 1986 semiconductor agreement, when for years it was held hostage to measurable criteria of market share.

Not the least reason that Kantor finally accepted a second-best outcome was the enormous collateral damage being caused by continuous pressure. As Richard Solomon notes, some *gaiatsu* is certainly helpful, but the approach adopted by Mickey Kantor was so remorselessly confrontational that it had begun to undermine basic confidence in the relationship. Anyway, it could be outmaneuvered and did not solve underlying problems.[27] The case against the strategy was convincingly made at the time by Jeffrey Garten, undersecretary of trade for international commerce and a lead negotiator in the auto talks. "A relationship between the world's two biggest trading nations that is characterized by one trade confrontation after another seems as anachronistic as the old gunboat diplomacy," he argued. It was time to move away from constant tension to calm cooperation.[28]

PRESSURES TO SETTLE

As the prospect of success or failure looms, pressures build up from domestic interests, from the opponent—and particularly, in high-profile negotiations, from the political echelon and the press. Under the stress of this decisive encounter, the mettle and nerves of negotiators are tested to the utmost. Character is bound to be important. But, above all, the negotiating resources and assumptions of the group are put to the test. Americans enjoy several advantages: ingenuity and an enterprising spirit, extraordinary resources, a strong institutional and informational base. Although the term "bureaucratic politics" is an American political science invention, it may surprise Americans to learn that turf wars notwithstanding, interagency coordination in international negotiation is on the whole much better in Washington than in any of the high-context countries discussed here. Where individualism fosters team play—loyalty to a superordinate interest —group-oriented, high-context officials may be too committed to their agencies of origin to work together in the common cause.

American negotiators do tend to display some flaws in the end game: an underestimation of others' glacial bureaucratic procedures, an impatience to settle, and the *paradox of superpower vulnerability*. With so many irons in the fire, the need to address so many interconnected issues, the U.S. ability to exert sustained pressure may be more limited than is apparent to the outsider. Invariably, however important the immediate question under discussion, the cooperation of the interlocutor will soon be needed by the United States on some other matter in some other forum. China has been particularly adept at linking one negotiation to another, convincingly able to argue that it was as much needed by the United States as the reverse.

From the tactical point of view, despite its many bargaining assets, the United States does not in consequence always have the upper hand in the end game. American habits of urgency may incline negotiators to premature concession in the wish to settle. It is hard enough negotiating the issues; bargaining against the clock compounds the difficulty. Worse, the American negotiator joins impatience to an overwhelming and barely concealed obligation to succeed; American culture, in the form of public opinion, career dictates, and government expectations, does not take kindly to failure. To add to these self-generated pressures there are sometimes congressionally mandated deadlines for reports or appropriation markups.[29]

Hence, in the final contest of wills, as their opposite numbers are well aware, American negotiators are vulnerable to delay. Whereas they must bring matters to a prompt conclusion, their non-Western opponents—or, indeed, anyone else free of stifling deadlines—can sit them out or, if necessary, credibly threaten to walk away from the bargaining table altogether. Freedom from time pressure is an enviable asset.

The definitive statement on the tendency of the American negotiator to give ground in the face of an obdurate rival was made many years ago by the U.S. delegate to the Panmunjom armistice talks for ending the Korean War. Looking back on his experience, Ambassador Arthur Dean ruefully observes the asymmetry of pressures on the two sides:

> Communists are in no hurry. They have no timetable. They think time is on their side and that Americans, being optimistic, friendly, truthful, constructive and inclined to believe and hope for the best, will become discouraged. They believe that at a long-drawn-out conference the American negotiators will be forced by American public opinion to give in, in order to have a successful conference. Impatience mounts as no progress is reported. People

ask: "What progress did you make today?" The Communists know this and utter rude, insulting, arrogant demands that the American negotiators stop their unconstructive stalling tactics.[30]

Alexis Johnson, the U.S. delegate at the ambassadorial talks with the People's Republic of China, described a similar experience: "During the almost four years that I was negotiating with the Chinese Communists at Geneva, between 1954 and 1958, what I found most annoying and frustrating was their supreme self-confidence that they need make no concessions of any kind and that if they just waited long enough we would be forced to make all the concessions to them."[31]

Now that some of the State Department papers on the ambassadorial talks are available to researchers, it is possible to document in greater detail the forces for concession to which Ambassador Johnson was subject. Although we are talking about something that happened over forty years ago, similar forces can be seen to be at work today. After a few weeks of negotiating with China for the repatriation of U.S. civilians, Johnson concluded, prematurely, that the Chinese refusal to agree to release all Americans on the mainland was irreducible. The talks had got under way on August 1. On August 18, the Chinese delegate made a great display of intransigence on the issue, resisting "persistent pressure" to provide assurances on the release of all the Americans. The battle continued for another two weeks, with Johnson pegging away with diminishing optimism.

According to Johnson's account, virtually the entire session of August 25 "centered around my continuing effort to obtain a definite statement on the definite period of time during which the remaining Americans would be released and Wang repeating this 'could never be done,' 'impossible' and repeating virtually verbatim his previous line in this regard." At the August 31 session, Johnson reported, the Chinese negotiator "showed no great sense of urgency," and Johnson doubted that the Chinese desire to move on to other matters was "strong enough to overcome their very strong reluctance to give up their position." He had already suggested that it would be difficult for the United States to maintain its original demands and suggested to the State Department that it might be "jeopardizing" the immediate release of more than half of the detained Americans by insisting that they all be freed. In its instructions of September 2, the State Department concurred, concluding that the agreed announcement was "as good as can be expected."[32] Glacial Chinese patience had won the day; valuable bargaining chips remained in their hands for future negotiations.

The American propensity for self-induced deadlines was also evident in the 1978 normalization talks with China.[33] With admitted hindsight, it is clear that the haste with which these negotiations were pursued by the Carter administration was particularly inappropriate because time was actually working to the detriment of the People's Republic of China. There were tactical reasons why the United States wanted an agreement by the end of 1978—the looming debate over ratification of the Panama Canal treaties, the strategic arms limitation talks with the Soviet Union, and involvement in the Egyptian-Israeli peace process—but these were not insurmountable. But there were weighty, indeed inescapable, strategic considerations behind China's wish for early normalization: its planned attack on Vietnam and the need to neutralize the danger of Soviet involvement. Following the publication of the agreement on December 15, 1978, formal diplomatic relations were established on January 1, 1979, paving the way for the visit by Deng Xiaoping to the United States at the end of the month. On February 17 the People's Liberation Army attacked Vietnam, Deng having cleverly obtained the appearance of U.S. complicity as a deterrent to Soviet intervention.

Nevertheless, despite the asymmetry of interest in a speedy resolution of the issue, China successfully concealed its own sense of urgency while the United States acted as though it faced an immutable deadline. At a meeting of top U.S. officials on June 20, 1978, it was first decided to aim for completion of the normalization negotiations by December 15, but the Chinese were not supposed to be informed of this target date. Secretary of State Vance argued that this timetable "would allow us to proceed with Peking at a reasonable pace and would have some negotiating advantages over a stretched-out process." However, National Security Adviser Zbigniew Brzezinski had already told Deng that President Carter was prepared to move as quickly as possible, and in September Carter openly stressed to the head of the People's Republic liaison office in Washington the desirability of a quick normalization. While the Chinese "hung tough" on their insistence that the United States terminate its arms relationship with Taiwan, Brzezinski made little attempt to conceal his own sense of urgency. He "told the Chinese Ambassador that if we missed this opportunity, we would have to delay normalization until far into 1979. The congressional schedule would be overloaded and we would have to move ahead on SALT and a possible meeting with Brezhnev." Brzezinski continued to be the main proponent of haste. Again on December 11, impatient with the slow pace of the Chinese response, he made the case for a speedy decision to Ambassador Chai.

The negotiating advantages to the Chinese of this artificially induced sense of urgency are obvious. It was made to appear, with no basis in the objective situation, that the United States was more eager for agreement than were the Chinese. As might be anticipated, there was a price to be paid for American impatience. The United States had concluded early that China would not be prepared to renounce officially its right to use force to reunify Taiwan with the mainland. Consequently, it was decided to settle on the device of an American statement of "interest in the peaceful resolution of the Taiwan issue," which would not be contradicted by a simultaneous Chinese statement. But on December 15, U.S. desires notwithstanding, the Chinese went ahead with a statement that did contradict the American position. The manner in which Taiwan would be brought "back to the embrace of the motherland," the People's Republic declared, "is entirely China's internal affair." It was a ringing slap in the face for Carter. To add insult to injury, in 1982 fresh negotiations on the problem of Taiwan produced a new agreement. In return for a remarkable U.S. commitment not to exceed past qualitative and quantitative levels of arms sales to Taiwan, China now pledged to seek a peaceful solution to unification. It had succeeded in selling the same horse twice.

All of the tendencies seen in these historical episodes, the Chinese ability to keep their nerve to the last minute, to push U.S. negotiators up against a deadline, to settle as late as possible, to "sell the same horse twice," and to exploit American impatience, are perennial features of the negotiating relationship.[34] Even as tough and experienced a negotiator as James Baker was disarmed by Chinese intransigence. In the November 1991 negotiations in Beijing, Baker was almost driven to distraction, although objectively an ostracized China was in the weaker position. Baker found his Chinese counterparts insistent in their demands, "a laundry list of concessions"— among them, the raising of sanctions, entry into the GATT trading system —and "utterly unyielding" in their willingness to meet U.S. needs on human rights, nuclear proliferation, and intellectual property. At one point, when Baker complained at Chinese intransigence, Premier Li Peng told him, "You should be happy that I am even seeing you." Baker wondered whether he should just walk out, but resisted the temptation. It was only on the third and final day, near the very end of a marathon meeting, that Foreign Minister Qian, "in the usual Chinese fashion," offered some miserly concessions. He had correctly judged Baker's imperative need (particularly in the light of President Bush's special interest in China) to return home with a document that could be presented as a "success." The rather threadbare understandings reached, however, on missile transfer, prison labor, intellectual property rights, human rights, and so on mostly unraveled in the final year of the Bush administration. Baker himself was under no illusion as to what had been achieved: "Eighteen hours of grueling negotiation over three days had finally yielded just enough to keep the trip from being characterized as a failure."[35] For China, the mere fact of the visit and the message of normality that had emerged from it—"business as usual"—could be rated real achievements.

Vulnerability to time pressure, impatience, and the need for political successes have also characterized U.S. negotiations with Mexico. Timothy Bennett felt that the American determination to solve problems led to a willingness to concede more than necessary in order to get a deal.[36] Gerry Bowers, who negotiated a 1992 memorandum of understanding with the Mexican government on behalf of a contractor for USAID, commented that he was always conscious that the meter was running in the talks.[37] Another State Department official admitted that Mexicans were better able to hold out for a more favorable bargain. In contrast to U.S. negotiators, Mexicans were "happy to go away without an agreement at a given session."

In high-profile negotiations, the tendency of U.S. negotiators to settle too early in the end game are compounded, David Newsom adds, by pressures from the media for public statements. "Once the press is aware that the formal meetings have ended, the demand for information is more than most politically sensitive officials can resist. One result is that statements are made about the outcome that may be premature and, in some cases, sufficiently offensive to the other side to derail the agreement."[38] In the very last phase of the NAFTA negotiations in 1992, White House aides spread the word that an agreement was on hand—and would be announced by President Bush the next day. This pulled the rug out from under the feet of U.S. trade representative Carla Hills, who was still negotiating, and was forced to make a number of substantive last minute concessions so as not to embarrass her president.[39]

In territorial disputes with Mexico the key to a solution has invariably been U.S. acceptance of the rival position, even when the American case was a reasonable one (which it arguably was not, in the Chamizal talks). Joseph Friedkin, with years of experience negotiating with Mexico, observed that the resolution of the Presidio-Ojinaga land dispute simply depended on the State Department giving in. It did try for a compromise at first, but the Mexicans remained adamant that the contested area—the result of bewildering and uncharted changes in the course of the Rio Grande—had to be transferred to them. Mexico, Friedkin continued, was always "very patient." In the Presidio-Ojinaga case they "felt that if it couldn't be solved to their satisfaction, they'd just leave it pending."[40]

In the 1979 gas talks, the United States, which was paying $2.29 per thousand cubic feet for new domestic gas, finally settled on a new price of $3.625 after weeks of weary haggling with Mexico. The final rounds of bidding went as follows. On August 9, the United States was offering $3.40; Mexico held out for $3.75. Both sides dug their heels in at this point. Then on August 29 and 30, Under Secretary of State Warren Christopher met with Foreign Minister Jorge Castaneda of Mexico. While the United States upped its offer to $3.50, Mexico stuck at $3.75. If Christopher had expected a reciprocal concession by Castaneda, he was disappointed. The Mexican proved able to hang in longer. The final agreed price of $3.625 predictably split the difference between the two latter bids.[41] According to Julius Katz, who had handled previous rounds of the negotiations, Christopher had indeed gone "over the edge," agreeing to an excessive price because of political considerations. In a haggle of this kind, Katz remarked, the United States is at an inevitable disadvantage. Because "you can't afford to fail," you say "Let's let them have it." Now it may be legitimate to trade a marginal monetary concession for a more highly valued political advantage. But it should be noted that in this case the political considerations impinged absolutely symmetrically on the two sides. Both President Carter and President López Portillo wanted an agreement in hand for their upcoming late September summit. Both welcomed the domestic benefits of a diplomatic success. Yet it was the American delegate who blinked first and proposed an unreciprocated concession on August 29.[42]

In the 1980–82 air service negotiations with Japan, the final outcome was the linear consequence of an error made at the outset. In its opening proposal the United States put forward a package that held nothing in reserve and put on the table almost everything on offer. Here was premature concession at its worst. Stubborn Japanese bargaining gained for Japan a major, unreciprocated concession in the final phase: the right to an all-cargo service to Chicago. The United States failed to achieve the objective that it had set its heart on—an additional landing point in Japan.[43] Obviously, one can never know if the Japanese delegation would ultimately have conceded the point in the face of reciprocal U.S. obduracy. But one thing is clear: having made major concessions at the beginning, the United States was left with insufficient bargaining chips at the end.

India's "geologic sense of time" and ready acceptance of delay were commented on by an experienced State Department official. He acknowledged
that the weakness of the American approach to negotiation lay in its domestically conditioned habit of working under self-imposed time constraints.
Officials jetting into Delhi from Washington for a few brisk days of talks
totally miscalculate the time required. Walter Bollinger, USAID's director
in India 1990–95, commented that Indians, with their 3,000-year perspective, are not worried if their procedures do not fit into the U.S. time frame.
Negotiating a program for the prevention of HIV-AIDS in Tamil Nadu,
he found himself laboring under a strong sense of urgency, and was deeply
frustrated by Indian bureaucratic politics and their serene assumption that
they had all the time in the world.[44]

In the 1995 U.S.-Indian aviation negotiations the U.S. penchant for
self-imposed deadlines had very clear consequences. The great subject of
contention in the talks, which went through three rounds, was the Air
India request for the so-called fifth freedom right to take on passengers in
London and fly them on to Chicago. India had been seeking the service,
linking two large ethnic Indian populations, for twenty years. This had
always been resisted by the United States, since the route was already ser-
viced by American, United, and British Airways. India was also interested
in landing rights at other U.S. cities. For its part, the United States wanted
expanded access to Indian cities and sought the right for United Airlines to
land at New Delhi on a new round-the-world service. On paper, then, the
equation seemed more or less symmetrical, except for one crucial U.S.
point of weakness that the Indian delegation was able to exploit to the full:
Before the conclusion of negotiations United Airlines *had already announced*
that its new flagship round-the-world service would be inaugurated on
December 15, 1995! This left the American delegation to the final round
of talks, held at the end of November in Delhi, without a leg to stand on.

At the instructions of the State Department, which was under strong
pressure from United Airlines and its political friends, U.S. negotiators
were obliged to settle for a last-minute deal, concluded on December 1,
highly advantageous to India. For the privilege of access to Madras, permission for Northwest to fly direct to India, but particularly United's landing rights in Delhi, a heavy price was paid: Air India gained access to *five*
new U.S. points and the gilt-edged right to operate *seven* weekly fifth-
freedom flights to Washington and Chicago! No wonder a spokesman for
American Airlines sourly commented: "We find it very frustrating . . . It is

one more example of our government giving vastly more authority to foreign carriers than U.S. airlines."[45]

Ambassador Eilts and others confirmed that Egyptians were equally tough negotiators for Americans to deal with. They would stick stubbornly to their positions and accept a compromise only with difficulty. Eilts's judgment is exemplified by Ellsworth Bunker's historic 1963 mission to mediate the cessation of Egyptian and Saudi intervention in the Yemeni civil war. Widely regarded as the greatest American negotiator of his generation, Ambassador Bunker faced a formidable opponent in President Nasser. The two men negotiated for three days after Bunker had already achieved a modification of the Saudi position. A key problem was the linkage of the suspension of Saudi aid to the royalists with the withdrawal of Egyptian forces. For three days Nasser did not yield an inch on this issue. Only at the close of their final meeting did the Egyptian president make a grudging concession in response to the American envoy's entreaties. "You know, Mr. President," Ambassador Bunker besought, "I have to be able to go back and say you actually withdrew some forces. Won't you give me just half a company? It isn't anything, half a company." Smiling somewhat, Nasser finally agreed.

Bunker had demonstrated rare judgment and patience, as subsequent events made clear. The fact is that half a company is not an independently viable military unit. One cannot withdraw half a company and leave it at that. The truth of the matter, as Bunker must have suspected, is that Nasser was prepared all along to withdraw at least a token force, knowing full well that without it there would be no agreement. He could not, however, give in too easily. When Bunker returned to Cairo from Jidda a week later, Nasser told him that he would like to withdraw two battalions within fifteen days of the commencement of disengagement and at least "one or two" companies simultaneous with the Saudi suspension of aid to the royalists. He had, in short, been holding out for reasons of tactics, not principle. A lesser negotiator than Ellsworth Bunker might have allowed himself to be discouraged.[46]

In the Bunker-Nasser encounter just described, the key to Bunker's success was a remarkable sensitivity to Nasser's psychological requirements. In a tour de force of creative negotiation, Bunker met each of the cultural requirements of high-context, face-salient interlocutors discussed in this chapter. He displayed infinite forbearance, being prepared to synchronize his negotiating pace with their more leisurely tempo. Like Kissinger years later, he patiently shuttled from Cairo to Jidda and back, allowing the task to dictate his timetable, and not the reverse. He also accommodated himself to the elliptical and implicit form of understanding preferred by Nasser. An oral assurance was all that was on offer. Most important was his shrewd willingness to allow Nasser to present his concession to Saudi Arabia as something of little importance, granted as a personal favor to the mediator. Had Bunker insisted on Nasser conceding two battalions and one or two companies up front, the agreement would have fallen through, for Nasser would have preferred proud intransigence to open compromise with his sworn enemies. By asking Nasser for half a company—"it isn't anything, half a company"—Bunker enabled the Egyptian leader to concede without loss of face. This was diplomacy of the highest order. In the following chapter we shall explore further the importance of face and form in concluding agreements with high-context cultures.

10

Face and Form

End Game II

OUTWARD APPEARANCES

In shame cultures like Egypt and the other interdependent, collectivistic societies discussed here, outward appearances are as important as substance. "Make your harvest look big," runs a popular Egyptian saying, "lest your enemies rejoice." Better to starve and have others think you are satisfied than to reveal a humiliating weakness. Low-context negotiators may find it difficult to understand this philosophy of life because it flies in the face of the Western concept of material rationality. Yet for their high-context negotiating partners, for an outcome to be acceptable, it must not only be good, it must also look good. Indeed, as we shall see, correct packaging may render palatable something otherwise unacceptable.

Legalistic U.S. negotiators do not display the obsession with face so characteristic of collectivistic cultures; better to get the fine print right. In a study of the role of face in negotiation, Stella Ting-Toomey and Mark Cole argue that negotiators from collectivistic backgrounds are concerned to honor face, whereas negotiators from individualistic cultures are adept at threatening face.[1] American diplomats are expected to behave honorably, that is, tell the truth; comport themselves with dignity; and negotiate within the framework of the law, the Constitution, and the accepted moral principles of the United States. Subject to those provisos, the achievement of compromise (that is, equitable distribution of payoffs between the parties) is thought to constitute an inherently honorable outcome; there is certainly nothing shameful in having facilitated an agreement by meeting one's opponent halfway. Because the successful conclusion of a negotiation is in itself highly desirable, loss of prestige (probably a better word in this context than face) would be felt to follow more from having "failed" to settle a problem than from some secondary flaw in the final accord. Hence the temptation to believe that any agreement is better than no agreement.

For the representatives of high-context cultures, the experience of international negotiation is fraught with considerations of face. The very structure of the situation, in which competing parties pit their wills and skills against each other, is uncongenial to societies that see social harmony, not confrontation, as the desired state of affairs. Beyond the matter being negotiated, there exists an entire psychological dimension in which pride of place is given to considerations of psychic, not material, gains and losses. "While the discussion of tangible issues such as territorial rights, boundaries, and tangible scarce resources represents the substantive level of verbal, or written diplomatic exchange," Ting-Toomey and Cole argue, "intangible issues such as national representation, status, pride, honor, power, dignity, and face often reflect the hidden dimension of the overt negotiation process."[2]

Precedence and status inevitably loom large, both in the mechanics of the talks ("the shape of the table") and in the outcome. To non-Western countries, any negotiation with the mighty United States is potentially redolent of challenges to national honor and perceived standing. When emotive topics like sovereignty, independence, and the defense of traditional values in the face of modernization are thought to be on the line, interlocutors of the United States may define success more in terms of resistance than agreement. To have withstood the United States may be perceived (or at least presented) as a prestigious outcome.

For Jesus Silva de Herzog, Mexican finance minister from 1982 to 1986 and ambassador to the United States since 1996, to negotiate with the United States is to take on an "empire." Inevitably, the preponderant fact was that "we begin in an unequal position. There is a powerful element and a weak one."[3] In these circumstances the thought of capitulation, the disgrace of being seen to have conceded cherished assets or bowed to American pressure, is a constant concern. Honor requires that any agreement be defensible in the eyes of the group. We are back to appearances and presentation.

A classic illustration of the salience of symbolism in the end game is provided by the U.S.-Japanese, Connally-Kashiwagi talks of December 1971, held against the background of serious U.S. balance-of-payments problems. After months of preliminary negotiations on exchange rates, the moment of truth arrived in Washington. For Finance Minister Mizuta of Japan, the prospect of being pressured into concessions was too much. He canceled a meeting with his American counterpart because of an "upset stomach" (later admitted to be fictitious). At the crucial encounter he was replaced by his deputy, Kashiwagi. Treasury Secretary Connally informed Kashiwagi that the United States insisted on a 17 percent upward revaluation of the yen and gave him until 10 A.M. the next day to reply.

Apparently unmoved by the ultimatum, Kashiwagi rejected the demand. Seventeen percent was unacceptable, he explained, because a Japanese finance minister had been forced to commit suicide in the 1930s after agreeing to a 17 percent revaluation. (Actually, the historical record was even bleaker: Finance Minister Junnosuke Inouye was assassinated in February 1932.) So it was the number that was taboo rather than the principle. Without more ado Connally suggested a revaluation of 16.9 percent, and Kashiwagi agreed. By proposing a substantively insignificant but symbolically crucial concession, the U.S. Treasury secretary had saved the honor of his counterpart.[4]

For China, as for Japan, considerations of face have long been decisive.[5] U.S.-Chinese relations amply demonstrate this point. Fortunately, American negotiators have been rather successful in addressing the issue. In the 1971–72 negotiations, face impinged on the diplomatic exchanges at various levels. First and most obvious, it was inherent in the very concept of an American presidential visit to Beijing, which, as many have pointed out, was uncannily reminiscent of past "pilgrimages" by "barbarians" to the Middle Kingdom. A Chinese leader did not visit the United States until 1979, following the formal normalization of diplomatic relations. The drafting of the announcement of the Nixon trip in July 1971 fully reflected Chinese requirements in this respect. The Chinese draft communiqué first submitted to Kissinger baldly implied that President Nixon was coming as a supplicant—that he had solicited an invitation. Put in this unembroidered way the text was unacceptable to the United States. But with only a slight alteration the communiqué that was finally agreed to carried very much the same implication. It read (Kissinger writes): "Knowing of President Nixon's expressed desire to visit the People's Republic of China, Premier Chou En-lai . . . has extended an invitation to President Nixon to visit China . . ." This wording left no doubt that the initial interest had come from the American, not the Chinese, side. The point is that from an American perspective (and within reason) the fact of the visit was perceived to be overwhelmingly more significant than the text of the invitation. Not so to the Chinese.

Chinese preoccupation with face was also reflected in the unique form of the crucial document that emerged from the Nixon visit, namely, the Shanghai communiqué. The initial American proposal, in Kissinger's words, "followed the conventional style, highlighting fuzzy areas of agreement and obscuring differences with platitudinous generalizations." This style, it transpired, was utterly unacceptable to the Chinese. If profound ideological differences were so easily papered over, what had been the purpose of China's years of struggle? At the express instructions of Mao, Zhou Enlai rejected the draft. "The communiqué had to set forth fundamental differences; otherwise the wording would have an 'untruthful appearance.'" Zhou's counterdraft set forth the Chinese position on the various issues in "extremely uncompromising terms," leaving room for the United States to insert its own contrary positions. This approach was utterly unconventional, but not only was it more truthful, it also ensured that neither side was seen to have sold out its principles for the sake of the rapprochement. The Shanghai communiqué, in fact, was a unique face-saving and also face-giving device. In substantive terms neither side made any concession to the other.[6]

Face, then, is very much about *facades*. The Shanghai communiqué was an elaborate artifice intended to free the parties to enter into a productive relationship. Above all, it ensured that neither side would be perceived to have lost, for such a perception would have been fatal for the continuation of the process. Sometimes honor is satisfied by a propitiatory formula, an original solution that effectively transcends the issue under contention or an ingenious device that either obscures reality or transforms it. All of these devices were resorted to at various times in the negotiations studied.

In the Tarapur negotiation with India of the early 1980s, one of the most contentious issues was the handling of nuclear waste. The United States insisted on intrusive safeguards to prevent a diversion of the material, while India rejected them as a violation of sovereignty. Nuclear waste, India argued, should either be returned to the United States or, if the latter did not want it, be left to India to do with as it saw fit. Finally, both sides agreed on a third option involving adoption of the French process of caramelization, whereby waste products are injected into liquid glass, which can then be safely stored. Thus here an ingenious "technical fix," not completely satisfactory to either side, but going some way to meet the requirements of each, provided the way out of the conundrum.[7]

In the sensitive 1986–87 talks for the sale of a U.S. supercomputer to India, the same safeguards-sovereignty dilemma arose. Here the United States government needed safeguards against undesirable end use (for instance, application to nuclear weapons development) or the transfer of secret computer technology to the Soviet Union. The Indian government, as always, resisted the imposition of an intrusive supervisory regime; it had to be able to go before the Indian Parliament and credibly prove that sovereignty had not been compromised, that India was not falling under the control of a foreign power. In the end, the Indians proved very pragmatic in evolving language that went some way toward meeting U.S. concerns. In a classified memorandum—the form of the agreement was essential to its acceptability—the Indian government agreed not to network (meaning that users had to go in person to the computer) and accepted more intrusive monitoring than they had ever consented to before. Thus a compromise was reached away from the spotlights.[8]

As a mediator in the Arab-Israeli peace process the United States has displayed exceptional sensitivity and deftness in devising formulas to meet the powerful need of Arab governments to protect their honor, both in the eyes of their own people and in the wider Arab community. Former secretary of state George Shultz uses the apt term "Middle East solution" to describe an arrangement whose most sensitive and controversial provisions are left "understood," because if made explicit they would be repudiated by the parties. "The Arabs," he acknowledges, "were able to proceed this way; it did not come naturally to Americans or Israelis, but it is a wise strategy in moments of possible progress in the Middle East."[9]

In the November 1973 negotiations for a binding cease-fire agreement after the Yom Kippur War, it was vital to conceal the perilous state of the Egyptian Third Army and the fact that its very survival depended on Israeli forbearance. The presence of Israeli troops on the main road to Cairo did not at all conform with the triumphant picture that Sadat was attempting to project to the world. Accordingly, in return for certain concessions to Israel, a corridor would be opened up along the Cairo-Suez road to supply the encircled Egyptian forces. Although the route passed through Israeli-controlled territory, this fact would be disguised by placing the checkpoints under United Nations control.

In order to save Egyptian face, it was vital to obscure the precise details of this and other arrangements. As Kissinger understood, "too many public concessions would hurt [Sadat's] position with his Arab brethren." Acknowledgment of Israeli control of the Cairo-Suez road would have been deeply embarrassing, and a detailed schedule for the resupply of the army "would have brought home its plight to every Arab." If the cease-fire humiliated Egypt, what chance would there be of progress toward a political settlement?[10] The cease-fire agreement devised by the United States ensured that Egypt's reputation was *mastourah* (covered up against public censure).

To meet Mexico's psychological requirements has often required considerable technical ingenuity and material expense on the American part. In 1973 Mexico's principled insistence on water of quality equal to that enjoyed by U.S. farmers was sidestepped by American agreement to create fresh water through desalination. Similarly, one of the key elements in the Chamizal settlement was the relocation of the course of the Rio Grande, at a cost of $43.6 million. In the final stage of the 1963 negotiation, President López Mateos of Mexico held out for more acreage than seemed feasible, given the lie of the land. He wished to be able to claim before his people, and history, that he had given away not even one square inch of territory. The solution of Boundary Commissioner Joseph Friedkin of the United States (who combined the talents of both diplomat and engineer) was a technical one. A new, deeper channel would be dug north of the Rio Grande's present course and set in concrete. This channel would not only solve the problem of flood control, it would also provide President López Mateos with the extra land that he needed to gild his achievement.[11]

The symbols of success are so important that in the 1982 debt talks the Mexican team actually preferred a materially inferior agreement to one that bore the misleading appearance of a greater concession on its part. The short-term solution suggested by the U.S. Treasury to Mexico's liquidity crisis was a $2 billion loan. Mexican oil, to be sold to the U.S. strategic reserve under a fixed-term, renewable contract, would be the collateral for half that sum. The quid pro quo from the American point of view would be the concessionary price paid for the oil. Instead of the world price of $32 per barrel, the United States proposed to pay only $28. Finance Minister Silva de Herzog of Mexico was dismayed by this proposal. The United States could not be permitted, Silva de Herzog argued, to appear to buy oil that still lay beneath Mexican soil. Doing so would entail the loss of the nation's patrimony. Moreover, a contract granting major price concessions to Washington was politically impossible. Despite the grave financial crisis, the president of Mexico could not give the impression of capitulating to his mighty neighbor.

The Mexican counterproposal was for a loan with interest charged but no mention of the price of the oil. When the American experts came back with an arrangement that would entail an effective interest rate of 35 percent, the Mexicans were outraged. The device finally hit upon by the Department of the Treasury to cover Mexican concerns was an interest rate that would not look usurious but would be topped up by a front-end fee, or bank service charge. In principle, this was much more attractive to the Mexicans. After some haggling, a figure of $50 million was agreed upon. Under this arrangement Mexico would, in fact, be paid $27.40 for its oil, less than the $28 first proposed! As Adhip Chaudhuri notes, "With all their threats and break-offs the Mexicans had actually ended up with a worse deal."[12] The point is, of course, that the front-end fee concealed from observers back home the real price concession that had been made.

For a Mexican negotiator any public whiff of surrender would torpedo an agreement. Herbert Brownell, former attorney general and special negotiator with Mexico, stresses that Mexicans could never "appear to be giving in to the United States." Brownell's counterpart in the 1972–73 Colorado salinity talks was concerned about this point. It could even be "somewhat useful to have a fight with the United States," Brownell wryly observes. Mexicans are so convinced of their past exploitation and so preoccupied by the asymmetry of the two sides that any agreement with Washington automatically comes under suspicion. Indeed, if an agreement can be presented as an American defeat, all Mexican psychological requirements are covered. "We got an agreement," a high-ranking Mexican official trumpeted at the end of the 1979 gas talks, "because the United States suddenly agreed to our final offers. It was as simple as that. We are very pleased."[13]

Whether the official's boast reflected genuine satisfaction at having gained the upper hand over U.S. negotiator Warren Christopher, or wishful thinking, is an important question but hard to answer. It may be argued that, because face equals facade, cosmetic or symbolic adjustments rather than genuine concessions are sufficient to requite the honor of one's rival; it was so with the classic 16.9 percent solution of the yen revaluation conundrum, and in the debt crisis a rather flimsy disguise satisfied Mexican pride. In the following section we shall consider how the form taken by the final agreement may reflect culturally conditioned needs and also serve face-saving purposes.

FORMS OF AGREEMENT

International understandings come in an assortment of shapes and sizes, ranging from written contracts of various degrees of specificity, publicity, and formality, via unilateral letters of intent, oral "gentleman's agreements," and more informal promises, to one-sided, but not contradicted, statements of "hopes and expectations." United States practice also distinguishes between a *treaty*, which requires ratification by the Senate, and an *executive agreement*, which requires only congressional review. The title of the contract —whether treaty, pact, convention, agreement, or so on—makes no difference to its binding character in international law. Informal, unwritten promises and understandings are accepted as an unavoidable expedient in the ongoing conduct of diplomacy, but are considered an undesirable form for expressing the outcome of a negotiation. Other sorts of accord such as communiqués and unilateral declarations are thought to be morally and politically binding, if not necessarily enforceable in a court of law. Only the "non-paper," or *bout de papier*, a document without attribution or signature, and conveyed to the other party to clarify a point during the course of negotiations, lacks binding force. In all other cases, *pacta sunt servanda:* agreements are to be honored.[14]

For face-saving purposes, informal, unwritten arrangements may be preferred by high-context negotiators. A formal treaty has a certain symbolic resonance as well as binding legal status. It is a solemn document signed at an appropriate ceremony, and it can be published for all to see. In short, it is an eminently public and tangible instrument. An informal arrangement lacks these weighty, irrevocable qualities of publicity. When an agreement is felt in some way to be discreditable or embarrassing, or to require unpleasant concessions, the unwritten understanding permits concealment, or at least minimization, of the accord. For those preoccupied by appearances there must be something psychologically reassuring about an agreement that has not been frozen in visible permanence, like a fly in amber.

American instincts and legal requirements, in contrast, militate against precisely those features of informal arrangements favored by high-context cultures. In the low-context U.S. tradition, obligations should be spelled out and (unintended) ambiguities resolved. Moreover, the Congress, a key player in the supervision of foreign policy, requires nothing less than strict precision in the international obligations of the United States.[15] International agreements should leave as little room for future misapprehension as possible; all the i's should be dotted and the t's crossed. Understandings based on the personal interpretation of the immediate negotiators are particularly suspect. Appeals to the wider relationship, which high-context individuals rate above any written document, are thought to be beside the point. All important transactions in the individualistic culture are based on contracts that explicitly set out the rights and duties of the parties and are backed up by the force of law, not by ties of sentiment. The tighter and more specific the accord, the less the likelihood, it is felt, of future misunderstandings. There should be no doubt what the signatories have actually committed themselves to. A good contract will try to cover all conceivable contingencies. As international business has expanded executives and officials, worldwide, have become accustomed to the need for contracts rather than handshakes, as was once the case. Even so, the high-context inclination is for simplicity. Mexican negotiators, who have had more experience than most with U.S. practices, were still initially taken aback in the NAFTA talks by the tendency to "micro writing" displayed by the American team.[16]

Given political realities, and for want of an alternative, American negotiators may occasionally reluctantly consent to less than watertight arrangements. Regretfully, the historical record demonstrates no simple link between clarity and specificity, and compliance. Ambiguous understandings may indeed be a source of endless trouble—or the only way out of diplomatic deadlock. Since in many instances they are the solution of choice for high-context negotiators, they are not to be rejected out of hand simply on doctrinaire grounds.

Military cooperation is an area of particular sensitivity, raising potent issues of sovereignty, independence, and alignment. When a formal defensive pact with the United States, with all it entails, is politically impossible, an informal arrangement may satisfy all the parties. In 1952, U.S.-Mexican negotiations for a military pact immediately broke down because Mexico was not prepared to undertake a formal obligation to commit its forces in hemispheric defense, let alone enter into a binding military alliance with the United States. Behind the scenes, however, Mexico was ready to be more helpful, and the United States discovered that it could gain in secret what it could not obtain publicly.[17]

This lesson has been repeated time and again. In June 1980 the Mexican oil well Ixtoc 1 blew out of control, spilling thirty thousand barrels of oil a day into the Gulf of Mexico. Robert Krueger, the U.S. coordinator of Mexican affairs, announced demands for compensation for the pollution of Texas beaches. Mexico immediately published a categorical and irritable rejection. Krueger's heavy-handed tactics injured Mexican pride rather than encouraging compliance. But what Mexico could never agree to in public was acceptable if done discreetly. Out of the limelight, a cleanup operation did get under way, coordinated by U.S. and Mexican officials. The Mexicans agreed to U.S. Coast Guard ships entering Mexican waters to help with the operation on a low-key basis. This agreement would never have been possible had it gotten into the press. Mexico even offered to send teams to help clean up Texas beaches, although the United States declined this offer.[18]

The terms of U.S.-Mexican agreements typically tread a fine line between the up-front specificity demanded by a vigilant U.S. Congress overseeing the expenditure of taxpayers' dollars, and the aversion to publicity of a Mexican government always conscious of the vigilance to a sellout of Mexican public opinion. In the February 1995 rescue of the peso, draconian conditions were imposed on the Mexican economy, including painful structural reforms, short-term interest rates of almost 50 percent, and the use of oil revenues as collateral for $20 billion of loans and loan guarantees. Wisely, the U.S. Treasury resisted calls to link the financial agreement to explicit political conditions, such as tighter Mexican control of illegal border crossing and drug smuggling. "Since we are engaged in both a financial transaction and an act of diplomacy, these businesslike agreements are also written with great respect for the traditions and future prospects of both nations," declared Deputy Treasury Secretary Frank N. Newman at the signing ceremony. Nevertheless, Mexico *separately and privately* pledged to strengthen border controls.[19] It is not known what else was promised (in itself a significant point), but improvements were soon seen to follow in a number of problem areas of U.S.-Mexican relations, such as extradition and narcotics.

What Mexico could offer of its own free will, as a gesture of good neighborliness, or in the form of a "gentleman's agreement" could not be obtained by an explicit arrangement. An agreement implies obligation, conditionality, a curtailment of sovereignty; a unilateral act is an expression of free will. In the Israel-Egypt disengagement talks brokered by the United States after the 1973 Arab-Israeli war, Sadat made this point to Kissinger. "He could not accept a formal obligation to clear and reopen the Suez Canal. But he could tell me that if he could do so as his own decision —if Israel would only stop demanding it—he would begin clearance operations as soon as both armies had reached the lines foreseen in the disengagement agreement."[20]

Much discreet U.S.-Egyptian cooperation in various security spheres has been made possible because it rested on informal arrangements. Landing rights for AWACS (Airborne Warning and Control System) planes, overflight rights in Egyptian air space, the joint "Bright Star" series of military exercises, and the use of Egyptian facilities in the 1981 Iran rescue mission were of this nature.[21]

The United States has sometimes run into trouble when pressing for more formal agreements; we have already seen an example in the ill-fated Ras Banas negotiations. Sadat's initial preference was for a rather general, indeed informal, understanding. The more detailed and formal the accord, the less likely it was to be acceptable. Only a low-profile, gentleman's agreement could evade Egyptian national sensibilities. The inescapable difficulty this posed for the United States was nicely put by Congressman Joseph Addabbo (D-N.Y.) following a visit of the House Subcommittee on Military Construction Appropriations to Egypt in 1981:

> If we are going to completely rebuild [Ras Banas]—we are talking about a billion dollars . . . In my meeting with President Sadat, he said no American flag, no agreement. Now, the American people, in our defense budget, with tax dollars, have gone to many bases. We have built bases in Libya, Vietnam, and Thailand. What guarantee do we have after we put in this untold millions of dollars . . . that they won't say, "thank you for building it. We will see you in 100 years and we will take over the bases."[22]

Strictly speaking, Addabbo's argument did not unambiguously strengthen the case for a formal guarantee. After all, the United States had been thrown off the Wheelus air force base in Libya despite the existence of an international agreement. Contracts, as *awase* negotiators know full well, cannot hold together an embittered relationship. Nor was it clear why Egypt would want to risk its partnership with the United States for a military camp it did not need at a godforsaken place like Ras Banas. But Addabbo was speaking as a representative and guardian of U.S. institutional and legal culture, and from this perspective it would have been inconceivable for the Congress to appropriate monies for the Ras Banas facility without some paper contract. For Sadat to imagine otherwise was unrealistic. Some things are nonnegotiable. Having said this, reports have appeared in the press of confidential arrangements allowing discreet U.S. access to Egyptian military facilities.[23]

On occasion, the United States has gone beyond the bounds of proper form and strayed into the undergrowth of excessive formalism. It was surely so with the Defense Department's insistence on a privileges and immunities agreement to cover its naval and military medical research unit. Given that the unit had been permitted to work in safety even after the severance of U.S.-Egyptian diplomatic relations in June 1967, it is hard to understand what added benefit staff could derive from this new document. Here was an unworthy imputation on Egyptian hospitality.

In the light of the culturally grounded expectations and needs of the two sides, some negotiations appear foredoomed to failure. Ras Banas is one example. Another is the 1962–63 U.S.-Indian talks on air defense. The idea of a "tacit air defense pact" was first raised by the Indian government in December 1962 just after the Chinese withdrawal from Indian territory. India would provide the airfields and ground support, and the United States would send in planes to defend Indian cities in the event of an emergency, that is, a renewal of hostilities with China. Ambassador Galbraith seized on the proposal with enthusiasm, seeing it as a "great opportunity to bring India into much closer working association with the Western community." At the very outset, therefore, negotiations were dogged by an irreconcilable inconsistency: India wished for a "tacit" arrangement, Galbraith for "a virtual alliance." Almost at once the project began to unravel. The moment American views of the scheme became known to the Indians, they recoiled in predictable horror. Members of Parliament and the opposition press warned that the policy of nonalignment was threatened. Under fire, Nehru denied the idea altogether.[24]

Sino-American relations have been dogged by both substantive and procedural problems. The United States has found it difficult, even when the basis of an understanding has existed, to find a form of agreement acceptable to the Chinese. Differing fundamentally on the Taiwan issue, yet wishing to cooperate pragmatically in other areas, the two countries have been obliged to resort to instruments of a lesser force than the solemn, binding international treaty. Examples are the 1972 Shanghai communiqué, the parallel statements normalizing relations of 1978, and the 1985 Nuclear Cooperation Agreement. In effect, the United States has accommodated itself to Chinese practice. As Stanley Lubman points out, in the Chinese tradition a contract represents the beginning of a relationship and not its consummation. It defines the desired outcome of a transaction rather than the rights and obligations of the parties toward each other. The Chinese do not expect all contingencies to be anticipated and are particularly loath to consider the possibility of a breakdown in the partnership. Whereas Americans demand specificity, the Chinese are content with rather general language. They also view American contracts as overcomplex and prefer a simplicity that Americans find unsatisfactory.[25]

One example of a very vague agreement, "rammed down Chinese throats" largely to accommodate congressional concerns, was the 1992 Chinese prison labor memorandum of understanding.[26] The agreement, in which China had no interest of its own, was intended to facilitate the implementation of U.S. laws banning the importation of prison-made products. Its terms were terse and vague, and inherently flawed in two basic respects. One was that the parties did not concur on what constituted "prison labor." The other was that the memorandum referred to the investigation and exchange of information on the violation and enforcement of "relevant laws and regulations of *either the United States or China*," implying that China was supposed to be aware of and adhere to domestic American rules. Accordingly, one of the four clauses, calling for officials to "meet *under mutually convenient circumstances* to exchange information" on the enforcement of and compliance with these rules, was so equivocal as to be capable of implementation only in the sort of atmosphere of cooperation and cordiality that had long since departed from the relationship.[27] Within a short time the memorandum had become a dead letter, a source of mutual irritation.

Japanese domestic custom is to rely on unwritten agreements. Legal documents are the exception to the rule. "Just a lot of words" is how Masao Kunihiro sums up his compatriots' attitude to contracts.[28] A simple lexical comparison demonstrates the point. The English term "contract," the official document containing the authoritative and legally binding text of the mutual obligations agreed upon by the signatories, is usually translated into Japanese by the word *keiyaku*. "Yet *keiyaku* has a narrower meaning than the word contract as it is used in the United States as a legal term. While contract is used in the United States to mean a legally enforceable promise or a set of promises with accompanying duties and rights, *keiyaku* implies just part of the process of negotiation, namely, the promissory stage, in which two parties agree to work together to create a mutually advantageous relationship. The implications of a transaction created by a *keiyaku* are unclear to Americans because much of the negotiation and most of the details of the transaction are intended to be filled in later."[29]

Disagreement over the meaning and obligatory character of agreements has been the blight of U.S.-Japanese relations. The irresistible force of the U.S. drive to open Japanese markets has collided with the immovable object of Japanese attachment to the status quo to produce understandings of exquisite ambiguity and dubious enforceability. Under political pressure to come up with something to show for their efforts U.S. negotiators, against their better judgment, have had to settle for the fuzzy forms of words, beloved of the Japanese, that preserve appearances, avoid a direct clash, and give a transitory appearance of success.[30]

A typical agreement of this kind was the July 1993 so-called Framework Agreement intended to launch negotiations in various fields linked by the common theme of reducing the imbalance of trade between the U.S. and Japan. The document agreed upon was really an agenda rather than a blueprint and contained such high-sounding but vague Japanese undertakings as "to achieve over the medium term a highly significant decrease in its current account surplus," and to "aim at significantly expanding Japanese government procurement of competitive foreign goods and services."[31] The understanding was immediately subject to contradictory interpretations. For his part, U.S. Treasury under secretary Lawrence Summers claimed that a "highly significant" reduction in the Japanese trade surplus meant "a number that's a little above 3% of gross national product and you do it over a few years and you're certainly below 2%." In contrast, Japanese vice minister for International Affairs of the Ministry of International Trade and Industry Sozaburo Okamatsu insisted that there was no specific understanding of what "highly significant" meant. "The U.S. team may have a number, 2%, but there is no agreement on a number," he told reporters. Holding up the text he pointed out: "A number isn't written on the paper."[32] Other Japanese officials openly dismissed the significance of the accord. "It doesn't have clear meaning," the vice minister of the Finance Ministry noted.[33] What it did was to provide President Clinton with a political success on his first visit to Tokyo, while postponing argument until later.

One of those arguments was over opening up the tightly restricted Japanese insurance market, the second largest in the world. In October 1994, as one of a series of pacts negotiated with the U.S. under the terms of the 1993 Framework Agreement, the Japanese government consented to implement a deregulation plan to expand sales opportunities for foreign companies. However, the understanding was that a so-called third sector of the market involving nontraditional products (such as personal accident, cancer, and sickness insurance), where foreign insurance companies had carved out something of a niche for themselves, would be opened up only *after* the traditional first and second sectors of the market had been liberalized. In the event Japan did precisely the opposite, targeting the foreign niche for initial deregulation, while protecting the major Japanese insurance companies in the primary sectors. What had gone wrong? According to former U.S. trade representative Clyde Prestowitz, the insurance pact "turned out to be a classic U.S.-Japan agreement. It was mostly oral. The written agreement was vague. Each side had a different view of what was agreed to." As a result, Japanese Ministry of Finance officials had orally briefed their own insurance industry executives with "a view of the deal that is completely at odds with the U.S. view. Thus, for the past several months the U.S. and Japanese negotiators have been locked in an argument over the meaning of the deal they signed 19 months ago."[34]

Disagreement over interpretation, rooted in ambiguity and tactical sparring, is not to be confused with deliberate violation. On the whole, Mike Smith noted, the Japanese did keep their agreements and, if you had the confidence of Japanese negotiators, they also honored their verbal undertakings.[35] Would that all the high-context negotiating partners of the United States maintained the same high standards of treaty observance. For the last great conundrum the cross-cultural negotiator has to face is in some ways the most perplexing: When is a deal a deal?

11

When Is a Deal a Deal?

Blurred boundaries

Relief that negotiations are at an end and that the agreement is signed and sealed may be quickly replaced by frustration. Instead of the automatic compliance that had been taken for granted an unpleasant realization dawns: one's high-context partners are not, or so it seems, keeping their side of the bargain.

The expectation that agreements are to be kept is the foundation-stone of Western diplomacy. *Good faith* negotiation, indeed, assumes that the entire object of the exercise is to reach an agreement that, by virtue of the voluntary commitment of the signatories, is then put into effect. Negotiation is viewed as a discrete, finite process that terminates with the conclusion of an accord. At this point the negotiators go home, having successfully completed the task in hand. The contract that has been agreed upon is satisfying, visible proof that a line has been drawn under the talks. Diplomats and their principals have achieved—more or less—what they set out to do and are now deserving of congratulation for a job well done. Appropriate professional and political credit is then bestowed.

After negotiation of the contract the parties are thought to have crossed over an invisible but highly significant boundary. The subsequent implementation stage constitutes a quite separate category of activity governed by the hallowed principle that contracts are to be honored. Without the well-founded belief that any agreement reached will be implemented, negotiation would seem to lose all point. Once the transaction is concluded, the fluid uncertainty of give-and-take, offer and counteroffer, argument and counterargument, is replaced by the structured certainty of a mutually acceptable text. If negotiation is considered to be a process of joint decisionmaking, as it often is in the American literature,[1] by definition, negotiation is decisive; its outcome is action. Arild Underdal rightly comments that for the decisionmaker (meaning *Western* decisionmaker!) "signing a contract implies committing oneself to a particular course of action (or abstaining from certain actions) . . . The official purpose of negotiation is to establish mutual commitments."[2]

According to the powerful and pervasive "either-or" Western conception of negotiation, a successful negotiation necessarily entails convergence on an agreement followed by implementation. If there is no agreement the parties either break off the talks or carry on talking. To have an agreement and continue negotiating—as though you did not have an agreement—would fly in the face of culturally grounded common sense about the boundaries between different categories. How disorienting, culturally shocking, to discover that other, non-Western societies may sometimes blur the boundary between negotiating and postnegotiating phases. In place of a clear-cut distinction they see nothing improper in a continuous process of interaction that never really ends. From this perspective a single accord is no big deal, certainly not a conclusion, but simply a benchmark. At every step of what Westerners assume to be the postnegotiation, "implementation phase" further talks are considered acceptable, because nothing is ever definitively closed.

(In the American system of government international treaties require the consent of the Senate [strictly speaking, according to the Constitution, treaties are to be ratified by the president following the approval of two-thirds of the Senate]. As a consequence, examples can be found of international agreements that have been reopened by the United States at the insistence of the Senate or that have been repudiated entirely. In 1978 U.S. diplomats were required to renegotiate certain unacceptable provisions of the Panama Canal treaties. Notoriously, in 1919 the Treaty of Versailles and the Covenant of the League of Nations were defeated in the Senate and never ratified. I would insist, however, that nonratification is very different from flawed implementation. Whereas the former is an unintended and exceptional consequence of the separation of powers, the latter is a recurrent, structural feature of high-context negotiating.)

There are various explanations for the phenomenon of unsatisfactory compliance: High-context legal traditions, grounded in the legally privileged status of the ruler, ascribed roles, and the priority of the collectivity, lack the low-context conception of contract as the crucial instrument binding together a society of free individuals. For high-context societies, an agreement is seen as a provisional step on a never-ending journey, yet another move in an open-ended relationship. High-context parties do not necessarily enter into a contract with a malicious intention to infringe it; rather, they lack the low-context conception of the centrality of contracts, or the connected assumption that a good agreement should guide future relations by covering every conceivable contingency. Viewing agreement as the beginning, not the end of an arrangement, it is simply assumed that, if the relationship is healthy, the contracting parties will be able to work out future differences in a cooperative, rather than litigious, spirit of *goodwill*. What use a watertight legal document should the partners lose confidence in each other or their interests diverge? This is very far from negotiating in bad faith, rather an expectation that talks will naturally continue throughout the course of a relationship.

There may also be a second factor blurring the sharp negotiation/implementation distinction: the phenomenon in high-context societies of *social desirability*, the tendency to subordinate accuracy to approval, to act to please others. In comparing low- and high-context cultures I have already mentioned the high-context dislike of unnecessary abrasion, the preference for forms of words that avoid offending or disappointing one's interlocutor. This tendency may sometimes result in promises being given that cannot be kept and arrangements being agreed to in the full knowledge that they are unlikely to be implemented. To someone brought up to the truth ethic and the sanctity of contracts, this behavior will be seen as frustrating and duplicitous, an infringement of the rules. But to the high-context negotiator it may be acceptable on various grounds. One motive may be to shake off, without unnecessary unpleasantness, an excessively persistent Western interlocutor who does not know when to take no for an answer and will not otherwise go away. Agreement is the line of least resistance. Another motive may be the wish to save the interlocutor's face. Pseudo-agreement (provided both sides are aware of the charade) may lead nowhere, but it preserves appearances and can be presented as a success. If low-context interlocutors obtusely take seriously a contrived facade of accord, that is their problem. Finally, agreement may be reached in a Micawber-like hope that "things will turn out all right in the end." Why, it is wondered, generate a crisis over some eventuality that may never arise and, if it does, can be worked out when the time comes by people of goodwill?

To sum up this section we may conclude that whereas low-context negotiators emphasize negotiating in good faith and religiously fulfilling the terms of contracts, high-context negotiators place the onus on maintaining the ongoing relationship—that subsumes any individual negotiation—on the basis of sincerity and goodwill.

China: Endless negotiation

The confusing effect of blurred cross-cultural boundaries between negotiation and implementation has been felt with greatest force in U.S.-Chinese relations. Again and again supposed agreements have come apart at the implementation stage, resulting in considerable ill-will on the American side. These include the 1992 memorandum of understanding on the use of prison labor, which became moribund after one visit in the spring of 1993 following which further access was denied; and the series of never quite consummated talks and understandings on the intellectual property question. Issues believed by the United States to be finally disposed of have repeatedly reappeared on the negotiating agenda in a seemingly endless succession of bargaining sequels.

The point was well made by former Commerce Department official Franklin Lavin, who noted ruefully that "the real negotiations with China often begin once the agreement is signed. For one thing, it is unclear to what extent China honestly desires to abide by its trade agreements. Beijing often considers itself to have entered into them under duress. After an agreement is reached, the Chinese attitude is never 'Thankfully that issue is resolved, and now we can both expand trade,' as it might be in other countries. Instead the response is more, 'The Americans have given us an impossible mess in this silly agreement, but at least they have left the country.'"[3] Chinese attitudes and conduct were described to me in very similar terms by other experienced U.S. negotiators. Mike Smith mused that Chinese negotiators promised to do the right things, but were not really convinced that they would have to deliver in the end. With immense civilizational arrogance they believed that the United States would soon pass from the scene.[4] A former ambassador to Beijing argued that it was easier for the Chinese to deal with American truculence than to change themselves. In the protracted intellectual property talks the Chinese would simply go through with a token shutdown of factories producing pirated products and put on a public show for the cameras of crushing illicit compact disks under the treads of bulldozers, without any real intention of compliance with agreements reached. It was a way of "kicking the problem down the road," hoping it would go away.

The major strategic question of nuclear proliferation, continuing over a decade, exemplifies all these tendencies. From the outset, ambiguous forms of words and irregular procedures, of the kind referred to in the previous chapter, have been resorted to in order to project the appearance of agreement even when a basic meeting of minds has been lacking. American eagerness for a successful conclusion to negotiations has often overridden a countervailing cautiousness and preference for greater specificity and conformity to accepted legal instruments. With hindsight, the unhappiness of congressional and other critics with ambiguous, less than watertight accords has proved itself to be largely justified.

In the 1985 Nuclear Cooperation Agreement the United States went further than in any other comparable accord to meet Chinese reluctance to pin itself down with conventional treaty commitments.[5] Permitting the sale and transfer of nuclear materials and equipment from the United States to the People's Republic, the agreement was concluded only after far-reaching American concessions were made over "consent rights" and "safeguards." In the past, the United States had required certain explicit commitments from its nuclear partners to ensure against the diversion of nuclear materials for the purpose of weapons production. Specifically, the cosignatory had to agree to request American consent before reprocessing spent U.S.-supplied fuel and also had to accept supervision of its reactors by the International Atomic Energy Agency (IAEA). Adherence to the Nuclear Nonproliferation Treaty was also expected and was particularly pertinent in this case, given China's historical assistance to Pakistan's nuclear weapons program.

China, however, was unwilling to make any formal commitments, although it had joined the IAEA, for two stated reasons: First, it argued that it was already a nuclear weapon state and was therefore not obliged under the terms of IAEA membership to accept supervision of materials provided by another nuclear weapon state. To do so would be to concede to the United States control over the future course of its nuclear weapons development. Second, it claimed that the Nuclear Nonproliferation Treaty was a discriminatory accord by which the great powers seek to maintain their own nuclear weapons monopoly. In the light of subsequent events it seems that there were two further motives: that China was reluctant to tie its hands irrevocably with a full-blown treaty and that in the final analysis it considered Pakistani development of nuclear weapons to be in its national interest as a useful threat against India.

To meet Chinese objections the United States abandoned many of its usual requirements. In place of "consent rights" Washington agreed to an elliptical and ambiguous provision in the treaty. Should China wish to reprocess fuel for peaceful purposes in the future, the parties would consult "immediately" with a view to reaching agreement. For its part, the United States would consider a Chinese request "favorably" and would avoid "hampering" the latter's nuclear program or refrain from inhibiting the "exploitation of nuclear energy for peaceful purposes." The balancing Chinese assurance was contained in a vague clause in which both parties agreed "to refrain from actions which either party believes would . . . adversely affect cooperation under this agreement." In the oversanguine American view, this assurance provided the United States with the equivalent of "consent rights," because China was supposedly well aware that illegitimate diversion of fuel would most certainly "affect cooperation under this agreement."

On the safeguards issue, the signatories agreed to "exchange information and visits." Here again the Reagan administration argued that such an exchange was the equivalent of formal international supervision, because nuclear exports would not be licensed unless the United States was satisfied that agreed arrangements came up to IAEA standards.

The nonproliferation aspect was in some ways the trickiest issue to resolve, because China refused any reference to the matter in the treaty at all! The best that could be achieved was an oral pledge made by Prime Minister Zhao Ziyang of China at a White House reception. Raising his champagne glass in a toast, Zhao stated: "We do not engage in nuclear proliferation ourselves, nor do we help other countries develop nuclear weapons."[6] The U.S. interpretation of this and other verbal Chinese assurances was contained in a classified State Department memorandum.[7]

Critics of the Nuclear Cooperation Agreement were dissatisfied that Chinese obligations were not explicitly spelled out in the text of the agreement. What if China declined in the future to agree with the U.S. interpretation? The ambiguity inherent in the accord would only foster misunderstanding and conflict. "There can only be one reason for these excursions into the netherworld of State Departmentese," Congressman Edward Markey (D-Mass.) scathingly charged. "The Chinese are not prepared to commit to what the American law requires."[8]

In the end, however, the treaty was ratified. Congressional concerns were met by a joint resolution requiring the president, in advance of the issue of an export license, to provide certain defined assurances. Reciprocal arrangements on end use would have to be satisfactory and additional information provided on China's nonproliferation policies. When the debate subsided and the contestants departed, a complex structure of overlapping understandings was in place. In addition to the international treaty, there were oral Chinese assurances, a classified State Department memorandum of interpretation, explanations to the Congress, and a congressional resolution. Unfortunately, it all proved fruitless: despite these efforts to satisfy Congress, in violation of its commitments China continued to help Third World countries, including Pakistan and Algeria, to develop nuclear weapons.[9] Congressman Markey had been right all along.

Hope, as they say, springs eternal in the human breast. For years China repeatedly rebuffed U.S. attempts to persuade it to come aboard the Missile Technology Control Regime (MTCR, an international agreement to prevent the spread of medium-range missiles). Eventually, in November 1991, Secretary of State Baker persuaded China to agree in talks in Beijing to a tortuous declaration in which it stated, not that it "will observe," but that "it intends to observe" the MTCR guidelines. This was further watered down in a clarification from the Chinese Foreign Ministry after the talks in which it said only that it "may consider observing" those guidelines. China also insisted on deleting references to specific countries to which it was thought to have supplied missile or nuclear technology in the past.[10] (This was not long after it was revealed that China was helping Algeria to build a nuclear reactor not subject to international safeguards.) In exchange for this fuzzy assurance Washington would lift some sanctions on the sale of high-technology equipment, imposed on missile proliferators according to a 1990 law.[11]

Following the Baker trip to Beijing, the Bush administration continued to press China to provide a written assurance of its promise to check the spread of ballistic missiles, noting that a verbal commitment was insufficient to satisfy Congress. This effort appeared to have borne fruit in January 1992 when Prime Minister Li Peng promised President Bush in person to furnish a written version, in the form of a letter, of the commitments given to Secretary Baker. Li's new promise temporarily relieved U.S. pressure on China. A report appearing in the *New York Times* claiming that China had continued to make various transfers to Syria and Pakistan was not brought up at their UN meeting by President Bush; on February 21 the Bush administration announced the selected lifting of sanctions, as agreed in November.[12]

Sadly, the Clinton administration soon detected Beijing to be in violation of the spirit of the 1991 declaration, having secretly sold components
of M-11 missiles to Pakistan. In August 1993 sanctions on U.S. high-
technology exports to China were reimposed. The parties were back to
square one.[13]

Remarkably, the United States has continued in its efforts to tie the
Chinese down to commitments that they are not interested in making and
that, on the basis of past performance, they may well violate. In May 1996
the Clinton administration decided not to impose sanctions on China for
exporting ring magnets to Pakistan, to be installed in equipment used for
enriching uranium to nuclear-weapons level, in contravention of China's
1985 IAEA commitments. Instead, the administration used the threat of
sanctions to extract a new promise from the Chinese "not to do it again."
However, China declined to acknowledge *in public* its supposed obligation
to desist from future transfers. The form taken by the understanding would
have been thought unacceptable in any other relationship: a statement
made by Washington, with the agreement of Chinese officials, explicitly
referring to a private promise made by Foreign Minister Qian Qichen to
Secretary Christopher. "They agreed we would issue that statement and . . .
[said] that was a correct statement," Christopher told a congressional subcommittee. "This is an important new agreement that moves China a step
further down the road toward the nonproliferation program."[14]

In all these cases the United States went the extra mile to meet Chinese
reluctance to enter into explicit, unambiguous, contractual obligations. It
certainly did this with reluctance and in full awareness of the risks
involved. Doubtless the political arguments seemed compelling: better a
flawed commitment that the Chinese could later be held to, than unre-
stricted Chinese proliferation. The goal has always been to draw China,
step by step, into a net of entangling obligations in the hope that at some
point it would accept the constraints and responsibilities of good international citizenship. So far this strategy has not worked, and critics of these
tortuous informal understandings have been repeatedly proved correct in
their claim that China has evaded specificity in order to provide itself with
ample scope for evasion while sidestepping the outright ignominy arising
from the violation of a more solemn treaty. Looseness of form has accurately reflected, in these cases, laxity of intention. In the final analysis the
outcome has been detrimental in a number of respects: the Chinese have
come to be viewed as notoriously unreliable; U.S. credibility has been dam-

aged; illicit technology has continued to flow; and the wider U.S.-Chinese relationship has suffered.

CONTRACTS JAPANESE-STYLE

U.S. relations with Japan, Mexico, and Egypt are immeasurably better than those with China, grounded in broadly commensurate interests and treaty ties rather than strategic divergence and unremitting friction. Nevertheless, analogous problems of blurred boundaries and sometimes lackadaisical compliance exist.

Japan and the United States can be observed to possess different conceptions of the nature of contract and the finality of negotiations. Japan assumes the primacy of relationships over outcomes, with important implications for the way in which it tackles infringements of contract. If Americans seek to protect themselves against failure by exhaustively anticipating future contingencies, the Japanese take as their point of departure the centrality of the continuing connection. Wagatsuma and Rosett put it well when they point out that "in the West contract is used to define rights and duties of the parties by detailed provisions when good will and trust have broken down, while the Japanese tend to insist upon the continuing effectiveness of good will and trust in every situation." Thus Japanese contracts contain such clauses as "if in the future a dispute arises between the parties with regard to the rights and duties provided in this contract, the parties will confer in good faith," or "will settle the dispute harmoniously by consultation."[15] This noteworthy departure from Western practice starkly reveals the key feature of Japanese contracts: that they are not intended to stipulate all commitments in detail, but to set up an ongoing relationship in which mutual obligations will be worked out as the need arises. Mushakoji Kinhide adds that *awase* logic ensures that in any event agreements are treated flexibly and broad-mindedly. "Japanese society operates by not making time exact and not paying strict attention to the provisions of contracts. Minor infringements are often overlooked (*ome ni miru*)."[16]

Americans do not take kindly to such a cavalier approach to contracts; infringements are not overlooked, but vehemently condemned as an unacceptable breach of trust. Donald Abelson, director of the Office of Trade Barriers in the Office of the U.S. Trade Representative, recalls with the horror of culture shock his own experience in this regard. In April 1979, Japan, together with the United States and other GATT (General Agreement on Tariffs and Trade) signatories, agreed on a standards code after years of negotiation. Before putting the code into law, Congress sought

prompt assurances that U.S. trading partners would do likewise. Sadly, as
Abelson notes, "in Japan quick agreements never seem to stick." After two
negotiating sessions, the Japanese delegation initialed an agreement,
"drank champagne and that was it." The document was never subsequently
signed or ratified. Later, Abelson continues bitterly, the Japanese government "threw that initialed document into the waste-basket." What was
assumed by the United States to be a firm commitment turned out to be
merely the first milestone on a long and weary road of further negotiation.[17] Abelson's interpretation of Japanese conduct in this case is understandable, though harsh. It was unrealistic to assume that the Japanese
government, with its tortuous, consensual decisionmaking procedures, could
provide prompt assurances about anything. And naturally the Japanese delegation took the easy way out: reluctant to disappoint their American interlocutors, they gave them the consent that was so urgently demanded by
an overlegalistic Congress. In light of what has been said so far, it is not at
all surprising that the quick fix produced to satisfy Congress required subsequent prolonged clarification. What to the Americans was an outrageous
infringement of the rules constituted socially desirable behavior for the
Japanese. After all, in the end everything did indeed work out for the best.

A last word on the subject can be given to Michael Donnelly. In his
study of U.S.-Japanese trade negotiations he rightly contrasts the American drive for closure with the Japanese tendency to inconclusiveness:

> Americans have come to favor clear goals, deadlines, and fairly definitive
> results. The Japanese tend to view definitive discussions (words such as "bar-
> gaining" or "negotiations" are not often used in Japan to describe these talks)
> as on-going and are reluctant to consider any single point in the discussion
> as terminal and definitive. Such a propensity reflects a more general habit in
> Japanese governing practices of maintaining a style of politics that permits
> constant monitoring and feedback about errors, successes, wrong interpre-
> tations and changing circumstances.[18]

MEXICO: UNKEPT PROMISES

Good relations with its southern neighbor, since 1994 a valued partner in
the North American Free Trade Agreement, are a vital national interest of
the United States, and it is only natural that every effort is made to downplay differences and play up successes in the relationship. Problems of
implementation certainly exist, arguably for reasons similar to those found
in the Chinese and Japanese cases—a less rigorous attitude to contracts, an

emphasis on relationships over outcomes, irresolute domestic enforcement. Yet it is precisely because the overall relationship is relatively sound that the United States is better able to work out its differences with Mexico (and Japan) than with China.

In the area of intellectual property it is a surprise to discover that the Mexican record of implementing agreements is hardly superior to that of China. However, the issue is not elevated to a make-or-break test of Mexican reliability, and rather than being addressed in angry declarations is tackled behind the scenes by quiet diplomacy. Still, in a 1996 report to the U.S. trade representative the International Intellectual Property Alliance complained that "Mexico has become one of the biggest piracy markets in the world," grossly failing to implement its own laws protecting copyright, in violation of NAFTA provisions. The Business Software Alliance claimed that four-fifths of all business software used in Mexico are unlicensed copies. In response to U.S. complaints, Mexico agreed that officials of the two countries would meet monthly to monitor the issue, but few pirates are prosecuted, and irregularities in domestic law enforcement, to put it delicately, remain legion.[19]

Despite this discouraging example, one lesson of U.S.-Mexican negotiating over the years is that perseverance may pay off. The 1978 Extradition Treaty is a case in point. For many years it proved a one-way street, with the United States agreeing unconditionally to extradite American citizens accused of crimes in Mexico, but Mexico declining to surrender a single one of its nationals wanted north of the border. Viewed with concern as a treaty violation by the U.S. Justice Department, this pattern of behavior can be understood as a clash of contending legal philosophies. Mexican legal thinking (grounded in the axiomatic Civil Code approach, as opposed to the empirical tradition of the common law) is to prefer to try its citizens at home for offenses committed abroad. National pride has also been an obstacle, though under the Mexican constitution extradition is permitted under "exceptional circumstances." In 1990 the Bush administration was so frustrated by Mexico's noncooperative attitude that it gave the green light to the abduction from Mexican soil of a doctor accused of complicity in the 1985 torture and murder of a U.S. drug enforcement agent. As understandable as this decision was, it triggered counterproductive outrage in Mexico. In angry response, President Salinas de Gortari threatened to suspend American drug-enforcement activities in Mexico unless the United States pledged itself in writing to prevent further abductions. Presidents Bush and Clinton were obliged to bow to this demand.[20]

To complicate matters, the extradition-abduction issue, with its emotive crime and national sovereignty connotations, became tangled up with the negotiation and ratification of NAFTA. In September 1992 a Mexican citizen, Serapio Zuniga Rios, kidnapped and brutally raped a four-year-old child in California. He then fled across the border, where he was arrested. When the Mexican authorities refused his extradition, a Florida congressman conditioned his vote for the trade accord on an assurance from the Mexican attorney general that Zuniga Rios would in fact be turned over to the United States. In the event, President Salinas personally promised to secure the extradition. It was, therefore, with particular shock and disappointment that the United States learnt some months later that Zuniga Rios had been tried and convicted in secret by a Mexican court.

On the eve of a meeting with Mexican officials Robert S. Gelbard, assistant U.S. secretary of state for narcotics and international crime issues, was highly critical of Mexican behavior. He commented that

> the Mexican government has known from the beginning that we have considered the Zuniga Rios case to be of fundamental importance. We thought we had complete assurances from the Mexican government . . . that this man would be extradited . . . If they are not prepared to extradite Zuniga Rios under the assurances we have gotten, under what circumstances are they going to extradite anyone?

A senior State Department official was scathing: "They lied to us. There was amazement, horror and real anger when we learned what they had done." Under California law, which provides protection against double jeopardy (being tried twice for the same offence), Zuniga Rios was now ineligible for extradition and trial.[21]

As is often the case in international relations, a fortuitous change of circumstances reshuffled the negotiating hand in favor of the United States. At the beginning of 1995, in fulfillment of President Bush's pledge to President Salinas, a U.S.-Mexican treaty, forbidding cross-border abductions of criminal suspects, came before the Senate. At this very moment the Clinton administration was called on to bail out, to the tune of $20 billion, the Mexican economy and the plummeting peso. The leverage was obvious. U.S. ambassador to Mexico James Jones was being indiscreet but frank when he stated: "If we're going to have the treaty pass, there have to be some indications that there will be a chance for extraditions. People must know that if heinous crimes are committed, you will not have a safe haven in either country."[22]

As already noted, the peso rescue package went through without any explicit political conditions being attached. However, specific requests for extradition soon began to be considered with much greater sympathy in Mexico City. In a landmark decision that was both a precedent and a face-saving compromise, a Mexican suspect with dual citizenship was *deported* by Mexico to the United States.[23] Within a short time, applications for the *extradition* of two Mexican citizens were approved by the Mexican authorities. In the one case the decision was justified on the grounds that a Mexican trial would (as in the Zuniga Rios affair) potentially violate the principle of double jeopardy. In the other case "the infamous nature of the crimes"—a quadruple murder—and the suspect's dual citizenship provided the "exceptional circumstances" required by the law.[24] It had taken eighteen years of persistence, but the Extradition Treaty was at last being enforced.

CONCLUSION: GRADUATED RECIPROCITY

In the Mexican case just considered, perseverance in the face of reluctance ultimately paid off. New circumstances and a close overall relationship gave Mexico some incentives for compliance. But it would be naive to overlook the immediate leverage presented to the United States by the peso crisis. Since the U.S. Justice Department had always declined, on legal grounds, to specifically tie its own agreement to Mexican extradition requests to Mexican behavior, an alternative inducement had to be sought. Mexico's economic plight, and its consequent dependence on U.S. assistance, provided this inducement. The conclusion is obvious: if high-context (or any other) negotiating partners have difficulty in complying with their treaty commitments, for whatever reason, some system of conditionality, preferably ongoing, has to be built into the original treaty design. In many areas of life continued good behavior is secured by tying reward to performance. Robert Axelrod has famously demonstrated how a "tit-for-tat" strategy induces cooperative behavior in repeated plays of the prisoner's dilemma (where players are otherwise obliged by the payoff structure to act uncooperatively in any single game).[25] If this logic is accepted, then it follows that a system of graduated incentives may also encourage treaty compliance—by an otherwise reluctant partner—over time.

Corroboration of this thesis is found in the recent experience of USAID, the foreign aid arm of the United States government. In both India and Egypt a system of *performance-based disbursement* has been successfully implemented in certain projects. This follows World Bank precedent, whereby pending "tranches" of financial aid may be made conditional on the recipient having met defined targets set for previous installments. In the face of a pattern of bureaucratic recalcitrance, glacial implementation, and unfulfilled promises, conditionality, though invariably much disliked by the recipient country, is effective in the simple Pavlovian sense that it rewards, and therefore reinforces, desirable behavior, and penalizes, therefore discourages, undesirable behavior.

In the past, aid disbursements for set project items were traditionally approved by USAID officials and the use to which monies were then put was subsequently—and laboriously—audited. Not only did this waste an inordinate amount of time on intrusive supervision and form pushing, it was also ineffective, in that once a payment had been made the stimulus to compliance declined. In place of this approach the big family-planning project in India has moved, at the district level, to tying packages of aid to set decreases in local fertility.[26]

A similar approach was adopted in Egypt. Here, development aid in the 1975–95 period of $19 billion achieved some successes. However, it has also been much criticized for discouraging needed economic reform because until recently money was not made conditional on performance. "You can make criticisms of the donors," noted one Western diplomat, "but we're only as good as our hosts, and I don't think the Egyptians have taken sufficient advantage of the money at their disposal."[27] Persistent problems were the gross inefficiency and overmanning of the massive state-controlled sector, a holdover from the Nasser era of state socialism, and Egyptian government reluctance to charge customers anything like economic prices for government-owned utilities such as water and electricity. Economic reforms were often promised, but never implemented. During the 1980s, the *New York Times* reported, "US aid officials tried to withhold funds out of dissatisfaction with the government's failure to carry out policy reforms,"[28] but they were overruled by the State Department on political grounds.

By the beginning of the 1990s, it was clear that the pattern of continuing Egyptian evasion was unsustainable. In 1991 there was a flurry of negative news stories in the American press. Under a new country director, USAID decided to make performance a key issue and to deliver "$200 million of the annual aid package in the form of a cash grant tied to the implementation of specific changes, such as removal of price controls and the sale of state industries to private investors." Failure to meet promised targets could result in monies being withheld.[29] So far, the Egyptian government, which much prefers aid without strings, has fought a rearguard action, giving ground reluctantly, appealing behind the back of USAID to sympathetic congressional supporters, procrastinating, and promising compliance at some future date. Nevertheless, there have been some results, for instance in the big Alexandria water project, where funding was conditioned on structural reforms. In the end, all will depend on the willingness of the U.S. government to withstand political pressure and persevere with its strategy over the long haul in the face of political pressures and changes of personnel.[30]

Graduated reciprocity is a good solution to the problem of blurred boundaries between negotiation and implementation presented in this chapter. Realistically, it acknowledges from the outset that automatic compliance cannot be assumed and that high-context cultures may drag their feet over implementation. It avoids the low-context tendency to turn a blind eye to minor infringements of an agreement, then lash out in an unwise spasm of anger when a certain level of frustration has been reached. Moreover, it accepts the valid point that in the final analysis agreements are not the end but the beginning of an arrangement, and that cooperation between sovereign states will ultimately depend on the quality of the relationship and not simply the terms of the contract. International cooperation on such ongoing matters as nuclear nonproliferation, respect for intellectual property rights, economic reforms by aid recipients, extradition, market liberalization, and so on, has come to rest, willy-nilly, on a system of endless negotiation. The hope that high-context partners of the United States would sign on the dotted line and unquestioningly comply has surely long since been punctured. It is, therefore, only prudent to recognize that cross-cultural differences about the finality of negotiation and the nature of contracts do exist and must be taken into account not only in the conduct of talks but also in the terms of agreements reached.

12

In Search of Harmony

Conclusions

Culture has been called "the hidden dimension," unseen, yet exerting a pervasive influence on the behavior of individuals, groups, and societies. From this premise it has been but a short step for researchers to recognize the potential for dissonance and misunderstanding in situations of intercultural communication. When interlocutors attempt to convey messages across linguistic and cultural barriers, nuances are filtered out, and dialogue distorted. Moves that are supposed to be coordinated fall out of step. What one culture takes to be self-evident, another may find bizarre. Concepts central to one culture are peripheral to another. The boundaries between ideas are drawn in different places.

Strangely enough, international negotiation has, implicitly or explicitly, been excluded by many political scientists from this general tendency. Yet few activities require such a synchronization of moves, conventions, and meanings across interlocutors as does negotiation. And indeed, in the cases investigated, involving the United States and a group of non-Western nations, it was seen that cross-cultural discrepancies may strongly affect the conduct and outcome of such talks.

Negotiation theorists' dismissal of the effect of culture springs from the assumption that there is a single, universal paradigm of negotiation and that cross-national differences are stylistic and superficial. In opposition to that contention, the existence of two quite different paradigms of negotiation was confirmed by this study. One is associated with the predominantly verbal and explicit, or low-context, communicatory style of the United States. In a nutshell, it is infused with the can-do, problem-solving spirit, assumes a process of give-and-take, and is strongly influenced by Anglo-Saxon legal habits. When theorists posit a universal paradigm of negotiation (usually involving such features as the "joint search for a solution," "isolating the people from the problem," and the "maximization of joint gains"), they are in effect proposing an idealized version of the low-context, problem-solving model. Notice the instrumental assumptions of rationality that underlie the paradigm: people are part of the problem, not the solution; each problem can be solved discretely; goals are defined in terms of material, not psychic, satisfactions.

The problems inherent in assuming a single, universally valid model of negotiation were demonstrated before the 1990–91 Gulf War, which followed the unprovoked Iraqi invasion of Kuwait. Roger Fisher, founder of the Harvard Program on Negotiation, whose *Getting to Yes* (written with William Ury) is a classic account of "win-win" negotiating, called in a series of newspaper articles for fair and sympathetic consideration of Saddam Hussein's reasonable needs and concerns. President Bush had to "make clear to Saddam the ways in which Iraq will be better off withdrawing from Kuwait." Iraq had "legitimate" concerns that had to be addressed, including its claim to Kuwaiti oil fields and cancellation of war debts, access to a deep-water port, call for withdrawal of U.S. and Western forces from the Gulf and a fairer distribution of Arab wealth, solicitude for the Palestinian cause, and right to a "fair process for dealing with its concerns." Both Iraq and the United States, Fisher argued, had "to try to convince the other of what ought to be done in the light of precedent, international law, or some other objective criterion. If agreement is reached, neither has given in to the arbitrary position of the other. Each can explain to constituents why the result is fair."[1] Fisher's recommendations are strikingly incongruous and, indeed, culture-bound. His projection of Western concepts of fair play, negotiation by reasoned persuasion, due process, and equity onto the Iraqi dictator are inappropriate to the point of naïveté. "Win-win," designed for a domestic American market, was totally unsuited to the requirements of compelling the brutal Iraqi leader to withdraw his army of occupation from Kuwait. It merely repeated the initial, erroneous assumption underlying the policy of conciliation that had tempted Saddam into the invasion in the first place: the belief he was a reasonable statesman who would prefer a peaceful, compromise outcome to war.

There exists another, quite different paradigm of negotiation just as self-consistent and valid in its own terms as that exemplified by Fisher's low-context, problem-solving approach. This alternative model, associated with a nonverbal, implicit, high-context style of communication, predominates in interdependent societies that display a collectivistic, rather than individualistic, ethos. This paradigm was found to mark the negotiating behavior of the non-Western states examined. In contrast to the results-oriented American model, it declines to view the immediate issue in isolation; lays particular stress on long-term and affective aspects of the relationship between the parties; is preoccupied with considerations of symbolism, status, and face; and draws on highly developed communication strategies for evading confrontation.

Putting the two paradigms together in the same room in an intercultural or interparadigmatic encounter produces some interesting reactions. American negotiators tend to be surprised by their interlocutors' preoccupation with history and hierarchy, preference for principle over nitty-gritty detail, personalized and repetitive style of argument, lack of enthusiasm for explicit and formal agreement, and willingness to sacrifice substance to form. They are frustrated by their partners' reluctance to put their cards on the table, intransigent bargaining, evasiveness, dilatoriness, and readiness to walk away from the table without agreement. Non-Western negotiators tend to be surprised by their interlocutors' ignorance of history, preoccupation with individual rights, obsession with the immediate problem while neglecting the overall relationship, excessive bluntness, impatience, disinterest in establishing a philosophical basis for agreement, extraordinary willingness to make soft concessions, constant generation of new proposals, and inability to leave a problem pending. They are frustrated by their American partners' occasional obtuseness and insensitivity; tendency to see things and present alternatives in black-or-white, either-or terms; appetite for crisis; habit of springing unpleasant surprises; intimidating readiness for confrontation; tendency to bypass established channels of authority; inability to take no for an answer; and obsession with tidying up loose ends and putting everything down on paper. Obviously, these are oversimplified depictions, but they do serve to highlight the main points of abrasion in the low-context–high-context encounter.

Insistence on the dichotomy may seem overstated in the light of contemporary patterns of interdependence and globalization. But its continuing relevance stems from the existence of an international trend to some cultural *convergence* at the same time as deep-seated *divergence* continues to exist. True, non-Western elites are increasingly familiar with American society and often the product of American universities. Tens of thousands of young people from all the countries considered are today studying in the United States. They go home possessing a superb command of English, a liberal education, and cosmopolitan professional skills. In some situations, such as the NAFTA talks, the shared language of liberal economics un-questionably facilitates a productive negotiation. In many cases the business and scientific communities can draw on shared, transnational assumptions. Nevertheless, home-grown political elites and their grassroots constituencies, the overwhelming majority after all, continue to set the dominant tone. In U.S.-Mexican relations, where cross-cultural convergence has progressed as far and as fast as anywhere, dissonance remains salient; not always, but frequently enough to be consequential. One of the reasons that the December 1994 peso crisis took the United States by surprise was the mis-taken belief on the part of Treasury Department officials that the gap between the two societies had vanished. However, outside the guild of Chicago- and Harvard-trained economists much remained unchanged.[2] In addition, noneconomic agencies on both sides, whether law enforce-ment or environmental officials, often lack international expertise and lin-guistic skills.[3] Stereotypes and misconceptions are resilient among the masses. Most important, culturally grounded structures of meaning shape expectations and behavior even when on the surface a common language has been acquired.

The historical record examined for this study provided persuasive evi-dence of the persistence of cultural influences on negotiating goals and behavior. National negotiating styles, as for instance Lucian Pye, Paul Kreisberg, Richard Solomon, and others confirm in their studies of China, are broadly predictable. This does not mean, though, that negotiating out-comes are determinate, a very different matter, since circumstances, inter-ests, and the distribution of power vary from case to case and from one period to another. Since the end of the Cold War, Japan has learned to say no, India to say yes. When overall Sino-American relations are healthy, general agreements, such as the 1978 normalization accord, tend to stick. When trust is absent, vague agreements, such as the 1992 memorandum on prison labor, quickly come unstuck.

Given that important proviso, the chemical compound obtained when high-context and low-context paradigms join in debate is seen to be highly volatile, as Paul Keating, Robin Raphel, and Mickey Kantor, among many others, have discovered. Communication lapses and behavioral asynchronies may simply be a nuisance or have serious diplomatic consequences. "Harmless" remarks by Keating and Raphel triggered major incidents. In other cases, cross-cultural incompatibilities contributed to the failure of negotiations. They seriously hindered the Ras Banas and General Motors negotiations with Egypt of the early 1980s, although there was potential for agreement in terms of significant shared interests and a good underlying relationship. In the Ras Banas affair the heavy-handed, legalistic approach of the Department of Defense frightened the Egyptians off when a low-key accord to establish a modest facility would have better met both sides' needs. As for General Motors, it was discouraged by the labyrinthine and far from pristine maneuvers of the Cairo bureaucracy. In the 1993–94 MFN negotiations the United States misread Chinese signals and made a fundamental misjudgment in linking the neuralgic topic of human rights with trade. The talks were doomed from the outset. Cross-cultural contradictions and sensitivities were also behind the unproductive discussions on intelligence and security between U.S. and Saudi officials in the prelude to the June 1996 Dahran terrorist bombing in which nineteen U.S. servicemen were killed. A combination of Saudi procrastination, lack of forthrightness, and ambivalence toward the U.S. presence, together with American fear of encroaching on Saudi sensibilities, fatally hamstrung contacts.[4] Yet the partners had a clear common interest in combating terrorism.

Cultural factors are not usually decisive by themselves but are amplified by situational factors. In the 1958 U.S.-Chinese ambassadorial talks over hostilities in the Taiwan Straits, at a time of widening Sino-Soviet discord, an opportunity to build upon overlapping interests was lost. Whereas Beijing insisted, in typical fashion, on prior U.S. agreement to a general renunciation of force, Washington pragmatically proposed to defuse hostilities step by step. Looking back from the vantage point of 1971, Mao surely hinted at past error when he told Nixon that the United States was right to propose tackling small issues before big ones. The earlier atmosphere of distrust had exacerbated the methodological gap between the parties. By 1971 a convergence of supreme national interests—primed by subtle diplomacy—diminished the impact of cross-cultural discordance.

A second result of dissonance is tactical rather than strategic: negotiations have proved productive, but U.S. negotiators have achieved less favorable terms than they might have otherwise. We saw that a common error of the United States was to offer premature concessions in the mistaken assumption that its opponent, driven by the same eagerness for compromise, would reciprocate in kind. This misjudgment placed the United States in an inferior position in the final round of negotiations. This tendency was observed in the 1955 civilian repatriation talks with China, when the United States made substantial concessions too soon and then, in the face of Chinese obduracy, decided not to insist on the immediate release of all civilian detainees held on the mainland. Equally, in believing that holding hostages would achieve political benefit, China (uncannily like Iran much later) sadly miscalculated the acute U.S. sensitivity to human rights issues, embittering relations. This discordant pattern has uncannily repeated itself over the years. In the 1956–57 air transport talks, Mexico achieved its major goals while the United States conceded its main objectives, having long since—one-sidedly—exhausted its bargaining assets. Demonstrating the consistency of these tendencies, despite a change of cast and circumstances, a similar pattern appeared in the 1980–82 air service negotiations with Japan: premature U.S. concessions in the face of Japanese reticence resulted in a final agreement more favorable to Japan. In the 1978 normalization talks with China, the United States naively informed the Chinese that its opening position was not its last word. Playing its hand closer to its chest, China withheld the assurance of a peaceful resolution of the Taiwan issue, only to use that very trump to obtain quite new concessions in 1982 discussions.

Together with premature concession, impatience in the end game has also been to U.S. detriment. In both the 1989 and 1991 Baker-Qian talks, conducted on the American side with stopwatch in hand because of a strong presidential commitment to speedy results, the United States gave away more than it received in return. At the end of the NAFTA talks, Carla Hills found herself obliged to negotiate final details with no cards after the White House had already announced the conclusion of an agreement. The most striking example of the American propensity for deadlines occurred in the 1995 aviation negotiations with India, when the basis for inevitably far-reaching concessions on the American part was laid by United Airlines' announcement that it was inaugurating its round-the-world service by a fixed date. In none of the cases mentioned here were the negotiators personally to blame for the self-induced pressure; they were acting on instructions from the political echelon. Responsibility was to be truly laid at the door of culturally ingrained habits of overeagerness.

The most frequent consequence of intercultural misunderstanding that we saw was undramatic but pernicious: a spillover effect spreading beyond the immediate negotiation and causing a loss of credibility and damage to the wider relationship. This phenomenon has notably haunted U.S.-

Japanese ties. On separate occasions in 1955, 1969, 1970, and 1987, the United States mistook polite Japanese reluctance to offend for actual compliance. Having failed to detect Japanese unhappiness, and foisted agreement on its unenthusiastic ally, it then completely miscalculated the ability of the Japanese political leadership to deliver the bureaucracy. Such spurious accord, reached without the requisite process of consensus building, was quickly repudiated in Tokyo. The result was an all-round loss of confidence, with angry Americans and embarrassed Japanese. In 1969 the culprit was President Nixon, who compounded cross-cultural insensitivity with classic prejudice, completely misinterpreting the hedged utterance of Prime Minister Sato of Japan ("I will do my best"). When this "promise" was not kept, Nixon privately accused Sato of being a liar. In 1987 President Reagan and his advisers felt that they, too, had been misled by Prime Minister Nakasone. Damage to U.S.-Japanese relations during the first Clinton administration was also caused by the overzealous adoption by U.S. trade representative Mickey Kantor of *gaiatsu*, pressure from the outside for internal reform. By the time the strategy was abandoned in 1995 the United States had concluded that it was achieving limited short-term results at the expense of the overall long-term relationship, a typically misplaced low-context trade-off.

Failure to interpret its negotiating partners' intentions because of cross-cultural misunderstanding has also sometimes deprived the United States of the ability to foresee future moves and hence to take necessary preventive or remedial action. During the last days of the shah, cultural limitations hindered the U.S. ability to read the situation in Iran correctly. An earlier misreading occurred in U.S.-Indian relations when Ambassador Allen misjudged Nehru's reaction to the 1954 U.S.-Pakistani arms deal. As a result, the American government was unprepared for the spasm of outrage that convulsed Indian opinion. Similarly, in 1962 Ambassador Galbraith failed to detect the reluctance behind Nehru's tepid response to the Anglo-American Kashmir mediation. In the circumstances of India's border war with China, Nehru could hardly dismiss Western proposals out of hand. But misplaced American pressure on India to make concessions to Pakistan dissipated the considerable credit accruing to the U.S. government as a result of its timely military assistance.

The same tendency to mistake politeness for agreement has repeated itself in U.S.-Egyptian relations. In 1977 the United States failed to grasp that behind President Sadat's lack of enthusiasm for a reconvening of the Geneva conference—"there was no rush"—lurked strong opposition to the

scheme. Overlooking the Egyptian president's growing sense of despera-
tion, the United States, albeit temporarily, lost complete control of the
Middle East peace process. Again in 1984, agreement was foisted on a reluctant Egypt for the passage of nuclear warships through the Suez Canal.
Having dragged its feet for years, the Egyptian government was loath to
turn the United States down flat. But, as in the Kashmir example, credit was
squandered and at the first opportunity Egypt repudiated the accord.

If cross-cultural dissonance can harm a relationship, the converse should
be equally true: that cross-cultural synchrony, based on careful attention to
the other side's psychological needs, should prove beneficial. This has indeed proved to be so. In the case of the "recalcitrant prime minister" Paul
Keating compounded the initial perceived insult to Malaysia by failing,
at first, to realize that in an Asian (high) context the right solution was a
speedy public apology. He might have learned from the example of Senator Mike Mansfield, a superb ambassador to Japan (1977–89). Following
a 1981 accident at sea, in which a U.S. nuclear submarine, the *George
Washington*, collided with a Japanese freighter, killing two Japanese sailors,
passions ran high in Japan. A speedy U.S. naval inquiry, acceptance of lia-
bility, and agreement to pay compensation, helped defuse the incident.
However, the critical step in finally disposing of the affair was taken by
Senator Mansfield. Delivering the final report to the Japanese foreign minister, he bowed low according to Japanese custom and apologized in full
view of press and television. "I wanted to let the whole nation know how
sorry the U.S. felt by adopting the Japanese manner of apologizing and
being sorry," he said. "I deliberately adopted something the Japanese would
understand. It was a small price to pay to bring an amicable settlement."[5]

Unless there are shared interests in reaching an accord, however, and a
healthy relationship following its conclusion, no amount of cross-cultural
sensitivity will help. Lee Sands, a China scholar, put his expertise to good
use in negotiating a 1995 intellectual property agreement with China. But
the deal reached was not self-enforcing and proved no better than the surrounding relationship.

In the negotiations studied, some U.S. negotiators made a major contribution by carefully cultivating close personal relationships with their foreign
counterparts. For example, in the 1962-63 Chamizal negotiation with Mexico, Ambassador Mann's long-standing friendship with Ambassador Tello
proved invaluable. It is significant that the two ambassadors did their best
work in informal settings. Many of the technical details were hammered
out by officials of the International Boundary and Water Commission,

who also had long experience of working together. Again in the 1973 Colorado River salinity talks the close Brownell-Rabasa relationship was a great help; the breakthrough in negotiations came in a conversation while the two were out for a stroll. The role of the personal touch strongly emerges in a survey of U.S.-Egyptian relations since 1973; all major political successes have been facilitated by it. The Egyptian-Israeli disengagement agreements of 1974 and 1975, and the accords of 1978 and 1979, seem hardly conceivable without the intimate Kissinger-Sadat and Carter-Sadat relationships. To complete the picture, it is worth recalling the personal rapport that obtained between President Lyndon Johnson and Prime Minister Indira Gandhi on the latter's successful trip to Washington in 1966, when the two concurred on a reform package for the Indian economy that included a painful devaluation of the rupee. This thawing of relations took place despite the continuing U.S.-Pakistan alliance. So much for purely objective factors in international politics.

The salience of "personal chemistry" in international affairs may, of course, be overstated. After all, the ongoing conduct of foreign policy is in the hands of a great many agencies and officials. National leaders and high officials are engaged only intermittently. Nevertheless, consultations at the highest level can play a crucial role. Communication between heads of state and foreign ministers brings information authoritatively and promptly to the attention of their respective governments. Commitments are made, directions indicated, agendas set. Where that communication is easy and unencumbered, it may not be possible to brush aside insurmountable differences, but misunderstanding of the other's intentions and gratuitous complications can be avoided. Moreover, without open channels of communication, opportunities to explore common interests may be missed.

A second factor facilitating harmony was the recognition by the United States that there may be certain points of inviolable dogma that are nonnegotiable as far as a high-context interlocutor is concerned. However, once such axioms are conceded in principle, it may be possible, in a pragmatic fashion, to arrive at a satisfactory agreement on concrete issues. This approach involves true cross-cultural accommodation, in that it reconciles the deep-seated needs of both sides. It was this approach that underlay the 1962 Kennedy-Mateos accord paving the way for a resolution of the Chamizal dispute. Once the United States recognized the justice of the Mexican claim (conceded by international arbitration in 1911), Mexico was prepared to be utterly pragmatic in its practical implementation. An identical strategy was followed in 1973, when President Nixon committed the United States to a "just solution" of the Colorado River problem, thereby acknowledging the responsibility of the United States to ensure that usable water reached Mexican farmers. Similarly, in the 1969 Okinawa bases negotiations the United States wisely conceded the principle of "home-level reversion"—the return of the Ryukyu and Bonin islands to Japanese administration—thereby guaranteeing both continued U.S. use of the bases and future military cooperation. The 1972 Shanghai communiqué was yet another example of a generalized framework beneath the philosophical awnings of which pragmatic cooperation could proceed. In this case, remarkably, points of difference were not plastered over. But the two countries' opposition to hegemony (that is, Soviet ambitions) was proclaimed and the yawning gap over the Taiwan issue was bridged with the ingenious U.S. acknowledgment "that all Chinese on either side of the Taiwan Straits maintain there is but one China."[6]

A final ingredient in reaching agreement with high-context negotiators was scrupulous regard for their heightened sensitivity in matters of face. Any whiff of humiliation would doom an agreement to perdition. To obtain the substance of accord it was essential to preserve appearances: to maintain —if necessary, contrive—the impression that the accord was an achievement of the other side, concluded on the basis of mutual respect and equal standing. Striking examples of this pattern were found in the 1971 Japanese devaluation and the 1982 Mexican loan. In the first instance, a 17 percent devaluation of the yen was impossible, but 16.9 percent devaluation was acceptable. In the second case, Mexico was ready to receive a lower effective price for its oil than it could otherwise have obtained, because it rested on a face-saving arrangement. The vital importance of face was also observed in the 1971–72 talks with China, for example, in the terms of the invitation to President Nixon; and in the 1973 negotiations for a cease-fire following the Yom Kippur War, when United Nations checkpoints on the Cairo-Suez road obscured the reality of the blockade of the Egyptian Third Army by Israeli forces. Finally, although it was not always feasible, something unacceptable as an explicit agreement might be palatable as an informal understanding. Over the years, many areas of cooperation, especially with Mexico and Egypt, have been assisted by this expedient. The February 1995 peso rescue package is an example. Political concessions were made by Mexico, but not in the main financial agreement.

It should be obvious by now that I do not believe that either Americans or their non-Western partners have a monopoly of wisdom when it comes to negotiation. As an outsider, I personally find much to commend in both the problem-oriented and relationship-oriented approaches. They are truly complementary. Learning that there is more than one way to go about things not only is enlightening but also enriches one's palette of alternatives. So it is neither possible nor desirable to lay down hard-and-fast, universal rules of how to negotiate. That depends on the issue, the situation, the opponent—and oneself.

Moreover, the proviso stated at the beginning of this monograph bears repetition: cross-cultural insight is not a panacea or substitute for consonant interests. Furthermore, prior to grasp of the cultural context must come the realization that negotiations do not take place in a vacuum. If negotiators are to succeed they must first have a good feel for the personal abilities, requirements, and freedom of maneuver of opposing delegates, as well as the political strengths and weaknesses, needs, and constraints of the government they represent.

Provided these reservations are borne in mind, there are certain obvious lessons to be drawn from this project. I present them here (for the benefit of the low-context individual faced by a high-context adversary) in the form of ten recommendations for the intercultural negotiator.

1. Prepare for a negotiation by studying your opponents' culture and history, and not just the issue at hand. Best of all, learn the language. Immerse yourself in the historical relationship between your two nations. It may explain more than you might expect.

2. Try to establish a warm, personal relationship with your interlocutors. If possible, get to know them even before negotiations get under way. Cultivating contacts and acquaintances is time well spent.

3. Do not assume that what you mean by a message—verbal or nonverbal—is what representatives of the other side will understand by it. They will interpret it in the light of their cultural and linguistic background, not yours. By the same token, they may be unaware that things look different from your perspective.

4. Be alert to indirect formulations and nonverbal gestures. Traditional societies put a lot of weight on them. You may have to read between the lines to understand what your partners are hinting at. Do not assume that they will come right out with it. Be ultra-careful in your own words and body language. Your partners may read more into them than you intend. Do not express criticism in public. Do not lose your temper. Anything that leads to the loss of face is likely to be counterproductive.

5. Do not overestimate the power of advocacy. Your interlocutors are unlikely to shift their positions simply in response to good arguments. Pressure may bring short-term results, but risks damaging the relationship. Facts and circumstances speak louder than words and are easier to comply with.

6. Adapt your strategy to your opponents' cultural needs. On matters of inviolable principle, attempt to accommodate their instinct for prior agreement with your preference for progress on practical matters. Where haggling is called for, leave yourself plenty of leeway. Start high, bargain doggedly, and hold back a trump card for the final round.

7. Flexibility is not a virtue against intransigent opponents. If they are concerned to discover your real bottom line, repeated concessions will confuse rather than clarify the issue. Nor is there merit in innovation for its own sake. Avoid the temptation to compromise with yourself.

8. Be patient. Haste will almost certainly mean unnecessary concessions. Resist the temptation to labor under artificial time constraints; they will work to your disadvantage. Allow your opponents to decide in their own good time. Their bureaucratic requirements cannot be short-circuited.

9. Be aware of the emphasis placed by your opponents on matters of status and face. Outward forms and appearances may be as important as substance. For face-conscious negotiators, an agreement must be presentable as an honorable outcome. On the other hand, symbolic gains may compensate them for substantive losses.

10. Do not be surprised if negotiation continues beyond the apparent conclusion of an agreement. Implementation is unlikely to be automatic and often requires continuing discussion. To assist compliance, it may help to build a system of graduated, performance-based incentives into the original contract.

Notes

1. PRELUDE

1. Harold Nicolson, *Diplomacy*, 3d ed. (London: Oxford University Press, 1969), chap. 10.

2. Joseph C. Grew, *Ten Years in Japan* (London: Hammond, Hammond, 1944), 241.

3. Ibid.

4. Ibid., 242.

5. Ibid.

6. U.S. Department of State, *Foreign Relations of the United States* (hereafter cited as *FRUS*), vol. 4, 1939 (Washington, D.C.: U.S. Government Printing Office, 1955), 455–462.

7. Robert S. McNamara, *In Retrospect: The Tragedy and Lessons of Vietnam* (New York: Vintage Books, 1996), 43, 322.

8. Gary Sick, *All Fall Down: America's Fateful Encounter with Iran* (London: I. B. Taurus, 1985), 34, 66.

9. Grew, *Ten Years in Japan*, 229–230.

2. NEGOTIATION

1. Edward Burnett Tylor, *Primitive Culture* (1871; New York: Harper and Row, 1958).

2. Clyde Kluckhohn, "The Study of Culture," in D. Lerner and H. D. Lasswell, eds., *The Policy Sciences* (Stanford, Calif.: Stanford University Press, 1951), 86.

3. Kevin Avruch and Peter W. Black, "The Culture Question and Conflict Resolution," *Peace and Change* 16 (1991): 27–30.

4. Clifford Geertz, *Local Knowledge* (New York: Basic Books, 1983), 75.

5. Avruch and Black, "The Culture Question and Conflict Resolution."

6. Robert A. Rubinstein, "Cultural Aspects of Peacekeeping: Notes on the Substance of Symbols," *Millennium* 22 (1993): 551.

7. For a good discussion on Sino-Japanese negotiations, see Ogura Kazuo, "How the 'Inscrutables' Negotiate with the 'Inscrutables': Chinese Negotiating Tactics *vis-à-vis* the Japanese," *China Quarterly* 79 (1979): 549.

8. Lucian Pye, *Chinese Commercial Negotiating Style* (Cambridge, Mass.: Oelgeschlager, Gunn, and Hain, 1982), 88–89.

9. For a review of the intercultural literature relevant to international relations, see Raymond Cohen, *Culture and Conflict in Egyptian-Israeli Relations: A Dialogue of the Deaf* (Bloomington: Indiana University Press, 1990), 8–13. See also idem, "International Communication: An Intercultural Approach," *Cooperation and Conflict* 22 (1987): 63–80; and idem, "Problems of Intercultural Communication in Egyptian-American Diplomatic Relations," *International Journal of Intercultural Relations* 11 (1987): 29–47.

10. Michael Weingarten, *Changing Health and Changing Culture: The Yemenite Jews in Israel* (Westport, Conn.: Praeger, 1992).

11. Laura Nader and Harry F. Todd Jr., eds., *The Disputing Process: Law in Ten Societies* (New York: Columbia University Press, 1978).

12. See, for example, Mara B. Adelman and Myron W. Lustig, "Intercultural Communication Problems as Perceived by Saudi Arabian and American Managers," *International Journal of Intercultural Relations* 5 (1981): 349–363; Pierre Casse and Surinder Deol, *Managing Intercultural Negotiations* (Yarmouth, Maine: Intercultural Press, 1985); Dean Allen Foster, *Bargaining Across Borders: How to Negotiate Business Successfully Anywhere in the World* (New York: McGraw-Hill, 1992); John L. Graham, "The Influence of Culture on the Process of Business Negotiations," *Journal of International Business Studies* 16 (1985): 81–96; Michael Kublin, *International Negotiating: A Primer for American Business Professionals* (New York: International Business Press, 1995); Robert M. March, *The Japanese Negotiator* (Tokyo: Kodansha International, 1988); John Pfeiffer, "How Not to Lose the Trade Wars by Cultural Gaffes," *Smithsonian* 18 (1988): 145–156; Pye, *Chinese Commercial Negotiating Style;* Oded Shenkar and Simcha Ronen, "The Cultural Context of Negotiations: The Implications of Chinese Interpersonal Norms," *Journal of Applied Behavioral Science* 23 (1987): 263–275; Rosalie L. Tung, "U.S.-China Trade Negotiations: Procedures and Outcomes," *Journal of International Business Studies* 13 (1982): 25–37; James R. Van De Velde, "The Influence of Culture on Japanese-American Negotiations," *Fletcher Forum* 7 (1983): 395–399; and Howard F. Van Zandt, "How to Negotiate in Japan," *Harvard Business Review* 48 (1970): 45–56.

13. Marie D. Strazar, "The San Francisco Peace Treaty: Cross-Cultural Elements in the Interaction between the Americans and the Japanese," in

R. P. Anand, ed., *Cultural Factors in International Relations* (New Delhi: Abinhav, 1981), 63–76.

14. Hiroshi Kimura, "Soviet and Japanese Negotiating Behavior: The Spring 1977 Fisheries Talks," *Orbis* 24 (1980): 43–67.

15. Michael Blaker, *Japanese International Negotiating Style* (New York: Columbia University Press, 1977).

16. Richard H. Solomon, *Chinese Political Negotiating Behavior, 1967–1984* (Santa Monica, Calif.: RAND Corporation, 1995).

17. Richard H. Solomon, *Chinese Political Negotiating Behavior: A Briefing Analysis* (Santa Monica, Calif.: RAND Corporation, 1985).

18. Raymond F. Smith, *Negotiating with the Soviets* (Bloomington: Indiana University Press, 1989), 5–6.

19. David D. Newsom, comments on the original ms. of this book, March 1997.

20. William Breer, interview by author, February 23, 1996; William Clark, Jr., interview by author, February 22, 1996.

21. Samuel W. Lewis, impromptu comments at a United States Institute of Peace work-in-progress seminar, Washington, D.C., November 10, 1988.

22. Glen Fisher, *International Negotiation: A Cross-Cultural Perspective* (Yarmouth, Maine: Intercultural Press, 1980).

23. E. C. Hendriks, "Research on International Business Negotiations: An Introduction," in C. Braecke and H. Cuyckens, eds., *Business Communication in Multilingual Europe: Supply and Demand* (Antwerp: ENCoDe/UFSIA, 1991), 169–186.

24. Kevin Avruch and Peter W. Black, "Conflict Resolution in Intercultural Settings: Problems and Prospects," in D. Sandole and H. van der Merwe, eds., *Conflict Resolution Theory and Practice: Integration and Application* (Manchester: Manchester University Press, 1993), 133, 134.

25. I. William Zartman and Maureen R. Berman, *The Practical Negotiator* (New Haven, Conn.: Yale University Press, 1982), 224–229.

26. Professor Mark Zacher of the University of British Columbia suggested this point.

27. Robert F. Goheen, "Openings and Impediments in U.S.-India Relations" (unpublished speech to the International Council of Tulsa, April 28, 1988).

28. Winfried Lang, "A Professional's View," in Guy Olivier Faure and Jeffrey Z. Rubin, eds., *Culture and Negotiation: The Resolution of Water Disputes* (Newbury Park, Calif.: Sage, 1993), 38–46.

29. Glen Fisher, *Mindsets* (Yarmouth, Maine: Intercultural Press, 1988), 68–69.

30. Gilbert Winham, "Practitioners' Views of International Negotiation," *World Politics* 32 (1979): 117, 119.

31. Newsom, comments on original ms.

3. INTERCULTURAL DISSONANCE

1. Lorand B. Szalay, "Intercultural Communication: A Process Model," *International Journal of Intercultural Relations* 5 (1981): 133–146.

2. Ibid., 135.

3. Ibid., 136.

4. Ibid., 140–141.

5. Geert Hofstede, *Culture's Consequences* (Beverly Hills, Calif.: Sage, 1980).

6. See, for example, Harry C. Triandis, Richard Brislin, and C. Harry Hui, "Cross-Cultural Training across the Individualism-Collectivism Divide," *International Journal of Intercultural Relations* 12 (1988): 269–289; Harry C. Triandis, Robert Bontempo, and Marcelo J. Villareal, "Individualism and Collectivism: Cross-Cultural Perspectives on Self-Ingroup Relationships," *Journal of Personality and Social Psychology* 54 (1988): 323–338.

7. Edward C. Stewart, *American Cultural Patterns* (Yarmouth, Maine: Intercultural Press, 1972), 68–72.

8. Edward T. Hall, *Beyond Culture* (New York: Anchor Books, 1976).

9. Stella Ting-Toomey, "Toward a Theory of Conflict and Culture," *International and Intercultural Communication Annual* 9 (1985): 71–86.

10. Edward T. Hall, *The Silent Language* (New York: Anchor Books, 1973), 157.

11. Ibid., 7.

12. *New York Times,* July 17, 1989.

13. Mushakoji Kinhide, "The Cultural Premises of Japanese Diplomacy," in Japan Center for International Exchange, ed., *The Silent Power: Japan's Identity and World Role* (Tokyo: Simul Press, 1976), 45–46.

14. Ibid., 40.

15. Stanley Hoffman, *Gulliver's Troubles, Or the Setting of American Foreign Policy* (New York: McGraw-Hill, 1968), 148.

16. Howard Raiffa, *The Art and Science of Negotiation* (Cambridge, Mass.: Harvard University Press, 1982).

17. Roger Fisher and William Ury, *Getting to Yes* (New York: Penguin, 1983).

18. Zartman and Berman, *Practical Negotiator,* 144.

19. *New York Times*, December 9, 1993.

20. *Foreign Broadcast Information Service* (hereafter cited as *FBIS*), *Southeast Asia*, November 23, 1993; emphasis added.

21. *FBIS, Southeast Asia,* November 24, 26, 1993.

22. *The Age* (Melbourne), December 13, 1993.

23. Hofstede, *Culture's Consequences*, 40.

24. *FBIS, Southeast Asia*, December 7, 1993.

25. Ibid., November 26, 1993.

26. Pushpa Thambipillai and J. Saravanamuttu, *ASEAN Negotiations: Two Insights* (Singapore: Institute of Southeast Asian Studies, 1985), 10–17.

27. *FBIS, Southeast Asia*, November 26, 27, 1993.

28. Ibid., December 2, 1993.

29. *The Age* (Melbourne), December 3, 1993.

30. Ibid.

31. *FBIS, Southeast Asia*, December 6, 1993.

32. Ibid., December 7, 1993.

33. Ibid., December 9, 1993.

34. Letitia Hickson, "The Social Contexts of Apology in Dispute Settlement: A Cross-Cultural Study," *Ethnology* 25 (1986): 285–287.

35. Ibid., 291.

36. *FBIS, Southeast Asia*, December 6, 1993.

37. *The Age* (Melbourne), December 13, 1993.

4. What Is Negotiable?

1. George P. Shultz, *Turmoil and Triumph: My Years as Secretary of State* (New York: Charles Scribner's Sons, 1993), 175.

2. *New York Times*, February 19, 1996.

3. Herb Cohen, *You Can Negotiate Anything* (Secaucus, N.J.: Lyle Stuart, 1980).

4. William J. Burns, *Economic Aid and American Policy toward Egypt, 1955–1981* (Albany: State University of New York Press, 1985), 152.

5. *Washington Post*, November 7, 1993; *Los Angeles Times*, April 19, 1994.

6. *Washington Post*, March 20, 1994.

7. Ibid., November 7, 1993.

8. *Los Angeles Times*, April 16, 1994.

9. *Jerusalem Post,* October 25, 1985.

10. Mohamed Riad, *The Struggle for Peace in the Middle East* (London: Quartet Books, 1981), 99.

11. Henry A. Kissinger, *The White House Years* (Boston: Little, Brown, 1979), 637.

12. *New York Times*, March 9, 1995.

13. Kenneth T. Young, *Negotiating with the Chinese Communists* (New York: McGraw-Hill, 1968), 348.

14. *FRUS*, vol. 14, pt. 1, 1952–54, 502.

15. Kissinger, *White House Years*, 689–690.

16. *Washington Post*, November 21, 1993, November 20, 1993.

17. BBC *Summary of World Broadcasts*, EE/D2511/G, pt. 3, January 16, 1996.

18. *FRUS*, vol. 2, 1950, 945.

19. John J. Jova, interview by author, January 13, 1989.

20. Kano Tsutomu, "Why the Search for Identity?" in Japan Center for International Exchange, *Silent Power*, 8, 9.

21. Leo J. Moser, "Cross-Cultural Dimensions: U.S.-Japan," in Diane B. Bendahmane and Leo Moser, eds., *Toward a Better Understanding: U.S.-Japan Relations* (Washington, D.C.: Foreign Service Institute, 1986), 22.

22. I. M. Destler et al., *Managing an Alliance: The Politics of U.S.-Japanese Relations* (Washington: Brookings Institution, 1976), 12–23.

23. Robert Angel, *Meeting the Japanese Challenge, 1969–1971: Balance-of-Payments Problems Force the Nixon Administration to Act*, Pew Program in Case Teaching and Writing in International Affairs, case 135, August 1988, 13–14.

24. *Washington Post*, November 19, 1993.

25. As reported in *U.S. News and World Report*, August 13, 1954.

26. Account based on interview with former State Department official. Also see U.S. Congress, House Committee on Appropriations, *Military Construction Appropriations for 1982: Hearings before the Subcommittee on Military Construction Appropriations*, 97th Cong., 1st sess., 1981, pt. 5 (Washington, D.C.: U.S. Government Printing Office, 1981).

27. William B. Quandt, *The United States and Egypt* (Washington, D.C.: Brookings Institution, 1990), 33.

28. Kissinger, *White House Years*, 326.

29. See Destler et al., *Managing an Alliance*, 23–25.

30. *FBIS, East Asia*, April 15, 1996, 12–13; *Washington Post*, April 16, 1996.

31. *FRUS*, vol. 6, pt. 2, 1951, 2142, 2153.

32. *FRUS*, vol. 11, 1952–54, 1710–1711, 1714–1715.

33. John Kenneth Galbraith, *Ambassador's Journal: A Personal Account of the Kennedy Years* (Boston: Houghton Mifflin, 1969), 393, 419, 423–424.

34. Robert F. Goheen, interview by author, April 6, 1989; Norman D. Palmer, *The United States and India: The Dimensions of Influence* (New York: Praeger, 1984), 234–235.

35. Dennis Kux, *India and the United States: Estranged Democracies* (Washington, D.C.: National Defense University Press, 1992), 440–441.

36. *Wall Street Journal*, July 21, 1992.

37. Associated Press, May 6, 1996.

38. *New York Times*, October 24, 1995; *Los Angeles Times*, October 25, 1995.

39. *Los Angeles Times,* March 19, 1996.

40. Surya Prakash Sinha, "The Axiology of the International Bill of Human Rights," in Pace University School of Law, *Yearbook of International Law* 1 (1989): 26.

41. Ibid., 28, 55.

42. Hermann F. Eilts, interview by author, October 17, 1988.

43. Ismail Fahmy, *Negotiating for Peace in the Middle East* (Baltimore: Johns Hopkins University Press, 1983), 188.

44. *Time,* October 21, 1985.

45. *Washington Post*, February 12, 1995.

46. Ibid., December 27, 1995.

47. Ibid., November 21, 1993.

48. *FRUS,* vol. 14, pt. 1, 1952–54, 478, 474–475, 479–480, 1030; vol. 3, 1955–57, 7, 23, 64–65.

49. Young, *Negotiating with the Chinese Communists,* 322–323.

5. SETTING OUT THE PIECES

1. Zartman and Berman, *Practical Negotiator,* chaps. 3, 4, 5.

2. Daniel Druckman, "Stages, Turning Points, and Crises: Negotiating Military Base Rights, Spain and the United States," *Journal of Conflict Resolution* 30 (1986): 327–360.

3. See Masao Kunihiro, "The Japanese Language and Intercultural Communication," 58, 61, and Kinhide, "Cultural Premises of Japanese Diplomacy," 45–46, in Japan Center for International Exchange, *Silent Power.*

4. Kinhide, "Japanese Diplomacy," 43–45.

5. I. William Zartman, "Prenegotiation: Phases and Functions," in Janice Gross Stein, ed., *Getting to the Table* (Baltimore: Johns Hopkins University Press, 1989), 5.

6. Brian W. Tomlin, "The Stages of Prenegotiation: The Decision to Negotiate North American Free Trade," in Stein, *Getting to the Table,* 18–43.

7. Zartman, "Prenegotiation," 10.

8. Kinhide, "Japanese Diplomacy," 44.

9. Angel, "Meeting the Japanese Challenge," 34–37.

10. *Economist,* October 27, 1984.

11. David A. Ralston et al., "Eastern Values: A Comparison of Managers in the United States, Hong Kong, and the People's Republic of China," *Journal of Applied Psychology* 77 (1992): 664–671.

12. Chas Freeman, interview by author, February 16, 1996.

13. Paul H. Kreisberg, "China's Negotiating Behaviour," in Thomas W. Robinson and David Shambaugh, eds., *Chinese Foreign Policy: Theory and Practice* (Oxford: Clarendon Press, 1994), 459–460.

14. Solomon, *Chinese Political Negotiating Behavior*, 2.

15. Shultz, *Turmoil and Triumph*, 396.

16. Ibid., 10.

17. Zbigniew Brzezinski, *Power and Principle: Memoirs of the National Security Adviser, 1977–1981* (New York: Farrar, Strauss, Giroux, 1983), 227.

18. *FBIS, China*, December 11, 1989, 1–4; Harry Harding, *A Fragile Relationship* (Washington, D.C.: Brookings Institution, 1992), 257.

19. Fisher, *International Negotiation*, 30–31.

20. Thomas Mann, telephone interview by Lewis Rasmussen, March 6, 1989; Joseph Friedkin, telephone interview by Lewis Rasmussen, March 16, 1989.

21. James A. Baker III with Thomas M. DeFrank, *The Politics of Diplomacy* (New York: G. P. Putnam, 1995), 43, 608.

22. Charles Roh, interview by author, February 21, 1996.

23. Hermann F. Eilts, interview by author, August 19, 1985.

24. John S. Badeau, *The Middle East Remembered* (Washington, D.C.: Middle East Institute, 1983), 189.

25. Joseph S. Sisco, interview by author, August 14, 1985.

26. Jimmy Carter, *Keeping Faith: Memoirs of a President* (New York: Bantam Books, 1982), 418. Quoted in Janice Gross Stein, "Prenegotiation in the Arab-Israeli Conflict: The Paradoxes of Success and Failure," in *Getting to the Table*, 194.

27. Clement Henry Moore, "Clientelist Ideology and Political Change," in Ernest Gellner and John Waterbury, eds., *Patrons and Clients in Mediterranean Societies* (London: Duckworth, 1977), 255–273.

28. Cohen, *Culture and Conflict*, 63.

29. Henry A. Kissinger, *Years of Upheaval* (Boston: Little, Brown, 1982), 640.

30. Ibid., 694.

31. Carter, *Keeping Faith*, 284.

32. Cyrus Vance, *Hard Choices* (New York: Simon and Schuster, 1983), 175.

33. Fisher, *International Negotiation*, 18.

34. D. Zhang and K. Kuroda, "Beware of Japanese Negotiation Style: How to Negotiate with Japanese Companies," *Northwest Journal of International Law and Business* (1989): 199.

35. Michael K. Blaker, "Probe, Push, and Panic: The Japanese Tactical Style in International Negotiations," in Robert A. Scalapino, ed., *The Foreign Policy of Modern Japan* (Berkeley: University of California Press, 1977), 60–61.

36. Personal communication.

37. Blaker, "Probe, Push, and Panic," 59–60.

38. Christopher S. Wendel, "Into the Pressure Cooker: The Strategic Impediments Initiative," Program on Negotiation at Harvard Law School, Working Paper Series 92-6, 1992, 5.

39. Blaker, "Probe, Push, and Panic," 60.

40. Kissinger, *White House Years,* 330–331.

41. William Breer, interview by author, February 23, 1996.

42. Wendel, "Into the Pressure Cooker," 15, 27.

43. Thomas P. Bernstein, *The Negotiations to Normalize U.S.-China Relations,* Pew Program in Case Teaching and Writing in International Affairs, case 426, August 1988, 23.

44. Mann, telephone interview.

45. Larman C. Wilson, "The Settlement of Boundary Disputes: Mexico, the United States, and the International Boundary Commission," *International and Comparative Law Quarterly* 29 (1980): 49.

46. Herbert Brownell and Samuel D. Eaton, "The Colorado Salinity Problem with Mexico," *American Journal of International Law* 69 (1975): 255–271.

47. J. Manuel Cervera, "The Mexico–United States Free Trade Agreement: An Analysis of Pre-Negotiation," Program on Negotiation at Harvard Law School, Working Paper Series 92-7, February 1992, 21, 25.

48. Steven Lande, interview by author, January 27, 1989.

49. *FRUS,* vol. 11, 1946, 993–996.

50. Account based on Richard B. Craig, "Operation Intercept: The International Politics of Pressure," *Review of Politics* 42 (1980): 556–580.

51. Patrick Lucey, telephone interview by author, January 31, 1989.

52. Robert Wilcox, interview by author, January 27, 1989.

53. Janice Gross Stein, "Getting to the Table: The Triggers, Stages, Functions, and Consequences of Prenegotiation," in *Getting to the Table,* 257.

6. LET THE CONTEST COMMENCE

1. Michael W. Donnelly, "On Political Negotiation: America Pushes to Open Up Japan," *Pacific Affairs* 66 (1993): 345.

2. Wendel, "Into the Pressure Cooker," 16.

3. For example, see *Aviation Week and Space Technology,* January 23, 1995, 42.

4. *Aviation Week and Space Technology,* September 12, 1994, 58–59; *FBIS, East Asia,* December 1, 1995, 4.

5. *FBIS, East Asia,* December 1, 1995, 6.

6. Leo J. Moser, "Negotiating Style: Americans and Japanese," in Bendah-mane and Moser, *Toward a Better Understanding*, 43.

7. Daniel M. Kasper, *Holding over Tokyo: U.S.-Japan Air Service Negotiations*, Pew Program in Case Teaching and Writing in International Affairs, case 104, 1988, 5. Dr. Kasper served on the American delegation.

8. Kreisberg, "China's Negotiating Behaviour," 462.

9. Chas Freeman, interview by author, February 16, 1996.

10. Kazuo, "How the 'Inscrutables' Negotiate," 541.

11. Brzezinski, *Power and Principle*, 225.

12. Ibid.

13. Ibid.

14. Bernstein, "Negotiations to Normalize U.S.-China Relations," 30–31.

15. Angel, "Meeting the Japanese Challenge," 30.

16. Kimura, "Soviet and Japanese Negotiating Behavior," 48.

17. Destler et al., *Managing an Alliance*, 109.

18. Wendel, "Into the Pressure Cooker," 19.

19. Fisher, *International Negotiation*, 41.

20. *FRUS*, vol. 6, 1943, 611, 613–614, 615.

21. Herbert Brownell, interview by author, January 19, 1989. See also Brownell and Eaton, "Colorado Salinity Problem."

22. Adhip Chaudhuri, *The Mexican Debt Crisis, 1982*, Pew Program in Case Teaching and Writing in International Affairs, case 204, 1988, 1, 6–7.

23. Ibid., 9–11; Peter Wallison, interview by author, January 18, 1989.

24. Carter, *Keeping Faith*, 340–341.

25. Hermann F. Eilts, interview by author, October 17, 1988.

26. *FRUS*, vol. 6, 1951, pt. 2, 2127.

27. Chester Bowles, *Promises to Keep: My Years in Public Life, 1941–1969* (New York: Harper and Row, 1971), 526.

28. William J. Barnds, "India and America at Odds," *International Affairs* 49 (1973): 379.

29. See Nemi C. Jain, "Some Basic Cultural Patterns of India," in Larry A. Samovar and Richard E. Porter, eds., *Intercultural Communication: A Reader*, 4th ed. (Belmont, Calif.: Wadsworth, 1988), 107.

30. Phyllis J. Rolnick, "Charity, Trusteeship, and Social Change in India," *World Politics* 14 (1962): 439–460.

31. Bernard S. Cohn, *India: The Social Anthropology of a Civilization* (Englewood Cliffs, N.J.: Prentice Hall, 1971), 131–132.

32. Paul Kreisberg, interview by author, February 5, 1989.

33. R. V. R. Chandrasekhara Rao, "Searching for a Mature Relationship," *Round Table* 263 (1976): 249–260.

34. Reuters World Service, New Delhi, May 12, 1995.

35. Kazuo, "How the 'Inscrutables' Negotiate," 532–534.

36. Solomon, *Chinese Political Negotiating Behavior,* 11.

37. Vance, *Hard Choices,* 82.

38. George T. Crane, *The Sino-U.S. Textile Trade Agreement of 1983: The Anatomy of a Trade Battle,* Pew Program in Case Teaching and Writing in International Affairs, case 109, 1988, 2–5.

39. Shenkar and Ronen, "Cultural Context of Negotiations," 270.

40. *Los Angeles Times,* June 13, 1996.

41. Doris Meisner, interview by author, January 25, 1989.

42. Timothy Bennett, interview by author, January 27, 1989.

43. Alan Riding, *Distant Neighbors: A Portrait of the Mexicans* (New York: Vintage Books, 1986), 281.

44. George W. Grayson, *The United States and Mexico: Patterns of Influence* (New York: Praeger, 1984), 81–82.

45. Edmund Glenn et al., "Cultural Styles of Persuasion," *International Journal of Intercultural Relations* 1 (1977): 52–66.

46. Solomon, *Chinese Political Negotiating Behavior,* 8.

47. Pye, *Chinese Commercial Negotiating Style,* 26–27, 41.

48. Ibid.

49. Young, *Negotiating with the Chinese Communists,* 166, 178.

50. Quoted in Solomon, *Chinese Political Negotiating Behavior,* 19.

51. Kissinger, *White House Years,* 745–746.

52. Mohamed Hassanein Heikal, *The Cairo Documents* (New York: Doubleday, 1973), 238.

53. Kissinger, *Years of Upheaval,* 215.

54. Ibid., 823, 825.

55. U.S. Department of State, *Bulletin* 71(1974): 92–93.

56. Eilts, interview.

57. William B. Quandt, *Camp David: Peacemaking and Politics* (Washington, D.C.: Brookings Institution, 1986), 136.

58. Charles Roh, interview by author, February 21, 1996.

59. Thomas Mann, telephone interview by Lewis Rasmussen, March 6, 1989.

60. *Washington Post,* September 6, 1979.

61. Account based on George W. Grayson, "The U.S.-Mexican Natural Gas Deal and What We Can Learn from It," *Orbis* 24 (1980): 573–607; and Julius Katz, interview by author, January 11, 1989.

62. Kinhide, "Japanese Diplomacy," 46.

7. ON TACTICS AND PLAYERS

1. I. William Zartman, "Negotiation as a Joint Decision-Making Process," *Journal of Conflict Resolution* 21 (1977): 619–638.

2. William B. Quandt, "A Strong Sense of National Identity," in Hans Binnendijk, ed., *National Negotiating Styles* (Washington, D.C.: Foreign Service Institute, 1987), 118–120.

3. Fuad I. Khuri, "The Etiquette of Bargaining in the Middle East," *American Anthropologist* 70 (1968): 700.

4. *New York Times*, June 17, 1996.

5. Kissinger, *White House Years*, 747.

6. Kissinger, *Years of Upheaval*, 829, 832.

7. Fisher, *International Negotiation*, 48.

8. Timothy Bennett, interview by author, January 27, 1989.

9. Adolfo Aguilar, interview by author, December 21, 1988.

10. *FRUS*, vol. 6, 1955–57, 707–708.

11. Ibid., 739–741. Agreement in *U.S. Treaties and Other International Agreements (UST)*, (1957), vol. 8, 306–316.

12. Daniel Druckman et al., "Cultural Differences in Bargaining Behavior: India, Argentina, and the United States," *Journal of Conflict Resolution* 20 (1976): 413–452.

13. *FRUS*, vol. 11, 1952–54, 1708, 1709.

14. Ibid., 1722, 1723.

15. Ibid., 1735.

16. Nathaniel B. Thayer and Stephen E. Weiss, "Japan: The Changing Logic of a Former Minor Power," in Binnendijk, *National Negotiating Styles*, 67–68.

17. Moser, "Negotiating Style," 46.

18. Destler et al., *Managing an Alliance*, 106.

19. *Los Angeles Times*, July 31, 1994.

20. Blaker, "Probe, Push, and Panic," 81.

21. Timothy J. C. O'Shea, *The U.S.-Japan Semiconductor Problem*, Pew Program in Case Teaching and Writing in International Affairs, case 139, September 1995, 25–30.

22. Senator Mike Mansfield, interview by author, February 15, 1996.

23. Thomas P. Rohlen, "Three Snapshots of Japan," in Bendahmane and Moser, *Toward a Better Understanding,* 18.

24. O'Shea, "Semiconductor Problem," 64.

25. Solomon, *Chinese Political Negotiating Behavior,* 6.

26. Shenkar and Ronen, "Cultural Context of Negotiations," 270.

27. Chas Freeman, interview by author, February 16, 1996.

28. Young, *Negotiating with the Chinese Communists,* 389.

29. Vance, *Hard Choices,* 79, 81–82.

30. Account based on *FRUS,* vol. 3, 1955–57, 9, 14.

31. Ibid., 76–77.

32. Ibid., 52, 59.

33. Ibid., 85, 86.

34. Baker, *Politics of Diplomacy,* 111–114.

35. Nancy Adler, *International Dimensions of Organizational Behavior* (Boston: Kent, 1986), chap. 6; Martin W. Simpson III, "Cultural Influences on Foreign Policy," in Charles F. Hermann, Charles W. Kegley, Jr., and James N. Rosenau, eds., *New Directions in the Study of Foreign Policy* (Boston: Allen and Unwin, 1987), 384–405.

36. David D. Newsom, comments on original ms. of this book, March 1997.

37. John McDonald at Jerusalem workshop, February 10, 1997.

38. Mike Smith, interview by author, February 20, 1996.

39. Gerard Bowers, interview by Frederick Williams, March 11, 1996.

40. Charles Roh, interview by author, February 21, 1996.

41. Lucius Battle, interview by author, August 13, 1985.

42. Hermann F. Eilts, interview by author, October 17, 1988.

43. Fahmy, *Negotiating for Peace,* 153, 52, 75.

44. Quandt, *Camp David,* 116.

45. Shultz, *Turmoil and Triumph,* 392–393.

46. Reuters, January 20, 1996.

47. Riding, *Distant Neighbors,* 474.

48. Grayson, "U.S.-Mexican Natural Gas Deal," 582, 586–588.

49. Baker, *Politics of Diplomacy,* 305–328.

50. *Los Angeles Times,* July 8, 1996.

51. O. P. Dwivedi and R. B. Jain, "Bureaucratic Morality in India," *International Political Science Review* 9 (1988): 208–209.

52. *Washington Post,* August 21, 1994.

53. N. Ram, "India's Nuclear Policy: A Case Study in the Flaws and Futility of Non-Proliferation," *IDSA Journal* 14 (1982): 504.

54. Paul Kreisberg, interview by author, February 5, 1989.

55. Eilts, interview.

56. Kissinger, *White House Years*, 1056.

57. Vance, *Hard Choices*, 117.

58. Chihiro Hosoya, "Characteristics of the Foreign Policy Decision-Making System in Japan," *World Politics* 26 (1974): 353–370.

59. Bendahmane and Moser, *Toward a Better Understanding*, 40.

60. Destler et al., *Managing an Alliance*, 15.

61. Kissinger, *White House Years*, 336–339.

62. Ellis S. Krauss, *Under Construction: U.S.-Japan Negotiations to Open Japan's Construction Markets to American Firms, 1985–1988*, Pew Program in Case Teaching and Writing in International Affairs, case 145, 1989, 25–26.

8. SOUNDS, SIGNALS, SILENCE

1. Baker, *Politics of Diplomacy*, 107.

2. Quoted in Kunihiro, "Japanese Language," 60–61.

3. Roger W. Benjamin, "Images of Conflict Resolution and Social Control: American and Japanese Attitudes toward the Adversary System," *Journal of Conflict Resolution* 19 (1975): 1, 23–37.

4. Interview by author with senior State Department official.

5. Richard Solomon (who served as assistant secretary of state for East Asian and Pacific Affairs, 1989–92), interview by author, February 26, 1996.

6. Interview by author, February 20, 1996.

7. *Chicago Tribune*, August 6, 1990.

8. Franklin L. Lavin, "Negotiating with the Chinese," *Foreign Affairs* 73 (1994): 19.

9. Ibid., 17, 20.

10. Joseph Friedkin, telephone interview by Lewis Rasmussen, March 16, 1989.

11. Herbert Brownell, interview by author, January 19, 1989.

12. Badeau, *Middle East Remembered*, 214.

13. Ibid., 75–77.

14. Lucius Battle, interview by author, August 13, 1985.

15. Interview by author with State Department official.

16. Palmer, *United States and India*, 22–23.

17. *FRUS*, vol. 11, 1952–54, 1645.

18. Ibid., vol. 8, 1955–57, 278.

19. Dick Wilson, "Where Trade Meets Culture: The United States, Europe, and Japan," *Pacific Review* 2 (1989): 279.

20. Clyde Haberman, "Japanese Have a Way (Out) with Words," *International Herald Tribune*, March 26–27, 1988.

21. *Economist*, September 14, 1985.

22. Kunihiro, "Japanese Language," 64.

23. Quandt, "National Identity," 119.

24. Interview by author with former State Department official.

25. Interview by author with State Department official.

26. Quandt, "National Identity," 119.

27. Galbraith, *Ambassador's Journal*, 385.

28. Craig, "Operation Intercept," 559–560, 564–565.

29. Masao Kunihiro, "U.S.-Japan Communications," in Henry Rosovsky, ed., *Discord in the Pacific: Challenges to the American-Japanese Alliance* (Washington, D.C.: Columbia Books, for the American Assembly, 1972), 167.

30. Krauss, "Under Construction," 40.

31. Richard Parker, interview by author, October 25, 1988.

32. See Bernard Reich, *Quest for Peace* (New Brunswick, N.J.: Transaction Books, 1977), 93.

33. Quandt, *Camp David*, 132, 92, 115.

34. Ibid., 124.

35. Harold Saunders, interview by author, October 27, 1988.

36. Fahmy, *Negotiating for Peace*, 206.

37. *FRUS*, vol. 11, 1952–54, 1738–39. Definite and indefinite articles restored to telegraphic style of original text.

38. Palmer, *United States and India*, 24.

39. Kissinger, *White House Years*, 878–882.

40. Richard M. Nixon, *The Memoirs of Richard Nixon* (London: Arrow Books, 1978), 525.

41. Oriana Fallaci, *Interview with History* (Boston: Houghton Mifflin, 1976), 161.

42. Kissinger, *White House Years*, 749.

43. Ibid., 779.

44. Ibid., 1073.

45. Ibid., 1061–1062.

46. I. Eibl-Eibesfeldt, "Similarities and Differences between Cultures in Expressive Movements," in R. A. Hinde, ed., *Nonverbal Communication* (Cambridge: Cambridge University Press, 1972), 297–314; P. Ekman, "Universals and Cultural Differences in Facial Expressions of Emotion," in J. Cole, ed., *Nebraska*

Symposium on Motivation, 1971 (Lincoln: University of Nebraska Press, 1971), 201–283; Aaron Wolfgang, ed., *Nonverbal Behavior: Perspectives, Applications, Intercultural Insights* (Lewiston, N.Y.: C. J. Hogrefe, 1984).

47. Fahmy, *Negotiating for Peace*, 42, 45, 48, 73, 157, 207, 237.

48. James W. Symington, *The Stately Game* (New York: Macmillan, 1971), 27.

49. Charles Thayer, *Diplomat* (London: Michael Joseph, 1960), 217.

50. Kissinger, *White House Years*, 699.

51. Ibid., 750.

52. Alexander M. Haig, *Caveat: Realism, Reagan, and Foreign Policy* (New York: Macmillan, 1984), 206, 207, 208.

53. *New York Times*, March 12, 1994.

54. Ibid., May 29, 1994.

55. *FBIS, China*, March 10, 1994.

56. Ibid., March 8, 1994.

57. *New York Times*, March 15, 1994.

58. *Washington Post*, March 13, 1994.

59. Bowles, *Promises to Keep*, 498.

60. Hermann F. Eilts, interview by author, August 19, 1985.

61. Patrick Lucey, telephone interview by author, January 31, 1989.

62. Kissinger, *Years of Upheaval*, 696; Shenkar and Ronen, "Cultural Context of Negotiations," 267.

63. Baker, *Politics of Diplomacy*, 106, 109–110.

64. Kunihiro, "U.S.-Japan Communications," 163; Bendahmane and Moser, *Toward a Better Understanding*, 17.

65. Umesao Tadao, "Escape from Cultural Isolation," in Japan Center for International Exchange, *Silent Power*, 28.

66. *Economist*, September 14, 1985.

67. *Wall Street Journal*, February 10, 1994.

68. Galbraith, *Ambassador's Journal*, 474.

69. Ibid., 406.

70. Kissinger, *White House Years*, 848; Dennis Kux, *India and the United States: Estranged Democracies* (Washington, D.C., National Defense University Press), 192, 395.

9. UNDER PRESSURE

1. Zartman and Berman, *Practical Negotiator*, 87–88.

2. Daniel Druckman, Jo L. Husbands, and Karin Johnston, "Turning Points in the INF Negotiations," *Negotiation Journal* 7 (1991): 56–60.

3. David D. Newsom, comments on original ms. of this book, March 1997.

4. Hermann F. Eilts, interview by author, August 19, 1985.

5. *Business Times*, February 17, 1994; *Washington Post*, February 18, 1994; *Wall Street Journal*, May 25, 1994.

6. John J. Jova, interview by author, January 13, 1989.

7. U.S. Congress, Senate Committee on Foreign Relations, *Situation in Mexico: Hearings before the Subcommittee on Western Hemisphere Affairs*, 99th Cong., 2d sess., 13 May, 17 June, and 26 June, 1986 (Washington, D.C.: U.S. Government Printing Office, 1986), 81, 89, 90–91, 49.

8. *Washington Post*, August 14, 1980, 32–33.

9. Cohen, "Egyptian-American Diplomatic Relations," 34–35.

10. John S. Badeau, *The American Approach to the Arab World* (New York: Harper and Row, 1968), 73.

11. Heikal, *Cairo Documents*, 204.

12. Bowles, *Promises to Keep*, 491.

13. Galbraith, *Ambassador's Journal*, 406, 447.

14. Ibid., 493, 494.

15. Vincent A. Auger, *Human Rights and Trade: The Clinton Administration and China*, Pew Case Studies in International Affairs, no. 168 (Washington, D.C.: Georgetown Institute for the Study of Diplomacy, 1995).

16. Chas Freeman, interview by author, February 16, 1996.

17. *Los Angeles Times*, December 17, 1994.

18. *Los Angeles Times*, March 6, 1995.

19. Ibid.

20. Diane Perry, "The United States, China, and Negotiations over 'Most Favored Nation' Status in 1994," Program on Negotiation at Harvard Law School, Working Paper Series 95-2, 1995, 8.

21. *Washington Post*, May 12, 1994.

22. *Atlanta Constitution*, January 9, 1992.

23. *Washington Post*, August 3, 1992.

24. *Los Angeles Times*, March 13, 1994; *Financial Times*, March 14, 1994.

25. *Crain's Chicago Business*, May 29, 1995.

26. *Wall Street Journal*, October 3, 1994; *Los Angeles Times*, October 2, 1994; *Financial Times*, October 12, 1994.

27. Richard Solomon, interview by author, February 26, 1996.

28. *Chicago Tribune*, August 7, 1995.

29. Newsom, comments on original ms.

30. Young, *Negotiating with the Chinese Communists*, 352.

31. Ibid.

32. *FRUS*, vol. 3, 1955–57, 46, 62, 64, 73–74, 75. Definite and indefinite articles restored.

33. Account based on Bernstein, "Negotiations to Normalize U.S.-China Relations."

34. See Kreisberg, "China's Negotiating Behaviour," 473; Lanvin, "Negotiating with the Chinese," 19–20.

35. Baker, *Politics of Diplomacy*, 590–594.

36. Timothy Bennett, interview by author, January 27, 1989.

37. Gerard Bowers, interview by Frederick Williams, March 11, 1996.

38. Newsom, comments on original ms.

39. *Washington Post*, September 3, 1992.

40. Joseph Friedkin, telephone interview by Lewis Rasmussen, March 16, 1989.

41. Grayson, "U.S.-Mexican Natural Gas Deal," 600–601.

42. Julius Katz, interview by author, January 11, 1989.

43. Kasper, "Holding Over Tokyo," sequel A, 1–2.

44. Walter Bollinger, interview by author, February 15, 1996.

45. *Aviation Daily, Journal of Commerce*, December 5, 1995.

46. Christopher J. McMullen, *Resolution of the Yemen Crisis, 1963: A Case Study in Mediation* (Washington, D.C.: Institute for the Study of Diplomacy, 1980), 32–37; Badeau, *Middle East Remembered*, 212.

10. FACE AND FORM

1. Stella Ting-Toomey and Mark Cole, "Intergroup Diplomatic Communication: A Face-Negotiation Perspective," in Felipe Korzenny and Stella Ting-Toomey, eds., *Communicating for Peace: Diplomacy and Negotiation* (Newbury Park, Calif.: Sage, 1990), 83.

2. Ibid., 78.

3. Jesus Silva de Herzog, interview by author, August 7, 1996.

4. Angel, "Meeting the Japanese Challenge," 45–46.

5. H. C. Hu, "The Chinese Concept of Face," *American Anthropologist* 44 (1944): 45–64.

6. Kissinger, *White House Years*, 751, 759, 781–782. On the concept of face giving, see Stella Ting-Toomey, "Intercultural Conflict Styles: A Face-Negotiation Theory," in Young Yun Kim and William B. Gudykunst, eds., *Theories in Intercultural Communication* (Beverly Hills, Calif.: Sage, 1988), 213–238.

7. Robert F. Goheen, interview by author, April 6, 1989; interview by author with State Department official.

8. Interview by author with State Department official.

9. Shultz, *Turmoil and Triumph*, 74–75.

10. Kissinger, *Years of Upheaval*, 641–654.

11. Robert Sayre, interview by author, January 30, 1989.

12. Roger S. Leeds and Gale Thompson, *The 1982 Mexican Debt Negotiations*, FPI Case Studies 4 (Washington, D.C.: Johns Hopkins Foreign Policy Institute, 1987), 25; Chaudhuri, "Mexican Debt Crisis," 10–11.

13. *Washington Post*, September 22, 1979; Herbert Brownell, interview by author, January 19, 1989.

14. I am grateful for several of the points in this paragraph to David D. Newsom.

15. Ibid.

16. Charles Roh, interview by author, February 21, 1996.

17. *FRUS*, vol. 4, 1952–54, 1327, 1328, 1330, 1351.

18. Interview by author with State Department official.

19. *Washington Post*, February 22, 1995.

20. Kissinger, *Years of Upheaval*, 825.

21. Interview by author with State Department official.

22. U.S. Congress, *Military Construction Appropriations*, 133.

23. Quandt, *The United States and Egypt*, 33 n. 28.

24. Galbraith, *Ambassador's Journal*, 439, 463, 476, 478.

25. Stanley B. Lubman, "Negotiations in China: Observations of a Lawyer," in Robert A. Kapp, ed., *Communicating with China* (Yarmouth, Maine: Intercultural Press, 1983), 60–61, 64–65, 67–68.

26. Richard Solomon, interview by author, August 19, 1996.

27. *U.S. Department of State Dispatch*, 3, August 17, 1992, 660, emphasis added; *New York Times*, August 8, 1992.

28. Kunihiro, "U.S.-Japan Communications," 159, 166.

29. Zhang and Kuroda, "Beware of Japanese Negotiation Style," 206.

30. Richard Solomon, interview by author, February 26, 1996.

31. *U.S. Department of State Dispatch*, 4, July 12, 1993, 494–496.

32. *Wall Street Journal*, July 15, 1993.

33. *Wall Street Journal*, July 13, 1993.

34. *Washington Post*, April 11, 1996; *Sacramento Bee*, July 6, 1996.

35. Mike Smith, interview by author, February 20, 1996.

11. When Is a Deal a Deal?

1. See, for example, I. William Zartman, "The Analysis of Negotiation," in I. William Zartman, ed., *The 50% Solution* (New Haven, Conn.: Yale University

Press, 1976), 7; Thomas R. Colosi, *On and Off the Record: Colosi on Negotiation* (Dubuque, Iowa: Kendall/Hunt, 1993), 1.

2. Arild Underdal, "The Outcomes of Negotiation," in Victor A. Kremenyuk, ed., *International Negotiation* (San Francisco: Jossey-Bass, 1991), 102.

3. Lavin, "Negotiating with the Chinese," 21–22. See also *Electronic Buyers' News*, May 27, 1996.

4. Mike Smith, interview by author, February 20, 1996.

5. The account is based on James Reardon-Anderson, *U.S.-China Nuclear Cooperative Agreement*, Pew Program in Case Teaching and Writing in International Affairs, case 110, 1989.

6. *Forbes*, June 4, 1984, 153.

7. Daniel Horner and Paul Leventhal, "The U.S.-China Nuclear Agreement," *Fletcher Forum* (winter 1987):113.

8. Reardon-Anderson, *U.S.-China Nuclear Cooperative Agreement*, 3.

9. Harry Harding, *A Fragile Relationship* (Washington, D.C.: Brookings Institution, 1992), 277; *Washington Post*, April 20, 1991.

10. Baker, *Politics of Diplomacy*, 589, 593–594; *Atlantic Journal and Constitution*, November 18, 1991.

11. *Washington Post*, February 9, 1992.

12. *Washington Post*, February 2, 22, 1992.

13. *New York Times*, August 28, 1993.

14. *Washington Post*, May 16, 1996.

15. Hiroshi Wagatsuma and Arthur Rosett, "Cultural Attitudes toward Contract Law: Japan and the United States Compared," *UCLA Pacific Basin Law Journal* 2 (1983): 83, 84.

16. Kinhide, "Japanese Diplomacy," 42–43.

17. Donald S. Abelson, "Experiencing the Japanese Negotiating Style," in Bendahmane and Moser, *Toward a Better Understanding*, 54, 56.

18. Donnelly, "On Political Negotiation," 3, 346.

19. *New York Times*, April 20, 1996.

20. *New York Times*, May 15, 1994.

21. *Los Angeles Times*, May 9, 20, 1994.

22. *Dallas Morning News*, January 29, 1995.

23. Robert Gelbard, testimony to the *Hearing of the House Western Hemisphere Affairs Subcommittee of the House International Relations Committee*, "Certification for Drug-Producing Countries in Latin America," March 7, 1996.

24. *New York Times*, May 2, 1996.

25. Robert Axelrod, *The Evolution of Cooperation* (New York: Basic Books, 1984).

26. Walter Bollinger, USAID director India (1990–95), interview by author, February 15, 1996.

27. The following account is based on *New York Times*, April 5, 1995.

28. *New York Times*, April 5, 1995.

29. Ibid.

30. Henry Bassford, USAID director Egypt (1991–94), interview by author, February 19, 1996.

12. In Search of Harmony

1. Roger Fisher and William Ury, *Getting to Yes* (Boston: Houghton Mifflin, 1981). Articles in *Christian Science Monitor,* October 15, 1990; *Boston Globe*, November 4, 1990; *Washington Post*, December 9, 1990; and *Atlantic Journal and Constitution*, December 16, 1990.

2. *Washington Post*, February 13, 1995.

3. Arturo Valenzuela, interview by author, February 16, 1996.

4. House Committee on National Security Staff Report, "The Khobar Towers Bombing Incident" (unpublished report, August 14, 1996); *Los Angeles Times*, June 27, 29, 30, July 2, 1996.

5. *Washington Post*, September 1, 1981; Mike Mansfield, interview by author, February 15, 1996. Also see Hiroshi Wagatsuma and Arthur Rosett, "The Implications of Apology: Law and Culture in Japan and the United States," *Law and Society Review* 20 (1986): 461–498.

6. Kissinger, *White House Years*, 1492.

Bibliography

Abelson, Donald S. "Experiencing the Japanese Negotiating Style." In Diane B. Bendahmane and Leo Moser, eds., *Toward a Better Understanding: U.S.-Japan Relations*. Washington, D.C.: Foreign Service Institute, 1986.

Adelman, Mara B., and Lustig, Myron W. "Intercultural Communication Problems as Perceived by Saudi Arabian and American Managers." *International Journal of Intercultural Relations* 5 (1981): 349–363.

Adler, Nancy. *International Dimensions of Organizational Behavior*. Boston: Kent, 1986.

Angel, Robert. *Meeting the Japanese Challenge, 1969–1971: Balance-of-Payments Problems Force the Nixon Administration to Act*. Pew Program in Case Teaching and Writing in International Affairs. Case 135, August 1988.

Auger, Vincent A. *Human Rights and Trade: The Clinton Administration and China*. Pew Case Studies in International Affairs, no. 168. Washington, D.C.: Georgetown Institute for the Study of Diplomacy, 1995.

Avruch, Kevin, and Black, Peter W. "The Culture Question and Conflict Resolution." *Peace and Change* 16 (1991): 27–30.

———. "Conflict Resolution in Intercultural Settings: Problems and Prospects." In D. Sandole and H. van der Merwe, eds., *Conflict Resolution Theory and Practice: Integration and Application*. Manchester: Manchester University Press, 1993.

Badeau, John S. *The American Approach to the Arab World*. New York: Harper and Row, 1968.

———. *The Middle East Remembered*. Washington, D.C.: Middle East Institute, 1983.

Baker, James A. III, with DeFrank, Thomas M. *The Politics of Diplomacy*. New York: G. P. Putnam, 1995.

Barnds, William J. "India and America at Odds." *International Affairs* 49 (1973): 371–384.

Bendahmane, Diane B., and Moser, Leo, eds. *Toward a Better Understanding: U.S.-Japan Relations*. Washington, D.C.: Foreign Service Institute, 1986.

Benjamin, Roger W. "Images of Conflict Resolution and Social Control: American and Japanese Attitudes toward the Adversary System." *Journal of Conflict Resolution* 19 (1975): 123–137.

Bernstein, Thomas P. *The Negotiations to Normalize U.S.-China Relations*. Pew Program in Case Teaching and Writing in International Affairs. Case 426, August 1988.

Binnendijk, Hans, ed. *National Negotiating Styles*. Washington, D.C.: Foreign Service Institute, 1987.

Blaker, Michael K. *Japanese International Negotiating Style*. New York: Columbia University Press, 1977.

———. "Probe, Push, and Panic: The Japanese Tactical Style in International Negotiations." In Robert A. Scalapino, ed., *The Foreign Policy of Modern Japan*. Berkeley: University of California Press, 1977.

Bowles, Chester. *Promises to Keep: My Years in Public Life, 1941–1969*. New York: Harper and Row, 1971.

Brownell, Herbert, and Eaton, Samuel D. "The Colorado Salinity Problem with Mexico." *American Journal of International Law* 49 (1975): 225–271.

Brzezinski, Zbigniew. *Power and Principle: Memoirs of the National Security Adviser 1977–1981*. New York: Farrar, Strauss, Giroux, 1983.

Burns, William J. *Economic Aid and American Policy toward Egypt, 1955–1981*. Albany: State University of New York Press, 1985.

Carter, Jimmy. *Keeping Faith: Memoirs of a President*. New York: Bantam Books, 1982.

Casse, Pierre, and Deol, Surinder. *Managing Intercultural Negotiations*. Yarmouth, Maine: Intercultural Press, 1985.

Chaudhuri, Adhip. *The Mexican Debt Crisis, 1982*. Pew Program in Case Teaching and Writing in International Affairs. Case 204, 1988.

Cohen, Herb. *You Can Negotiate Anything*. Secaucus, N.J.: Lyle Stuart, 1980.

Cohen, Raymond. "International Communication: An Intercultural Approach." *Cooperation and Conflict* 22 (1987): 63–80.

———. "Problems of Intercultural Communication in Egyptian-American Diplomatic Relations." *International Journal of Intercultural Relations* 11 (1987): 29–47.

————. *Culture and Conflict in Egyptian-Israeli Relations: A Dialogue of the Deaf.* Bloomington: Indiana University Press, 1990.

Cohn, Bernard S. *India: The Social Anthropology of a Civilization.* Englewood Cliffs, N.J.: Prentice Hall, 1971.

Colosi, Thomas R. *On and Off the Record: Colosi on Negotiation.* Dubuque, Iowa: Kendall/Hunt, 1993.

Craig, Richard B. "Operation Intercept: The International Politics of Pressure." *Review of Politics* 42 (1980): 556–580.

Crane, George T. *The Sino-U.S. Textile Trade Agreement of 1983: The Anatomy of a Trade Battle.* Pew Program in Case Teaching and Writing in International Affairs. Case 109, 1988.

Destler, I. M.; Sato, Hideo; Clapp, Priscilla; and Fukui, Haruhiro. *Managing an Alliance: The Politics of U.S.-Japanese Relations.* Washington, D.C.: Brookings Institution, 1976.

Donnelly, Michael W. "On Political Negotiation: America Pushes to Open Up Japan." *Pacific Affairs* 66 (1993).

Druckman, Daniel. "Stages, Turning Points, and Crises: Negotiating Military Base Rights, Spain and the United States." *Journal of Conflict Resolution* 30 (1986): 327–360.

Druckman, Daniel; Benton, A. A.; Ali, F.; and Bagur, J. S. "Cultural Differences in Bargaining Behavior: India, Argentina and the United States." *Journal of Conflict Resolution* 20 (1976): 413–448.

Druckman, Daniel; Husbands, Jo L.; and Johnston, Karin. "Turning Points in the INF Negotiations." *Negotiation Journal* 7 (1991): 56–60.

Dwivedi, O. P., and Jain, R. B. "Bureaucratic Morality in India." *International Political Science Review* 9 (1988): 205–214.

Eibl-Eibesfeldt, I. "Similarities and Differences between Cultures in Expressive Movements." In R. A. Hinde, ed., *Nonverbal Communication.* Cambridge: Cambridge University Press, 1972.

Ekman, P. "Universals and Cultural Differences in Facial Expressions of Emotion." In J. Cole, ed., *Nebraska Symposium on Motivation, 1971.* Lincoln: University of Nebraska Press, 1971.

Fahmy, Ismail. *Negotiating for Peace in the Middle East.* Baltimore: Johns Hopkins University Press, 1983.

Fallaci, Oriana. *Interview with History.* Boston: Houghton Mifflin, 1976.

Fisher, Glen. *International Negotiation: A Cross-Cultural Perspective.* Yarmouth, Maine: Intercultural Press, 1980.

————. *Mindsets.* Yarmouth, Maine: Intercultural Press, 1988.

Fisher, Roger, and Ury, William. *Getting to Yes.* New York: Penguin, 1983.

Foster, Dean Allen. *Bargaining Across Borders: How to Negotiate Business Successfully Anywhere in the World.* New York: McGraw-Hill, 1992.

Galbraith, John Kenneth. *Ambassador's Journal: A Personal Account of the Kennedy Years.* Boston: Houghton Mifflin, 1969.

Glenn, Edmund; Wikmeyer, D.; and Stevenson, K. "Cultural Styles of Persuasion." *International Journal of Intercultural Relations* 1 (1977): 52–66.

Graham, John L. "The Influence of Culture on the Process of Business Negotiations." *Journal of International Business Studies* 16 (1985): 81–96.

Grayson, George W. "The U.S.-Mexican Natural Gas Deal and What We Can Learn from It." *Orbis* 24 (1980): 573–607.

———. *The United States and Mexico: Patterns of Influence.* New York: Praeger, 1984.

Haig, Alexander M. *Caveat: Realism, Reagan, and Foreign Policy.* New York: Macmillan, 1984.

Hall, Edward T. *The Silent Language.* New York: Anchor Books, 1973.

———. *Beyond Culture.* New York: Anchor Books, 1976.

Harding, Harry. *A Fragile Relationship.* Washington, D.C.: Brookings Institution, 1992.

Heikal, Mohamed Hassanein. *The Cairo Documents.* New York: Doubleday, 1973.

Hendriks, E. C. "Research on International Business Negotiations: An Introduction." In C. Braecke and H. Cuyckens, eds., *Business Communication in Multilingual Europe: Supply and Demand.* Antwerp: ENCoDe/UFSIA, 1991.

Hoffman, Stanley. *Gulliver's Troubles, or the Setting of American Foreign Policy.* New York: McGraw-Hill, 1968.

Hofstede, Geert. *Culture's Consequences.* Beverly Hills, Calif.: Sage, 1980.

Horner, Daniel, and Leventhal, Paul. "The U.S.-China Nuclear Agreement." *Fletcher Forum* 11 (1987): 105–122.

Hosoya, Chihiro. "Characteristics of the Foreign Policy Decision-Making System in Japan." *World Politics* 26 (1974): 353–370.

Hu, H. C. "The Chinese Concept of Face." *American Anthropologist* 44 (1944): 45–64.

Japan Center for International Exchange, ed. *The Silent Power: Japan's Identity and World Role.* Tokyo: Simul Press, 1976.

Kamel, Mohamed Ibrahim. *The Camp David Accords.* London: KPI, 1986.

Kapoor, Ashok. *International Business Negotiations: A Study in India.* New York: New York University Press, 1970.

Kasper, Daniel M. *Holding over Tokyo: U.S.-Japan Air Service Negotiations.* Pew Program in Case Teaching and Writing in International Affairs. Case 104, 1988.

Kazuo, Ogura. "How the 'Inscrutables' Negotiate with the 'Inscrutables': Chinese Negotiating Tactics *vis-à-vis* the Japanese." *China Quarterly* 79 (1979): 529–552.

Khuri, Fuad I. "The Etiquette of Bargaining in the Middle East." *American Anthropologist* 70 (1968): 698–706.

Kimura, Hiroshi. "Soviet and Japanese Negotiating Behavior: The Spring 1977 Fisheries Talks." *Orbis* 24 (1980): 43–67.

Kinhide, Mushakoji. "The Cultural Premises of Japanese Diplomacy." In Japan Center for International Exchange, ed., *The Silent Power: Japan's Identity and World Role.* Tokyo: Simul Press, 1976.

Kissinger, Henry A. *The White House Years.* Boston: Little, Brown, 1979.

———. *Years of Upheaval.* Boston: Little, Brown, 1982.

Kluckhohn, Clyde. "The Study of Culture." In Daniel Lerner and Harold D. Lasswell, eds., *The Policy Sciences.* Stanford, Calif.: Stanford University Press, 1951.

Krauss, Ellis S. *Under Construction: U.S.-Japan Negotiations to Open Japan's Construction Markets to American Firms, 1985–1988.* Pew Program in Case Teaching and Writing in International Affairs. Case 145, 1989.

Kreisberg, Paul H. "China's Negotiating Behaviour." In Thomas W. Robinson and David Shambaugh, eds., *Chinese Foreign Policy: Theory and Practice.* Oxford: Clarendon Press, 1994.

Kublin, Michael. *International Negotiating: A Primer for American Business Professionals.* New York: International Business Press, 1995.

Kunihiro, Masao. "U.S.-Japan Communications." In Henry Rosovsky, ed., *Discord in the Pacific: Challenges to the American-Japanese Alliance.* Washington, D.C.: Columbia Books, for the American Assembly, 1972.

———. "The Japanese Language and Intercultural Communication." In Japan Center for International Exchange, ed., *The Silent Power: Japan's Identity and World Role.* Tokyo: Simul Press, 1976.

Kux, Dennis, *India and the United States: Estranged Democracies.* Washington, D.C.: National Defense University Press, 1992.

Lakos, Amos. *International Negotiations: A Bibliography.* Boulder, Colo.: Westview Press, 1989.

Lang, Winfried. "A Professional's View." In Guy Olivier Faure and Jeffrey Z. Rubin, eds., *Culture and Negotiation: The Resolution of Water Disputes.* Newbury Park, Calif.: Sage, 1993.

Lapid, Yosef. "The Third Debate: On the Prospects of International Theory in a Post-Positivist Era." *International Studies Quarterly* 33 (1989): 235–254.

Lavin, Franklin L. "Negotiating with the Chinese." *Foreign Affairs* 73 (1994).

Leeds, Roger S., and Thompson, Gale. *The 1982 Mexican Debt Negotiations.* FPI Case Studies 4. Washington, D.C.: Johns Hopkins Foreign Policy Institute, 1987.

Lubman, Stanley B. "Negotiations in China: Observations of a Lawyer." In Robert A. Kapp, ed., *Communicating with China.* Yarmouth, Maine: Intercultural Press, 1983.

March, Robert M. *The Japanese Negotiator.* Tokyo: Kodansha International, 1988.

McMullen, Christopher J. *Resolution of the Yemen Crisis, 1963: A Case Study in Mediation.* Washington, D.C.: Institute for the Study of Diplomacy, 1980.

McNamara, Robert S. *In Retrospect: The Tragedy and Lessons of Vietnam.* New York: Vintage Books, 1996.

Meyer, Gail E. *Egypt and the United States: The Formative Years.* Cranbury, N.J.: Associated University Presses, 1980.

Moore, Clement Henry. "Clientelist Ideology and Political Change." In Ernest Gellner and John Waterbury, eds., *Patrons and Clients in Mediterranean Societies.* London: Duckworth, 1977.

Moser, Leo J. "Cross-Cultural Dimensions: U.S.-Japan." In Diane B. Bendahmane and Leo Moser, eds., *Toward a Better Understanding: U.S.-Japan Relations.* Washington, D.C.: Foreign Service Institute, 1986.

———. "Negotiating Style: Americans and Japanese." In Diane B. Bendahmane and Leo Moser, eds., *Toward a Better Understanding: U.S.-Japan Relations.* Washington, D.C.: Foreign Service Institute, 1986.

Nixon, Richard M. *The Memoirs of Richard Nixon.* London: Arrow Books, 1978.

O'Shea, Timothy J. C. *The U.S.-Japan Semiconductor Problem.* Pew Program in Case Teaching and Writing in International Affairs. Case 139, September 1988.

Palmer, Norman D. *The United States and India: The Dimensions of Influence.* New York: Praeger, 1984.

Perry, Diane. "The United States, China, and Negotiations over 'Most Favored Nation' Status in 1994." Program on Negotiation at Harvard Law School, Working Paper Series 95-2, 1995.

Pfeiffer, John. "How Not to Lose the Trade Wars by Cultural Gaffes." *Smithsonian* 18 (1988): 145–156.

Pye, Lucian. *Chinese Commercial Negotiating Style.* Cambridge, Mass.: Oelgeschlager, Gunn, and Hain, 1982.

Quandt, William B. *Camp David: Peacemaking and Politics.* Washington, D.C.: Brookings Institution, 1986.

———. "Egypt: A Strong Sense of National Identity." In Hans Binnendijk, ed., *National Negotiating Styles.* Washington, D.C.: Foreign Service Institute, 1987.

Raiffa, Howard. *The Art and Science of Negotiation.* Cambridge, Mass.: Harvard University Press, 1982.

Ralston, David A., et al. "Eastern Values: A Comparison of Managers in the United States, Hong Kong, and the People's Republic of China." *Journal of Applied Psychology* 77 (1992): 664–671.

Ram, N. "India's Nuclear Policy: A Case Study in the Flaws and Futility of Non-Proliferation." *IDSA Journal* 14 (1982): 445–538.

Rao, R. V. R. Chandrasekhara. "Searching for a Mature Relationship." *Round Table* 263 (1976): 249–260.

Reardon-Anderson, James. *U.S.-China Nuclear Cooperative Agreement.* Pew Program in Case Teaching and Writing in International Affairs. Case 110, 1989.

Reich, Bernard. *Quest for Peace.* New Brunswick, N.J.: Transaction Books, 1977.

Riad, Mohamed. *The Struggle for Peace in the Middle East.* London: Quartet Books, 1981.

Riding, Alan. *Distant Neighbors: A Portrait of the Mexicans.* New York: Vintage Books, 1986.

Rohlen, Thomas P. "Three Snapshots of Japan." In Diane B. Bendahmane and Leo Moser, eds., *Toward a Better Understanding: U.S.-Japan Relations.* Washington, D.C.: Foreign Service Institute, 1986.

Rolnick, Phyllis J. "Charity, Trusteeship, and Social Change in India." *World Politics* 14 (1962): 439–460.

Rubinstein, Robert A. "Cultural Aspects of Peacekeeping: Notes on the Substance of Symbols." *Millennium* 22 (1993): 551.

el-Sadat, Anwar. *In Search of Identity.* London: Fontana, 1977.

Shultz, George P. *Turmoil and Triumph: My Years as Secretary of State.* New York: Charles Scribner's Sons, 1993.

Shenkar, Oded, and Ronen, Simcha. "The Cultural Context of Negotiations: The Implications of Chinese Interpersonal Norms." *Journal of Applied Behavioral Science* 23 (1987): 263–275.

Simpson, Martin W. III. "Cultural Influences on Foreign Policy." In Charles F. Hermann, Charles W. Kegley, Jr., and James N. Rosenau, eds., *New Directions in the Study of Foreign Policy.* Boston: Allen and Unwin, 1987.

Sinha, Surya Prakash. "The Axiology of the International Bill of Human Rights." *Yearbook of International Law,* vol. 1. Pace University School of Law, 1989.

Smith, Raymond F. *Negotiating with the Soviets.* Bloomington: Indiana University Press, 1989.

Solomon, Richard H. *Chinese Political Negotiating Behavior: A Briefing Analysis.* Santa Monica, Calif.: RAND Corporation, 1985.

———. *Chinese Political Negotiating Behavior, 1967–1984.* Santa Monica, Calif.: RAND Corporation, 1995.

Stein, Janice Gross, ed. *Getting to the Table: The Process of International Prenegotiation.* Baltimore: Johns Hopkins University Press, 1989.

―――. "Getting to the Table: The Triggers, Stages, Functions, and Consequences of Prenegotiation." In idem, *Getting to the Table.* Baltimore: Johns Hopkins University Press, 1989.

Stewart, Edward C. *American Cultural Patterns.* Yarmouth, Maine: Intercultural Press, 1972.

Strazar, Marie D. "The San Francisco Peace Treaty: Cross-Cultural Elements in the Interaction between the Americans and the Japanese." In R. P. Anand, ed., *Cultural Factors in International Relations.* New Delhi: Abinhav, 1981.

Symington, James W. *The Stately Game.* New York: Macmillan, 1971.

Szalay, Lorand B. "Intercultural Communication: A Process Model." *International Journal of Intercultural Relations* 5 (1981): 133–146.

Tadao, Umesao. "Escape from Cultural Isolation." In Japan Center for International Exchange, ed., *The Silent Power: Japan's Identity and World Role.* Tokyo: Simul Press, 1976.

Thayer, Charles. *Diplomat.* London: Michael Joseph, 1960.

Thayer, Nathaniel B., and Weiss, Stephen E. "Japan: The Changing Logic of a Former Minor Power." In Hans Binnendijk, ed., *National Negotiating Styles.* Washington, D.C.: Foreign Service Institute, 1987.

Ting-Toomey, Stella. "Toward a Theory of Conflict and Culture." *International and Intercultural Communication Annual* 9 (1985): 71–86.

―――. "Intercultural Conflict Styles: A Face-Negotiation Theory." In Young Yun Kim and William B. Gudykunst, eds., *Theories in Intercultural Communication.* Beverly Hills, Calif.: Sage, 1988.

Ting-Toomey, Stella, and Cole, Mark. "Intergroup Diplomatic Communication: A Face-Negotiation Perspective." In Felipe Korzenny and Stella Ting-Toomey, eds., *Communicating for Peace: Diplomacy and Negotiation.* Newbury Park, Calif.: Sage, 1990.

Tomlin, Brian W. "The Stages of Prenegotiation: The Decision to Negotiate North American Free Trade." In Janice Gross Stein, ed., *Getting to the Table.* Baltimore: Johns Hopkins University Press, 1989.

Triandis, Harry C.; Bontempo, Robert; and Villareal, Marcelo J. "Individualism and Collectivism: Cross-Cultural Perspectives on Self-Ingroup Relationships." *Journal of Personality and Social Psychology* 54 (1988): 323–338.

Triandis, Harry C.; Brislin, Richard; and Hui, C. Harry. "Cross-Cultural Training across the Individualism-Collectivism Divide." *International Journal of Intercultural Relations* 12 (1988): 269-289.

Tsutomu, Kano. "Why the Search for Identity?" In Japan Center for International Exchange, ed., *The Silent Power: Japan's Identity and World Role*. Tokyo: Simul Press, 1976.

Tung, Rosalie L. "U.S.-China Trade Negotiations: Procedures and Outcomes." *Journal of International Business Studies* 13 (1982): 25–37.

Tylor, Sir Edward Burnett. *Primitive Culture*. New York: Harper and Row, 1958. Original ed. 1871.

Underdal, Arild. "The Outcomes of Negotiation." In Victor A. Kremenyuk, ed., *International Negotiation*. San Francisco: Jossey-Bass, 1991.

U.S. Congress, House Committee on Appropriations, *Military Construction Appropriations for 1982: Hearings before the Subcommittee on Military Construction Appropriations*, 97th Cong., 1st sess., 1981, pt. 5. Washington, D.C.: U.S. Government Printing Office, 1981.

U.S. Congress, Senate Committee on Foreign Relations, *Situation in Mexico: Hearings before the Subcommittee on Western Hemisphere Affairs*, 99th Cong., 2d sess., 13 May, 17 June, and 26 June 1986. Washington, D.C.: U.S. Government Printing Office, 1986.

U.S. Congress. House International Relations Committee, *Hearing of the House Western Hemisphere Affairs Subcommittee of the House International Relations Committee*, "Certification for Drug-Producing Countries in Latin America," March 7, 1996.

U.S. Department of State. *Foreign Relations of the United States*, vols. 6, 1943; 9, 1945; 11, 1946; 2, 1949; 2, 1950; 6, pts. 1 and 2, 1951; 4, 11, 1952–54; 3, 6, 8, 1955–57. Washington, D.C.: U.S. Government Printing Office, different dates.

Vance, Cyrus. *Hard Choices*. New York: Simon and Schuster, 1983.

Van De Velde, James R. "The Influence of Culture on Japanese-American Negotiations." *Fletcher Forum* 7 (1983): 395–399.

Van Zandt, Howard F. "How to Negotiate in Japan." *Harvard Business Review* 48 (1970): 45–56.

Weingarten, Michael. *Changing Health and Changing Culture: The Yemenite Jews in Israel*. Westport, Conn.: Praeger, 1992.

Wendel, Christopher S. "Into the Pressure Cooker: The Strategic Impediments Initiative." Program on Negotiation at Harvard Law School, Working Paper Series 92-6, 1992.

Wilson, Larman C. "The Settlement of Boundary Disputes: Mexico, the United States, and the International Boundary Commission." *International and Comparative Law Quarterly* 29 (1980): 38–53.

Winham, Gilbert. "Practitioners' Views of International Negotiation." *World Politics* 32 (1979): 111–135.

Wolfgang, Aaron, ed. *Nonverbal Behavior: Perspectives, Applications, Intercultural Insights.* Lewiston, N.Y.: C. J. Hogrefe, 1984.

Young, Kenneth T. *Negotiating with the Chinese Communists.* New York: McGraw-Hill, 1968.

Zartman, I. William. "Negotiation as a Joint Decision-Making Process." *Journal of Conflict Resolution* 21 (1977): 619–638.

———. "Prenegotiation: Phases and Functions." In Janice Gross Stein, ed., *Getting to the Table.* Baltimore: Johns Hopkins University Press, 1989.

Zartman, I. William, and Berman, Maureen R. *The Practical Negotiator.* New Haven: Yale University Press, 1982.

Index

Abelson, Donald, 207, 208
Acheson, Dean, 142
Achille Lauro affair, 62
Act
    Battle, 115, 116
    Nuclear Nonproliferation, 96
    Taiwan Relations, 157
Addabbo, Joseph, 193
Afghanistan, 97
Agency for International Aid
    (USAID), 62–63, 124, 129,
    130, 178, 180, 211–212
Agreement
    Framework, 172–173, 195–197
    Nuclear Cooperation, 194, 203,
    204
    Status of Forces, 85
    U.S.-Canada Free Trade, 68–69
agreements, international, 189–197,
    190, 201
Algeria, 205
Ali, Kamal Hassan, 144–145
Ali, Mohammed, 150
Allen, George, 58, 116, 149, 150,
    160, 221
Anderson, Robert, 144

APEC. *See* Asia-Pacific Economic
    Cooperation forum
apology, role of, 41–42, 222
appearance, outward, 183–189
Arabs, and Israel, 68, 187
argument, use of, 136–142, 226
Art and Science of Negotiation
    (Raiffa), 38
ASEAN. *See* Association of South-
    east Asian Nations
Asia-Pacific Economic Cooperation
    (APEC) forum, 38–39
Association of Southeast Asian
    Nations (ASEAN), 39, 40–41
Astoria affair, 4–6, 10
Australia, 30, 38–43
authority, lines of, 123–133

Badeau, John, 74, 141, 167
Baker, James, 73, 121–123, 127,
    136–137, 151, 159, 177–178,
    205, 220
Bangladesh, 91
bargaining, 110, 111–113, 115
Battle, Lucius, 167
Ben Gurion, David, 144

Bennett, Timothy, 99, 114, 178
Bollinger, Walter, 180
bout de papier. See non-paper
Bowers, Gerard, 124, 178
Bowles, Chester, 93, 142, 158, 160, 168
Boxer Rebellion, 121, 122
Breer, William, 16, 77, 85
Brill, Kenneth C., 48
Brownell, Herbert, 80, 91, 140, 189, 223
Brzezinski, Zbigniew, 72, 87, 88, 176
Bundy, McGeorge, 47
Bunker, Ellsworth, 141, 181–182
Bush, George, 36, 51, 73, 74, 127, 156, 178, 205, 209
Business Software Alliance, 209

Camp David Accords, 74–75, 92, 104
Canada, 30, 68
Carter, Jimmy, 58, 61, 89
    and China, 87, 156, 176–177
    and Egypt, 74, 75, 92, 126, 147–149, 223
    and Mexico, 100, 127, 159, 179
Castaneda, Jorge, 179
Chai Zemin, 72, 176
China, Nationalist, 156–157
    see also Taiwan
China, People's Republic of
    agreements with, 194–195, 202–207, 218
    Algeria and, 205
    ambassadorships to, 101, 119, 175, 219
    appeals to principle by, 101–103
    arms proliferation and, 51
    concessions by, 98–99, 175
    cultural dissonance and, 21–22
    decisionmaking in, 125, 131–132
    dissent in, perceptions of, 63
    face in, 14, 185–186
    human rights and, 46, 51, 61, 63–65, 157–158, 170–171, 220
    IAEA and, 203–204
    implementation and, 202–207
    intellectual property rights and, 6, 99, 111–112, 134, 169–170, 202–203, 222
    internees in, as pawns, 64–65, 98
    and Japan, 97–98
    MFN status of, 157–158, 170–171, 219
    and the MTCR, 205–206
    negotiating style in, 16, 78, 86–88, 97–99, 101, 107, 118–123, 124, 151–153, 169, 177
    normalization negotiations in (1978), 71, 78, 87–88, 119, 176–177, 185, 194, 220
    nuclear nonproliferation agreements and, 203–205
    and Pakistan, 203, 204, 205, 206
    political choreography in, 151–152, 155–156
    prison labor and, 194–195, 202
    relationships in, and negotiation, 71–72, 93, 103
    repatriation of civilians from (1954–55), 64, 98, 120, 175, 220
    Soviet Union and, 176
    status and, 36, 46, 50–51, 63–64, 92–93, 122
    and Syria, 205
    Tiananmen Square and, 63, 72, 121, 136–137
    trade policy and, 51, 98, 111, 139, 153, 169–171
    Vietnam and, 150–151, 153, 176
    see also Taiwan
Chou En-lai. *See* Zhou Enlai

Christopher, Warren, 88, 136, 157, 161, 179, 189, 206
Clark, William, 16
Clinton, Bill, 50, 74, 142, 209
  and China, 48, 49, 51, 157–158, 170, 206
  and Japan, 142–143, 172, 196, 221
coercion, deadlock and, 164–166, 168–169
Commission
  Binational, 73
  International Boundary and Water, 72–73, 140, 188, 222–223
  U.S.-Mexico, for Border Development and Friendship, 72–73
communication, nonverbal, 25–28, 154–160, 225
compliance, 191, 199–202
Comprehensive Test Ban, 97
compromise, 113, 164, 183–184
concessions
  American perceptions of, 108, 109, 113, 119
  Arabic terms for, 108–109
  Chinese perceptions of, 72, 118, 121, 122
  Egyptian, 92
  Japanese perceptions of, 86
  and reciprocity, 83, 121
  symbolic, 185
confrontation, 165–166
Confucianism, 137, 159
Connally, John, 70, 184–185
Constantine, Thomas, 52
contract, 190–191, 201
contradiction, 142–146
Cook, Peter, 41
copyright, 209
  see also China, intellectual property rights and
Cortines, Ruiz, 114, 115
Cray computers, 58–59, 187

culture
  high-context, 19, 31–33, 36, 68, 69, 75–81, 201, 217
  individualistic, 29–30, 36, 106, 125
  as information, 12
  low-context, 31, 33, 36–37, 65–66, 69, 84, 201, 216
  and misunderstanding, 17
  nature of, 10–14, 21
  and nonverbal communication, 154
  perceptions and, 13
  political, 14, 123
  relationship-oriented, 29, 30–31, 36, 106
  shame-oriented vs. guilt-oriented, 32, 33, 75–76
  trends toward convergence in, 217–218
  values and, 54
  see also language

deadlock, breaking, 164–173
deal, perceptions of, 199–213
Dean, Arthur, 174–175
debate, 29–30, 136
de la Madrid, Miguel, 73
Deng Xiapong, 71, 72, 88, 98, 156, 176
Díaz, Porfirio, 46
dissonance, cross-cultural (intercultural), 25–43, 39–43, 46–47, 62, 101, 133
Dulles, John Foster, 102, 116, 132, 142, 144, 167

Egypt
  agreements with, 192
  bureaucracy in, 125, 130–131, 144
  cross-cultural dissonance and, 143, 144–145, 147–149, 219
  face and, 183, 187–188
  food aid for, 167

Egypt *(cont.)*
  General Motors in, 130–131, 219
  general principles and, 103
  human rights and, 61–63
  and Israel, 17, 74–75, 103, 104,
      112, 144, 148, 187, 192, 221,
      223, 224
  and the legacy of colonialism in,
      36, 49, 54, 65, 74
  military assistance and, 54–56
  negotiating style and, 17, 111,
      124, 154–155, 181
  and the NPT, 50
  personal relationships, 73–74,
      141, 223
  Ras Banas affair in, 55–56, 145,
      193, 219
  Saudi Arabia and, 141
  sovereignty and, 54–56, 65, 90
  and the Soviet Union, 166–1167
  status and, 46, 49–50
  Suez Canal and, 144, 167, 192,
      222
  as a supplicant, 92
  and USAID, 211, 212–213
  U.S. military presence in, 111, 131,
      144–145, 166, 192, 193, 222
  and the Yemen, 181
Eilts, Hermann, 61, 73, 92, 104, 130,
      144, 165, 181
Eisenhower, Dwight D., 53, 142, 149
end use, U.S. policy on, 57–59, 187,
      205
Enron Corporation, 7, 136
ethos, individualistic vs. interdepen-
      dent, 28–31
Evans, Gareth, 41

face, 14, 30, 164, 183–189, 226
  and international agreements, 190,
      201, 224
  language and, 142–143, 146–153

loss of, 31–32, 76, 109, 133
Fahmy, Ismail, 61–62, 75, 125–126,
      148–149, 154
Fang Lizhi, 137
Fattah, Ali Abdel, 63
Fisher, Glen, 17, 20, 22, 72, 90, 113
Fisher, Roger, 38, 216
Flanigan, Peter, 117
Ford, Gerald, 98
Freeman, Chas, 71, 87, 119, 169
Friedkin, Joseph, 73, 140, 178–179,
      188
frontality, 31, 37, 69

Galbraith, John Kenneth, 58,
      145–146, 160, 168, 194, 221
Gamasay, Muhammed Abdul Ghani
      al, 144
Gandhi, Indira, 93, 96–97, 127,
      141–142, 150–151, 158, 223
Gandhi, Rajiv, 59
Garten, Jeffrey, 173
GATT. *See* General Agreement on
      Tariffs and Trade
Gavin, John, 52, 92, 165
Gelbard, Robert S., 210
General Agreement on Tariffs and
      Trade (GATT), 99, 138, 207
General Motors, 130–131, 219
Getting to the Table (Stein), 68, 82
Getting to Yes (Fisher and Ury), 38,
      216
Ghorbal, Ashraf, 147
Glenn, Edmund, 100, 137
Glenn, John, 126
Goheen, Robert, 20, 58, 96
Grew, Joseph, 5–6, 8, 20

haggling, place of, 110–111, 118
Haig, Alexander, 55, 156–157
Han Xu, 136–137, 159
Hashimoto, Ryutaro, 143

Hata, Tsutomu, 160
Hay, John, 121
Henderson, Loy, 93
Hills, Carla, 73, 178, 220
Hirohito, Emperor, 6
history, attitudes toward, 35–36, 54
Ho Chi Minh, 93
honor, 30, 111, 112, 186
Hosokawa, Morihiro, 53–54, 172
Huang Hua, 87, 119

IAEA. *See* International Atomic
    Energy Agency
identity, cultural, and language, 13
Ikeda, Hayato, 57
implementation, 67, 68, 199–213, 226
India
    air defense pact (1962–63) and,
        194–195
    bureaucracy in, 128–130
    and China, 58, 145, 167, 168, 221
    civil avaiation agreement (1995),
        and, 138, 180–181, 220
    food aid for, 57, 93, 167–168
    Hindu ethic in, 94
    history and, 36
    military assistance for, 58
    moralism and, 94–97
    negotiating style and, 17, 106, 115,
        124, 128–129, 160, 180, 218
    nonalignment policy of, 57, 97
    and the NPT, 96, 97
    personal ties and, 29, 142
    power station in, 7
    sovereignty and, 57–59, 93–94
    status and, 46, 47–49, 92, 94, 95
    supercomputers for, 58–59, 187
    as a supplicant, 93
    Tarapur reactor and, 58–59, 96, 186
    thorium nitrate from, 57–58, 111,
        115–116, 127, 129–130
    and USAID, 211, 212

see also Kashmir; Pakistan
Inouye, Junnosuke, 185
International Atomic Energy Agency
    (IAEA), 203–204, 207
International Bill of Human Rights, 61
International Intellectual Property
    Alliance, 209
Iran, 7, 50, 54–55, 221
Iraq, 50, 127
Ismail, Hafez, 103
Israel
    and the Arabs, 68, 187
    and Egypt, 17, 74–75, 103, 104,
        112, 144, 148, 187, 192, 221,
        223, 224
    negotiating style of, 92, 124
    and the NPT, 50

Japan
    air traffic agreements and, 84–85,
        85–86, 117, 179, 220
    apology to, from the U.S., 222
    compromise in, 116–118
    concessions from, 185
    confrontation and, 137, 165, 173
    contracts in, 195–197, 207–208
    decisionmaking in, 125, 131,
        132–133
    face in, 14
    financial market reform in (1984),
        70–71
    fishing disputes and, 15, 89
    gaiatsu and, 171–172, 173, 221
    GATT and, 207–208
    history and, 36, 185
    insurance market in, 172–173,
        196–197
    language in, and cross-cultural
        dissonance, 142–143, 146, 218
    lost territories and, 56
    monetary crisis in (1971), 70, 89,
        184–185, 224

Japan *(cont.)*
  negotiating style in, 16, 36, 37, 68,
    69–71, 76–78, 84–86, 88–90,
    106, 107, 116, 117, 124, 137,
    138–139, 159–160, 208
  the "Nixon shock" (1971) and, 53
  nuclear weapons and, 56
  perceptions of negotiation in, 68
  relationships in, 29
  and the San Francisco peace
    treaty, 15
  semiconductor negotiations,
    117–118
  status and, 46, 52–54, 65, 71
  Status of Forces Agreement
    (1995–96) and, 85
  strategic impediments initiative
    (SII), 77–78, 84
  textiles negotiations (1970) and,
    77, 89, 117
  trade policy and, 53, 77, 89, 111,
    117, 134, 138–139, 143,
    171–173, 195–197
  see also Okinawa
Jiang Zemin, 51
Johnson, Alexis, 64–65, 120–121, 175
Johnson, Lyndon B., 47, 68, 158
  and Egypt, 103, 125, 141, 167
  and Indira Gandhi, 93, 141–142,
    223
Jones, James, 210
Jova, John, 52, 165

Kamel, Mohamed, 75
Kantor, Mickey, 76, 218, 221
  and China, 169
  and Japan, 53, 159–160, 165, 173
Kashmir, 48, 145–146, 160, 168, 221
Katz, Julius, 105–106, 179
Keating, Paul, 39–43, 218, 222
Kennedy, John F., 79, 102, 141, 168,
    223

Khan, Ayub, 145
Kissinger, Henry, 132, 151–152
  and China, 51, 98, 102–103, 112,
    153, 156, 185, 186
  and Egypt, 49, 74, 75, 103, 112,
    125–161, 155, 187, 192, 223
  and Japan, 56, 77
Kleindienst, Richard, 81, 146
Klinghoffer, Leon, 62
Korea, 28, 101, 151, 174–175
Kreisberg, Paul, 95
Kreuger, Robert, 191

Lande, Steve, 80
language
  and culture, 13, 14, 31–33, 77,
    142–143, 195, 225
  indirect, 146–153
  nonverbal, 25–28, 154–160, 159–
    160, 225
  semantic assumptions and, 26–28,
    39–40, 42, 71, 108
Lavin, Franklin, 139–140, 202
law, perceptions about, 31, 135–142,
    144–145
leadership, powers of, 125–131
League of Nations Covenant, 200
Le Duc Tho, 151
Lee Teng-Hui, 78
Lehr, Deborah, 169–170
Levin, Burt, 170
Lewis, Samuel, 16–17, 20
Libya, 50, 193
Li Peng, 177, 205
López Mateos, Adolfo, 79, 188
López Portillo, José, 100, 105–106,
    127, 179, 223
Lucey, Patrick, 59, 81, 105

MacArthur, General Douglas, 52–53
McNamara, Robert, 7
McNamar, Tim, 92

Mahathir Mohamad, 38–43
Malaysia, 38–43, 222
Malone, James, 130
Mann, Thomas, 73, 79, 105, 222–223
Mansfield, Mike, 118, 222
Mao Tse-tung, 152–153, 155–156, 186, 219
Markey, Edward, 204, 205
Meisner, Doris, 99
Mexico
  agreements with, 191–192
  air transport agreements and, 80–81, 114–115, 220
  Chamizal boundary dispute (1962–63), 73, 78–79, 105, 140, 187, 188, 222–223
  Colorado River and, 79–80, 90–91, 111, 140, 187, 189, 223, 224
  confrontation and, 165, 166–167
  cultural dissonance and, 6, 143, 146, 218
  debt crisis in (1982), 91, 188–189, 224
  drug traffic and, 52, 60, 81, 113, 146
  and extradition, 209–211
  gas exports from, 100, 105–106, 126–127, 166, 167, 179, 189
  GATT and, 99
  general principles and, 104, 105
  immigration from, 81, 99
  implementation and, 6, 208–211
  intellectual property and, 209
  negotiating style in, 90–92, 99–100, 113, 124, 178
  personal relationships, 72–73, 78–81, 140
  peso crisis (1995) in, 46, 59, 90, 192, 210–211, 218, 224
  Presidio-Ojinaga dispute with, 178–179

  relevance of history to, 36, 114, 189
  sovereignty and, 59–60, 65, 90
  status and, 46, 51–52, 114, 184, 188
  U.S. military presence in, 59, 60, 191
Meyer, Armin, 45
MFN. See most-favored nation status
Missile Technology Control Regime (MTCR), 205–206
Mitterand, François, 36
Miyazawa, Kiichi, 45–46
Mizuta, Mikio, 70, 185
Moser, Leo, 85, 116
most-favored nation (MFN) status, 157–158, 219
Motorola Corporation, 171–172
Moussa, Amr, 50
MTCR. See Missile Technology Control Regime
Mubarak, Hosni, 49, 50, 56, 62, 130, 144, 145

NAFTA. See North America Free Trade Agreement
Nakasone, Yasuhiro, 133, 221
Nasser, Gamal Abdel, 54, 74, 103, 125, 126, 141, 144, 166–167, 181–182
negotiation
  adaptive (awase), 38, 133–134
  on broad principles, 100–106
  by non-diplomats, 22–23, 85
  and decisionmaking, 123–133, 200
  end game in, 67, 163–164, 173–182, 219
  from the high moral ground, 94–100
  in good faith, 16, 199, 202
  ideal, 68, 76
  limits on, 46–66, 68, 223–234
  literature on, 38

negotiation *(cont.)*
  manipulative *(erabi)*, 36, 38, 136
  middle game in, 67, 107–108
  models of, 17–19, 25–28, 67–68
  nonverbal communication and,
    154–160
  paradigms of, 110–112, 215–216
  persuasion and, 100–101
  styles of, 16–17, 36–38, 76–78
  war and, 68
  "win-win," 133–134, 216
  see also implementation; pre-
    negotiation
Nehru, Jarwaharlal, 116, 142, 194
  and conditional U.S. aid, 57, 93,
    167
  and Kashmir, 168, 221
  and Pakistan, 145–146, 149, 160,
    221
  and U.S. end-use regulations, 58
Nepal, 17
Newman, Frank N., 192
Newsom, David, 16, 22, 114, 124,
    165, 178
Nicolson, Harold, 4, 23
Nixon, Richard M.
  and China, 52, 56, 152–153, 185–
    186, 219, 224
  and Egypt, 158
  and India, 142, 150–151, 158–160
  and Japan, 89, 132, 143, 147, 221
  and Mexico, 80, 223
Noburu, Takeshta, 143
non-paper *(bout de papier)*, 190
nonratification, 200
North America Free Trade Agree-
    ment (NAFTA), 133, 210, 218
  copyright and, 209
  cultural dissonance and, 21, 191
  and Mexico's status, 46, 52, 59, 91
  negotiation style and, 73, 104
  prenogiations and, 80

pressures to settle and, 178, 220
NPT. *See* Treaty, Nuclear Nonpro-
    liferation

Okamatsu, Sozaburo, 196
Okinawa, 56–57, 65, 85, 89, 133–134,
    224
Open Door policy (China), 121
Operation Intercept (1969), 146

Pakistan
  and China, 203, 204, 205, 206
  and India, 48, 145–146, 150, 160,
    168
  and the U.S., 51, 96, 145–146,
    149–151, 160, 221
Palestine Liberation Organization
    (PLO), 49, 62, 149
PEMEX. *See* Petroleos Mexicanos
People's Republic of China. *See*
    China
Pepsi Cola Corporation, 129
Peres, Shimon, 74
Perry, Commodore Matthew, 52, 85
Perry, William, 60
Petroleos Mexicanos (PEMEX), 106,
    126
Pickering, Thomas, 48
Pillai, Sir Naravana Raghavan, 116
PLO. *See* Palestine Liberation
    Organization
Poindexter, John, 144
postnegotiation, 200
power, perceptions of, 113, 125–127
prenegotiation, 67–82
prestige, and compromise, 184
Prestowitz, Clyde, 196
pride, as a stumbling block, 47–49,
    65
prime minister, "recalcitrant," 38–43,
    222
protocol, 49, 155, 158, 184

Qian Qichen, 72, 121–123, 177, 206, 220

quotas, and trade with Japan, 139

Rabasa, Emilio, 91, 140, 223
Rahmat, Mahomed, 39, 40
Raiffa, Howard, 38
Rao, P. V. Narasimha, 49
Raphel, Robin Lynn, 47–49, 218
Reagan, Ronald, 73, 133, 156, 157, 204, 221
Regan, Donald, 70–71
relationships
    and agreements, 201, 202, 207
    assumptions about, 14–15, 129
    culture and, 12
    dependency (amae), 15, 46, 65, 77, 89–93, 106, 207
    intercultural, 14–17
    negotiations as mending, 69
    and payoffs, 38
    personal, 32, 69–75, 110, 138, 140–141, 217, 222–223, 225
remedy, symbolic, 49, 50
Riad, Mohamed, 49, 147
Rogers, William, 49, 136, 166, 167
Roh, Charles, 73, 104, 124
Rohlen, Thomas P., 132
Roosevelt, Franklin D., 5, 90
Roosevelt, Kermit, 144
Rusk, Dean, 147

Sadat, Anwar, 55, 92
    and Israel, 68, 127, 148, 187, 221–222
    and Jimmy Carter, 74, 223
    and Kissinger, 49, 74, 75, 103, 112, 155, 192, 223
    and the Suez Canal, 144, 192
Saito, Hirosi, 4–6
Salinas de Gortari, Carlos, 73, 209, 210
Sánchez Vargas, Julio, 81

sanctions, U.S., 169–170, 172–173, 206
Sands, Lee, 160–170, 222
Sato, Eisaku, 53, 77, 89, 132–133, 143, 147, 150, 221
Saudi Arabia, 127, 141, 181, 219
Saunders, Harold, 148
Schlesinger, James, 105, 126, 166
Scowcroft, Brent, 72
Serrano, Díaz, 106
Serra Puche, Jaime, 73
Shanghai communiqué, the, 102, 103, 112, 151–152, 186, 194, 224
Shastri, Lal Badhur, 158
Shattuck, John, 157
Shekhar, Chandra, 59
Shigemitsu, Mamoru, 132
Shultz, George, 45–46, 74, 126, 159, 160, 187
SII. See Japan, strategic impediments initiative
Silva de Herzog, Jesus, 91, 184, 188
Singh, V. P., 59
Sisco, Joseph, 74
Smith, Mike, 124, 139, 197, 202
Smith, Raymond, 16, 20
Snow, Edgar, 155–156
Solarz, Stephen, 48
sovereignty, 45, 54–60, 65–66
Soivet Union, 15, 16, 166–1167
Sri Lanka, 17
status, 88, 184
    equality and, 83, 88
    negotiation and, 45–54, 226
Stein, Janice Gross, 68
Summers, Lawrence, 196
supplication, as a posture, 42, 88–94
surprise, antipathy toward, 75–81
Syria, 50, 149, 205

Taiwan, 51, 65, 71, 78, 98, 102–103, 119, 156, 176–177

Talbott, Strobe, 48, 49
Tello, Manuel, 73, 79, 105, 222–223
Thatcher, Magaret, 143
Thurston, 80–81
time, concepts of, 33–36, 114, 118, 133–134, 163–164, 180
timing, 32–33
trade, international, and diplomacy, 168–173
treaties, 190, 200
Treaty
    Extradition, 209–211
    Nuclear Nonproliferation (NPT), 50, 96, 97, 203
    San Francisco (1951), 15
    of Versailles, 200
Truman, Harry S., 142, 155

United Nations Organization, 50, 187, 224
United States
    aid with conditions from, 57, 63, 166–168, 211–213
    bargaining by, 64, 84
    and Canada, 68–69
    concessions from, 179, 204, 219–220
    decisionmaking in, 200
    foreign policy of, 37–38
    human rights and, 60–61, 63–64, 219
    individualism in, 29
    military presence of, 54–57, 59
    misinterpretation by, 147
    negotiating style of, 36–38, 45–46, 83–84, 101, 106, 107–108, 113, 124, 135–136, 174, 208
    and pressure to settle, 34–35, 36, 114, 173–179, 180, 220
    Public Law 480, 167
    status and, 46–47, 64–65, 83, 88

trade law, Special 301 provisions, 169, 172
Ury, William, 38, 216
USAID. See Agency for International Aid

Vance, Cyrus, 75, 98, 119, 131–132, 136, 148, 176
Versailles conference (1919), 77
Vietnam, 7, 151–152, 153, 176

Wallison, Peter, 92
Wang, 64, 120–121
War
    Arab-Israeli (1967), 49
    Gulf (1990–91), 59, 127, 131, 133, 216
    Indo-Pakistani (1971), 160
    Korean, 174–175
    Vietnam, 151
    Yom Kippur (1973), 49, 61, 75, 103, 154, 187, 224
Wei Jingsheng, 157, 158
Weizman, Ezer, 74
Wilcox, Robert, 81
Wilson, Pete, 165
Wisner, Frank, 49
Woodcock, Leonard, 87–88
World Bank, the, 211
World Trade Organization, 46, 170

Yasuya, Uchida, 77
Yeltsin, Boris, 142
Yemen, 181
Yeutter, Clayton, 118

Zhao Ziyang, 204
Zhou Enlai, 71, 102, 112, 151–152, 156, 159, 185, 186
Zuniga Rios, Serapio, 210

Raymond Cohen is professor of international relations at the Hebrew University of Jerusalem. He was a fellow at the United States Institute of Peace in 1988–89 and again in 1996, where he conducted much of the research for *Negotiating Across Cultures*. A specialist in the areas of diplomatic negotiations and intercultural communications, Cohen has published articles in numerous journals and is the author of four other books: *Culture and Conflict in Egyptian-Israeli Relations; Theatre of Power; International Politics: Rules of the Game;* and *Threat Perception in International Crisis*. He has studied at Oxford University and Lancaster University, and received his Ph.D. in international relations from the Hebrew University.

Jennings Randolph Program for International Peace

This book is a fine example of the work produced by senior fellows in the Jennings Randolph fellowship program of the United States Institute of Peace. As part of the statute establishing the Institute, Congress envisioned a program that would appoint "scholars and leaders of peace from the United States and abroad to pursue scholarly inquiry and other appropriate forms of communication on international peace and conflict resolution." The program was named after Senator Jennings Randolph of West Virginia, whose efforts over four decades helped to establish the Institute.

Since 1987, the Jennings Randolph Program has played a key role in the Institute's effort to build a national center of research, dialogue, and education on critical problems of conflict and peace. More than a hundred senior fellows from some thirty nations have carried out projects on the sources and nature of violent international conflict and the ways such conflict can be peacefully managed or resolved. Fellows come from a wide variety of academic and other professional backgrounds. They conduct research at the Institute and participate in the Institute's outreach activities to policymakers, the academic community, and the American public.

Each year approximately fifteen senior fellows are in residence at the Institute. Fellowship recipients are selected by the Institute's board of directors in a competitive process. For further information on the program, or to receive an application form, please contact the program staff at (202) 457-1700.

Joseph Klaits
Director

Negotiating Across Cultures

This book is set in Adobe Caslon; the display type is Gill Sans. Hasten Design Studio designed the book's cover, and Joan Engelhardt designed the interior. Pages were made up by Helene Y. Redmond. Frances Bowles prepared the index. The book's editor was Nigel Quinney.